Globalization and the Middle East

The Royal Institute of International Affairs is an independent body which promotes the rigorous study of international questions and does not express opinions of its own. The opinions expressed in this publication are the responsibility of the authors.

The Research and Studies Division is the specialized unit at the Crown Prince Court of the Emirate of Abu Dhabi responsible for conducting research and studies of political and economic developments of a local, regional and international nature of significance to the Emirate and the promotion of its welfare. The opinions expressed in the publications of the Division are those of the authors alone and not necessarily of the Crown Prince Court.

Globalization and the Middle East

Islam, Economy, Society and Politics

Edited by Toby Dodge and Richard Higgott

THE ROYAL INSTITUTE OF
INTERNATIONAL AFFAIRS
Middle East Programme

in association with
Division of Research and Studies
Crown Prince Court of Abu Dhabi

© Royal Institute of International Affairs, 2002

Published in Great Britain in 2002 by
Royal Institute of International Affairs, 10 St James's Square,
London SW1Y 4LE
(Charity Registration No. 208 223)

Distributed worldwide by
The Brookings Institution, 1775 Massachusetts Avenue NW,
Washington DC 20036-2188, USA

British Library Cataloguing in Publication Data
A CIP catalogue record for this book is available from the British Library.

ISBN 1 86203 133 9 *Hardback*
ISBN 1 86203 134 7 *Paperback*

Typeset in Times by Koinonia
Printed and bound in Great Britain by the Chameleon Press Limited
Cover design and photography by Matthew Link

Contents

Acknowledgments

This volume is the result of a joint endeavour between the Research and Studies Division of the Crown Prince Court of Abu Dhabi and the Middle East Programme of the Royal Institute of International Affairs (RIIA), at Chatham House in London. Since 1997 the two organizations have held an annual international symposium on contemporary issues facing the peoples of the region. A symposium on 'Globalization: Trends, Implications and Responses' was held in Abu Dhabi in November 2000. Its aim was to bring experts on globalization from industry, the media and academia together with those who specialize in the interaction between globalization and the culture, politics and economics of the Middle East. The result was two days of very productive discussions focusing on the nexus between the Middle East and the global economy. The papers presented at the symposium acted as the catalyst for this book. All those present agreed that a more detailed examination of the issues raised was needed. Acting on this advice, Toby Dodge and Richard Higgott invited nine academic experts on the Middle East, some from the region and some from the UK, to build on the original themes raised at the seminar in the light of their own expertise and events since November 2000. This resulted in the nine essays contained in this volume, which together address one of the dominant issues facing the Middle East at present.

The editors would like to thank all those who took part in the symposium, especially those who presented papers: Professor Abdul Khalik Abdullah, Abdulmalik Al Hamar, Nik Gowing, Yoshiki Hatanaka and Roger Rainbow. We are particularly grateful to H.H. Sheikh Sultan Bin Khalifa Al Nahayan for making the whole project possible. For guiding the endeavour from the inception to the completion of the work, special thanks are due to H.H. Sheikh Saeed Bin Saif Al Nahayan. Dr Iskandar Bashir is thanked for his coordination of the project and facilitation of continued cooperation between the participating institutions. The staff of the Research and Studies Division of the Crown Prince Court are to be thanked for organizing the symposium and assisting in the production of the book.

We would also like to thank Dr Ali Ansari, Dr Maha Azzam, Professor Fred Halliday and Professor Rodney Wilson for submitting additional chapters for the book in the light of recent events.

At Chatham House many thanks are due to Dr Rosemary Hollis for

Acknowledgments

overseeing the series of seminars that preceded the event in Abu Dhabi and for offering valuable advice and guidance to the editors as they brought the book to publication. Dr Kim Mitchell, Margaret May and Matthew Link are to be thanked for supplying the technical publishing expertise. Finally the editors would like to thank Emma Brigham and Robert Lowe for their excellent administrative support.

February 2002   T.D.
                                                                       R.H.

Contributors

Dr Ali M. Ansari is Lecturer in the Political History of the Middle East at the Institute for Middle Eastern and Islamic Studies, University of Durham and an Associate Fellow of the Middle East Programme at the Royal Institute of International Affairs (RIIA). He holds a PhD in Politics from the School of Oriental and African Studies (SOAS), University of London. His recent publications include 'The Myth of the White Revolution: Mohammad Reza Shah, "Modernisation" and the Consolidation of Power', *Middle Eastern Studies* (Vol. 37, No. 3, 2001); *Iran, Islam and Democracy: The Politics of Managing Change* (RIIA, 2000); 'Iranian Foreign Policy under Khatami: Reform and Reintegration', in A. Ehteshami and A. Mohammadi (eds), *Iran and Eurasia* (Ithaca, 2000); 'The Iranian Revolution 20 Years on', *Politique Etrangère* (Vol. 65, No. 1, 2000); and 'The Military Balance in the Caspian Region', in H. Amirahmadi (ed.), *The Caspian Region at a Crossroad: Challenges of a New Frontier of Energy and Development* (St Martin's Press, 2000). He will publish a history of modern Iran with Longman and a book on the political evolution of Iran with Routledge in 2003.

Dr Maha Azzam is a writer and analyst of Middle East politics. She has a DPhil from Oxford University. She worked at the International Institute for Strategic Studies, became a MacArthur Fellow at the Programme on Peace and International Cooperation and was a Research Fellow at the Royal United Services Institute for Defence Studies (RUSI), London, where she subsequently set up and headed the Programme on Security and Development in Muslim States from 1995 to 1999. Her main area of research and writing is on political Islam in the Middle East and the domestic politics and regional security issues of the region. Recent publications include 'Recent Developments among Islamist Groups in North Africa', in *Political Islam and Civil Society in North Africa: Four Approaches* (Stiftung Wissenschaft und Politik, 1998); 'Gender and the Politics of Religion in the Middle East', in Mai Yamani (ed.), *Feminism and Islam: Legal and Literary Perspectives* (Ithaca, 1996); 'Egypt: The Islamists and the State under Mubarak', in Salam Sidahmed and Anoush Ehteshami (eds), *Islamic Fundamentalism* (Westview Press, 1996); 'Islamism', in Alex Danchev, *Fin de Siècle: The Meaning of the Twentieth Century* (Tauris Academic Studies, 1995). Her latest book, *The International Political Attitudes and*

Policies of the Egyptian Muslim Brotherhood, will be published by the Council on Foreign Relations in 2002.

Dr Toby Dodge is an Associate Research Fellow of the Middle East Programme at RIIA. He received his PhD from the Politics Department at SOAS, on the transformation of the international system and the creation of the Iraqi state. He also taught Middle East Politics and International Relations at SOAS. He is now working on the political implications of globalization for the Middle East and the transformation of Iraq under sanctions. His most recent publications include 'The Social Ontology of Late Colonialism: Tribes and the Mandated State in Iraq', in Faleh Jabar and Hosham Dawod (eds), *Tribes and Power: Nationalism and Ethnicity in the Middle East* (Saqi, 2002); 'Iraq: Smart Sanctions and Beyond', *The World Today*, Vol. 57, No. 3, June 2001); and 'Iraq, Fragile Future', *The World Today* (Vol. 56, No. 1, January 2000). In 2003 he will publish a book on Iraq under sanctions with RIIA/Blackwell and one on the political evolution of Iraq with Routledge.

Professor Fred Halliday is Professor of International Relations at the London School of Economics and Political Science. His books include *The World at 2000: Perils and Promises* (Palgrave, 2001); *Nation and Religion in the Middle East* (Saqi, 1999); and *Islam and the Myth of Confrontation: Religion and Politics in the Middle East* (I.B. Tauris, 1996).

Professor Richard Higgott is Professor of International Political Economy and Director of the Economic and Social Research Council Centre for the study of Globalisation and Regionalisation at the University of Warwick. He has held previous chair-level appointments at the University of Manchester and in the Research School of Pacific and Asian Studies at the Australian National University, where he was Director of Graduate Studies in Foreign Affairs and Trade. He is the author/editor of 13 books or monographs and some 100 refereed articles and book chapters in the areas of international politics and development studies. Recent publications include *Non State Actors and Authority in the International System* (co-ed.) (Routledge, 2000); and, as co-editor with A. J. Payne, *The Political Economy of Globalisation*, 2 vols (Edward Elgar, 2000).

Dr Rosemary Hollis is Head of the Middle East Programme at RIIA where she is responsible for formulating and directing research projects and analysis on political, economic and security issues in the Middle East and North Africa. She gained her PhD in Political Science at George Washington

University. She taught Political Science and International Relations at George Washington University and was head of the Middle East Programme at RUSI. Her recent publications include *Managing New Developments in the Gulf* (ed.) (RIIA and Crown Prince Court Abu Dhabi, 2000); 'Barcelona's First Pillar: An Appropriate Concept for Security Relations?', in Sven Behrendt and Christian-Peter Hanelt (eds), *Security in the Middle East* (Bertelsmann, 2000); 'Sanctions or Dialogue?', in J. Mitchell (ed.), *Companies in a World of Conflict* (RIIA/Earthscan, 1998); and *Oil and Regional Developments in the Gulf* (ed.) (RIIA and Crown Prince Court, Abu Dhabi, 1998).

Dr Ali Tawfik Sadik is Director of the Economic Policy Institute, Arab Monetary Fund, United Arab Emirates. He received his PhD in Economics from North Carolina State University. He has held a number of economic and professional posts in Lebanon, Saudi Arabia, the USA, Kuwait and the United Arab Emirates. He previously worked for the Organisation of the Arab Oil Producing and Exporting Countries as a Senior Economist. He has produced over fifty studies in the areas of oil, fiscal, monetary and development policies, published in professional journals and books and edited seven books, the most recent of which is *Globalization and Managing National Economies* (2001).

Professor Rodney Wilson is Professor of Economics at the Institute for Middle Eastern and Islamic Studies, University of Durham. He was Chairman of the Council of the British Society for Middle Eastern Studies (1996–2000) and currently serves as Chairman of the Academic Committee of the Institute of Islamic Banking and Insurance in London. In 1998 he was a Visiting Fellow at the Islamic Research and Training Institute of the Islamic Development Bank in Jeddah. His recent books include *The Political Economy of the Middle East* (edited with Tim Niblock) (Edward Elgar, 1999); *Economics, Ethics and Religion: Jewish, Christian and Muslim Economic Thought* (Macmillan, 1997, reprinted 1998 and 2001); and *Economic Development in the Middle East* (Routledge, 1995). Recent articles include 'The Implications for Employment Conditions of Foreign Direct Investment in Saudi Arabia: Lessons from the Saudi Arabian Basic Industries Corporation' (with Abdullah Al-Salamah), *Managerial Finance* (Vol. 27, No. 10/11, 2001); 'New Regionalism and GCC Trade: New Directions', in Kevin Lawler and Hamid Seddighi (eds), *International Economics: Theories, Themes and Debates* (Prentice Hall, 2001); 'Business Ethics: Western and Islamic Perspectives', in Khaliq Ahmad and AbulHasan M. Sadeq (eds), *Ethics in Management and Business: Islamic and Main-*

stream Perspectives (ASEAN Academic Press, 2001); and 'EU–GCC Economic Relations: Towards a Free Trade Agreement and Beyond', in Christian-Peter Hanelt, Felix Neugart and Matthias Peitz (eds) (Bertelsmann Foundation, 2000).

Dr Mai Yamani is Associate Research Fellow of the Middle East Programme at RIIA and Research Associate at the Centre of Islamic and Middle Eastern Law at SOAS. She gained her DPhil in Social Anthropology at Oxford University. She taught social anthropology and sociology at the King Abdul Aziz University, Jeddah and was a Research Fellow at the Centre for Cross-Cultural Research on Women at Oxford University and Academic Adviser to the Centre for Contemporary Arab Studies at Georgetown University. Her most recent publications include *Changed Identities: The Challenge of the New Generation in Saudi Arabia* (RIIA, 2000); 'Muslim Women and Human Rights', in Eugene Cotran and Adel Omar Sherif (eds), *Democracy, the Rule of Law and Islam* (Kluwer Law Int., 1999); and 'The New Generation in the GCC: the Case of Saudi Arabia', in R. Hollis (ed.), *Oil and Regional Developments in the Gulf* (RIIA and Crown Prince Court, Abu Dhabi, 1998). Her latest book, *The Cradle of Islam: Hijazi Identity and the Making of Saudi Arabia,* will be published in 2002.

Introduction: '9/11', Islam, the Middle East and globalization

Toby Dodge

Since the attacks on the Pentagon and the World Trade Center in the United States on 11 September 2001, many thousands of words have been written in the Western media about the relationship between Islam, the Middle East and globalization. Much of this commentary has, of necessity, been quickly produced and speculative in nature. It has for the most part followed the lead given by former American Assistant Secretary of State James Rubin. Speaking on British television in the immediate aftermath of the assault, Rubin argued that this was not only a strike against America, but also an attack on civilization itself. In targeting the World Trade Center the perpetrators had attacked 'the centre of Western civilization where all the countries of the world trade in finance, industry, in all sorts of products'.[1] In the media, proposed responses to this 'attack on civilization' ranged from the ahistorical assertion of a Euro-centric liberalism calling for 'the restoration of religion to the sphere of the personal – its depoliticization' to calls for a new and active American imperialism based on the mandate system set up in the immediate aftermath of the First World War.[2]

What is striking and, on reflection, disturbing about this reportage was the lack of any historical or sociological understanding displayed by the media pundits when discussing the issues at stake.[3] In the rush to print and judgment it has proved all too easy to resort to clichéd stereotypes in the place of thoughtful and reasoned analysis. It is ironic that Samuel Huntington's 'clash of civilizations' thesis, largely pilloried on publication as post-Cold War paranoia, served as supposed intellectual analysis in the

---

[1] James Rubin, speaking on the BBC's Newsnight, 11 September 2001. Transcript available at *www.news.bbc.co.uk.*

[2] On the depoliticization of Islam see Salman Rushdie, 'On Islam versus Islamism', *The Guardian*, 3 November 2001: 'If terrorism is to be defeated, the world of Islam must take on board the secularist-humanist principles on which the modern is based.' On calls for an apparently liberal imperialism, see Niall Ferguson, 'Welcome the new imperialism', *The Guardian*, 31 October 2001.

[3] This is even more striking in that Ferguson is a Professor of History at Oxford University and should be acquainted with the very mixed heritage in the Middle East deriving from the mandate system.

aftermath of the attacks on New York and Washington.[4] The paucity of reasoned and historically grounded analysis makes it all the more important that those academics who have spent their professional lives studying and explaining the Middle East to a wider audience should take a central role in examining the nexus between Islam, globalization and the Middle East.

All but one of the chapters that make up this book were commissioned and largely drafted before the events of 11 September 2001. The analysis contained here is the outcome of many years of academic study and debate and not therefore a knee-jerk reaction to events as they have unfolded since that date. The chapters were born of a genuine concern among academics specializing in the study of the Middle East that a reasoned and nuanced debate had not taken place about the ongoing interaction between the cultural, political and economic effects of globalization and the states and societies of the Middle East. The events of 11 September highlight the prescience of this concern.

Most of the chapters in the book are the result of a series of workshops organized over the past two years across the Middle East and in London by the Middle East Programme of the Royal Institute of International Affairs, central among them a symposium, 'Globalization: Trends, Implications and Responses', held at the Crown Prince Court in Abu Dhabi in November 2000. The chapters by Toby Dodge, Richard Higgott, Rosemary Hollis, Ali Sadik and Mai Yamani originate from presentations at that event. Ali Ansari, Maha Azzam and Rodney Wilson were also asked to contribute chapters to the volume to make it more comprehensive. Finally, in the aftermath of 11 September, Fred Halliday kindly agreed to add an overview summing up the challenges and opportunities faced by the region in a globalized world.

In equating civilization with capitalism on the night of the attacks on America, James Rubin inadvertently highlighted the main issue at the heart of globalization and its effects on the Middle East. The primary cause of the current wave of globalization identified in the growing literature on the subject has been the phenomenal expansion in the size and influence of capital markets and the development of global manufacturing processes. Although the contributions in this book range across the Gulf region and the wider Middle East, focusing on politics, economics and society, they all take as their central theme the possible disjuncture between the history and culture of Middle Eastern societies and the remorseless advance in

---

[4] The thesis was first set out in Samuel P. Huntington, 'The Clash of Civilizations?', *Foreign Affairs*, Vol. 72, No. 3, 1993, pp. 22–49 and then expanded in Samuel P. Huntington, *The Clash of Civilizations and the Remaking of the World Order* (New York: Simon and Schuster, 1996). For criticisms see 'Responses to Huntington', *Foreign Affairs*, Vol. 72, No 4, 1993, pp. 2–26. See also Chapter 1 below.

global markets. The contributions as a whole provide a useful antidote to the 'top-down' approaches of the vast majority of international relations writing on the subject. In this book globalization is understood not primarily as a worldwide phenomenon transforming the Middle East but as a dialectical process in which the states and societies of the Middle East have a very definite proactive as well as reactive role to play.

The volume has been divided into three parts. A primary aim was to place the Middle East's experience of globalization into as wide a global context as possible. The three chapters in the first part do this by examining the social science literature on globalization and its relations to the Middle East, assessing the indigenous experience of globalization in historical perspective and considering how the region fits into the foreign policy concerns of Europe and the United States. Part II details the interaction between the states of the Gulf region and the cultural, economic and political forces of globalization. The final part takes a broader comparative look at the effects of globalization on the Arab states of the region.

In seeking to understand the dialectical interaction between the economics, politics, society and religion of the area and the forces of globalization, it is important to recognize the unique position of Israel. Economically and politically it offers a fascinating case study of a state's interaction with the global economy. The most industrialized country in the region, it is the most integrated into the world economy. However, this very fact sets it apart from its Arab neighbours. Its specific interaction with the dynamics of globalization demands much fuller explanation, which is outside the scope of this volume.

In Chapter 1, Toby Dodge and Richard Higgott set out the broad parameters within which debates on globalization and the Middle East are enacted. Developing the theme of local and international interaction, they contrast globalization with 'glocalization'. Glocalization is the hostile and sometimes violent reaction to the perceived threat of global capitalism. Religious and communal movements specific to a region deploy the technological fruits of globalization to fight against its negative effects, the weakening of specific cultures and identities. This chapter contrasts understandings of globalization in the developed North with those in the underdeveloped South. In the developing world and across the Middle East globalization is not seen as a universal or multi-causal process. Instead it is widely believed to be the re-empowerment of Western states, specifically the United States, in the aftermath of the Cold War. For the South, globalization has brought in its wake greater vulnerability to political and economic actors external to the region. Dodge and Higgott conclude by arguing that although globalization is a universal phenomenon, its causal effects are mediated by the geographic and cultural specificities of the societies with which it interacts.

In Chapter 2, Fred Halliday investigates the homogenization and fragmentation at the heart of globalization's interaction with the Middle East. He argues persuasively that the Middle East is not a region shaped by the atavistic forces of old but is instead very much the product of the modern world. The Middle East, far from being peripheral to the world economy, has suffered from its 'differential integration' into world markets. Over the nineteenth and twentieth centuries Middle Eastern societies have been transformed by the nature of this integration. People's lives have been revolutionized by economic change, rapid population movements and mass urbanization. Opponents of this hurried and disorientating modernization have deployed the religious certainties of Islam to rally populations badly let down by the secular promises of state-driven development. Halliday points out that although such redoubtable foes of Western domination such as Khomeini and Qadhdhafi have used Islamic rhetoric to rail against neo-imperialism, their calls for independence are part of a very modern political discourse. Islamic opposition to globalization draws on many of the same themes as nationalist left-wing opponents elsewhere in the developed and developing world. In short, he argues that the states and societies of the Middle East 'exist in the modern world, a world both globalizing and unequal' and their 'reaction to this process may be shaped only partially by religion, if at all'.

Rosemary Hollis, in Chapter 3, highlights the diminishing position of the Middle East in an increasingly globalized international system. For many years those living in the Middle East themselves and the great powers with interests in the area saw the region as distinct and in need of special attention. Hollis argues that the dynamics of globalization have the potential to marginalize the Middle East politically and economically. As the political and economic integration of developed countries continues apace, foreign policy-makers in Western Europe and the United States have begun to view the Middle East from a much wider perspective. Policy issues arising in the region that in the past might have been dealt with on a country-by-country basis are now handled in the multilateral institutions (the European Union, the United Nations Security Council or the World Trade Organization, for example) that have come to dominate international relations. Taking Britain's attitude to the Middle East as her main example, Hollis identifies a move away from the 'perceived historical responsibilities' of the post-colonial past to a new attitude in which the Middle East has a minor role in a set of global policy objectives. At the core of these policy objectives is the continued strength of the transatlantic link. Noting that there are not many votes to be won on Middle East issues, Hollis predicts that British foreign policy will continue to pursue influence in Washington as opposed to a regional policy in the Middle East. The result will be a foreign policy much more sensitive to US aims and objectives. The current 'war on terrorism' has confirmed this prediction. Although the personnel, finance and ideology behind the attacks of 11 September originated in the Middle East, the response quickly became global in its targets and ambitions. Once again the region has been subsumed in global responses to global problems.

The second part of the book, addressing the challenges that globalization poses for the states of the Gulf region, starts with a chapter by Ali Sadik that brings together a broad macroeconomic analysis of globalization with very detailed and valuable economic data from the states of the Gulf Cooperation Council (GCC). Sadik puts in perspective the position of the GCC within the world economy and details the policies needed for these economies to benefit from globalization. The economies of the GCC collectively produce less than one per cent of the world's income and contain half of one per cent of the world's population. These economies are also characterized by their vulnerability to the instabilities of the global economy, especially fluctuations in the demand for oil. Sadik argues that GCC governments have responded to their position within the world economy by liberalizing their trade regimes. However, as in the rest of the economies of the region, trade within the GCC bloc is low when compared with other regional blocs such as NAFTA and the EU. Sadik concludes that the export volatility and declining income levels of the past decade can be reversed only if the GCC states become much more competitive. For this to happen they 'need to exploit the interaction between trade, technology and productivity growth … in order to harness the benefits that globalization promises'.

In the aftermath of '9/11', the 'al-Jazira syndrome' has been transformed from a localized phenomenon affecting the states and societies of the Middle East to an issue of global importance impacting on the foreign policy decisions of the United States. In Chapter 5 Mai Yamani, in her extremely prescient contribution, explains the al-Jazira syndrome and why it has revolutionized the Arab media, mobilizing popular opinion and potentially threatening governments of the region. The influence of the Qatar-based al-Jazira satellite television channel is the culmination of a decade-long growth in globalized transnational Arab electronic media. Yamani argues that the advent of satellite television, especially the highly professional output of al-Jazira, heralds a new stage in the development of 'the imagined community of Arabs' which is crucial for the growth of Arab nationalism. The frank political discussions broadcast on al-Jazira have highlighted the dull and censored output of national government-controlled television. Yamani argues they have also encouraged trans-state communication among Arabs, enhancing the relative importance of a pan-Arab identity. She focuses on al-Jazira's coverage of the al-Aqsa Intifada that began in September 2000. However, what she has to say is equally, if not more, applicable to the US 'war on terrorism' in the aftermath of 11 September. By broadcasting high-impact visual images of Palestinian suffering, al-Jazira circumvented state control of the media and helped fuel a sense of moral outrage among those Arabs who had access to satellite television. The 'Arab street', popular opinion across the region, was mobilized by comparatively unfettered access to news of Palestinian suffering. Yamani argues that this has resulted in the creation of a new public sphere where Arabs are able to 'share in the painful experiences of the intifada'. The development of this pan-Arab extra-territorial identity has powerful ramifications for non-democratic states trying to control their population's access to information.

The final contribution in Part II is by Ali Ansari. In Chapter 6 he develops one of the central themes of the book, that of the interaction between the local and the international at the heart of globalization. He contrasts globalization with the historical experience of imperialism, arguing that the former allows for much greater reciprocity, especially in the field of cultural consumption. Taking Iran as his case study Ansari argues that massive emigration in the wake of the 1979 revolution and the continued need for trade during the Iran-Iraq war overcame the isolationist strands of some of Khomeini's preaching. Today all political factions in the struggle for power in Iran use the Internet to promote their cause. At the core of the political debate is the role of Islam and Iran in the world. Ansari argues that in the key battleground of culture there is a growing realization that the best way forward is to engage with the forces of globalization, attempting to reshape them in a way that suits Iranian society. Iranian intellectuals, at the heart of the current conflict, seek to understand Western ideas, especially political philosophy, and then refashion them in a way that will appeal to the Iranian population they are seeking to win over to their cause. The hoped-for result is the growth of a cosmopolitan Islamic philosophy, confident enough to engage with the secular forces of globalized culture, taking what it finds useful and rejecting the rest.

Moving away from the specifics of the Gulf, Part III takes a more broadly comparative approach, assessing how globalization has affected the culture, economics and politics of the Arab states in the wider region. Chapter 7, by Maha Azzam, analyses in detail the religious and political philosophy of several important Arab Islamic activists. She points out that contemporary assertions of political Islam are themselves 'part of the struggle with modernity, and both an outcome of it and a response to it'. The thinkers espousing political Islam may deploy a rich historical legacy but they are guided by very modern ideological approaches. They have capitalized on the fact that the majority of Muslims in the Middle East have not seen an improvement in their economic situation over the past decade and may feel more insecure and vulnerable to the uncertainties of the market than they did in the immediate aftermath of independence. Azzam makes the powerful point that the Westernization of Muslim societies is nothing new but has been a continuous process for the past century. What separates today's Islamists from their predecessors is the speed and reach of the globalization to which they are reacting and the poor economic performance across the region on which they are capitalizing. In societies where the defence of religious principles is a powerful rallying call, attacks on a secularizing globalization have struck a chord with many. Azzam concludes that radical Islamic groups are the product of modern political dynamics. The social space in which they operate and the support they garner are as much about the governmental policies of political repression and economic failure as about a desire to return to a re-imagined Islamic past.

Toby Dodge, in Chapter 8, examines the liberal economic assumptions behind much of globalization theory. These focus on the rise of a supposedly transnational economic and political culture in the aftermath of the Cold War. This is understood to bring in its wake the transformation of the state and its relations with society. The growth in the power and reach of financial markets undermined the autonomy of states everywhere, forcing them to adopt neo-liberal, market-friendly policies. But Dodge makes the point that markets in both the developed and the developing world bear the historical legacy of having been created by the governments within whose territory they operate. In the Arab states this historical legacy has left a weak and state-dependent bourgeoisie. The economic autonomy of these states was certainly curtailed by both the collapse of the oil price in the mid-1980s and the growing domination of the United States in the mid-1990s. However, the republican regimes of the *Mashreq* (the Arab world east of Libya) did not conform to the predictive logic of liberal globalization theory. Economically they reduced their role in the domestic markets, cutting back on subsidies and welfare programmes. The regimes in Syria, Egypt and Iraq have fought hard to preserve their autonomy from both society and the international system and as a result they 'brought the bourgeoisie back in'. Faced with an economic crisis, these regimes sought new sources of revenue by allowing the indigenous capitalists to become junior members of the ruling elite. This has brought about not the birth of liberal democracy but instead the rise of a liberal authoritarianism. The state has retreated from the economic sphere in order to guarantee its continued domination of the political. This process has been marked by continued if not increased repression of those within society who are brave enough to voice dissent.

The final chapter, by Rodney Wilson, compares and contrasts the effects of economic globalization on two key states: Egypt and Saudi Arabia. Like many authors in this volume, Wilson places contemporary globalization in its historical context, arguing that although states in the Middle East have had their economic sovereignty constrained this is nothing new. He argues that this still leaves the states of the region with 'much freedom of manoeuvre and discretion'. Developing a theme common to the book as a whole, Wilson identifies the growth of 'global communities of difference' that under globalization have been reinvigorated and invested with 'new meaning by a diverse array of trans-border solidarities'. The community of difference on which Wilson focuses consists of Islamic economists trying to develop indigenous theories of economics to combat the negative effects inherent in globalization. Wilson contrasts the prescriptions of Islamic economists with those of the Saudi and Egyptian governments. He concludes that globalization has forced a different, rather than reduced, role on Arab governments. States have become very skilled in protecting the vested interests of the national economic elites whose support is crucial for the regimes to remain in power. His conclusion may stand for the book as a whole: 'In a region with long experience of the rise and fall of many external civilizations, globalization, which many there equate with Americanization, may be only a passing phase.'

In the aftermath of '9/11', 'Islam' was placed at the heart of the analysis: key to explanations and hoped-for solutions. According to a variety of pundits Islam had declared war against America, globalization and civilization itself. A much deeper historical perspective is needed for a more nuanced understanding of the causes and consequences of the 11 September attacks. In the Middle East, in the period immediately preceding these events, globalization had to interact with states in the midst of both financial and political crises. As a result unpopular regimes in the region faced political opposition movements calling for a 'return' to Islamic forms of government and drawing their support from those sections of the population that have benefited least from the Middle East's interaction with global markets. This does not represent a set of societies or a culture seeking to avoid modernity but a population that has suffered from economic decline and political mismanagement turning to those who appear to offer a political alternative to corruption and repression. The nature of political repression in the Middle East meant that the mosque or religious charitable organizations offered the only vestiges of civil society. They acted as one of the few areas within society not repressed or co-opted by the state. It is hardly surprising, then, that political opposition to the ruling regimes coalesced around those promoting a religious message. The United States, in building its coalition to fight global terrorism, has turned to the very states in the Middle East that have experienced economic failure and political suppression. In return for joining the coalition various states, not least Egypt, have been granted further licence to ignore human and democratic rights. If the coalition built to eject Iraq from Kuwait is any precedent, then they will also be granted generous debt relief. Pakistan and Turkey have been among the early beneficiaries of US appreciation. In short, America's war against terrorism may not tackle the root causes of the resentment that resulted in the attacks; in the long run it may even have deepened them.

PART I
The Middle East in Global Perspective

1 Globalization and its discontents: the theory and practice of change in the Middle East

Toby Dodge and Richard Higgott

Introduction

In September 1999, the British supermarket chain Sainsbury's launched its first shop outside Britain and the US. The store was one of a hundred that the company opened in and around Cairo in less than two years. At the time, Sainsbury's venture into the Egyptian consumer market was heralded as a triumph of globalization. Starting in Egypt, but with plans to expand across the Middle East, one of Britain's leading companies was exporting mass retail consumerism into the heart of what had previously appeared to be a very different culture. Sainsbury's, unrestrained by artificial barriers to trade, could now sell to the individual consumer wherever she or he had the money to buy what was desired.

Within two years the triumphant tone of those promoting this as an example of globalization appeared to have been misplaced. By May 2001, Sainsbury's had sold its 81.1 per cent stake in its Egyptian venture back to its local partners, with an estimated loss of £100–150 million.[1] The company said it had decided to focus on its core business in Britain in order to boost profits. Its chairman cited the 'hostile environment' of Egypt's retail sector, along with the 'deterioration of the trading environment in the Middle East', as aggravating factors. 'There are lessons to be learned from our experiences in Egypt. We tried to do too much, too soon.'[2]

Sainsbury's had run into unforeseen political obstacles in Cairo and across the wider Middle East. Initially the supermarket's policy of aggressive pricing caused resentment among owners of small shops. The small traders enlisted the help of local mosques in their battle with the multinational

---

[1] See Andrew Murray-Watson, 'Sell-off sees Sainsbury on the rise', *The Financial Times*, 10 April 2001.

[2] Sainsbury's Chief Executive Peter Davis, quoted by Simon Bowers, 'Protests force Sainsbury's out of Egypt with £125m loss', *The Guardian*, 10 April 2000; Niveen Wahish, 'Clearing its shelves?', *Al-Ahram* weekly on-line, 21–27 December 2000; and Aziza Sami, 'Supermarketing hysterics', *Al-Ahram* weekly on-line, 19–25 April 2001.

giant. The result was preaching that equated shopping at Sainsbury's with adultery and drug-trafficking.[3] But the problems for Sainsbury's became much more serious when there was renewed violence between Palestinians and Israelis in autumn 2000. Although not connected to the conflict, Sainsbury's, as a potent symbol of Western consumerism, suffered from the general rise in the political temperature. The General Egyptian Committee for the Boycott of Zionist and American Products organized a boycott of Sainsbury's, and some of its stores suffered violent attacks.[4]

Sainsbury's brief but expensive experiment in Middle Eastern retailing proved to be not a triumph but a sobering lesson of 'glocalization'. 'Glocalization' involves the cultural and historical sensibilities specific to a region that are amplified and disseminated by global technology but that often act in opposition to the universalizing forces of globalization. This example raises important questions about globalization's effects on the developing world and, more specifically, the interaction between the politics, economy and culture of the Middle East and the international forces of globalization.

Globalization: a framework for understanding

As the example of Sainsbury's and Egypt highlights, globalization has become the most overused and underspecified concept in the lexicon of modern social science. It has become a key ideological catchword that has replaced the notion of the 'Cold War' as an organizing principle of international life. As such its utility, indeed its very existence, is contested, argued about and often resisted. But although it is faddish and its usage is overburdened with ideological baggage, it is certainly real; and although there are historical continuities with ages gone by, globalization does mark a break with the past.

Globalization is a multifaceted and complex phenomenon. Reducing it to a set of simple arguments for and against could do harm to reality. The most readily identified aspect of globalization in the economic domain has been the increasing level of global trade integration and the rapid growth in the movement of capital that occurred in the closing decades of the twentieth century. Turnovers in currency markets now far exceed the global stocks of foreign exchange reserves, and have been a major source of global financial instability in recent years.

[3] See Mona Eltahawy, 'Pyramid Selling', *The Guardian*, 13 April 2000.
[4] See Sami, 'Supermarketing hysterics', and Amira Howeidy, 'Secure a victory and move on', *Al-Ahram* weekly on-line, 26 April–2 May 2001.

In political and social affairs the trends towards globalization are more complex but no less significant. There is much talk about the globalization (or often Americanization) of culture (MacWorld) but, conversely, we are also witnessing the 'glocalization' of many sectors of society as they attempt to re-establish local identities weakened by globalization. New technologies, notably the Internet, not only advance economic interdependence but also make possible the empowerment, or at least stir the aspirations, of minorities around the globe. These new identities accompany and complicate but do not eradicate existing nationalisms. Labour migration both to and from Europe and around the developing world, along with modern air travel, ensure the continuous expansion of 'hybrid peoples' with multiple identities. Globalization should be seen as a set of complex and contingent economic, technological, political, social, cultural and behavioural processes and practices that increasingly transcend jurisdictional and territorial barriers. These processes lack uniformity and are not inevitable or irreversible. As events in Seattle in 1999 and or in Genoa in 2001 have shown, economic processes driven by globalization and states' attempts to regulate them are generating increasing resistance by the very manner of their development.

It is within the Third World, which has 80–85 per cent of the world's population, that globalization's rhetorical promise of improved economic circumstances succeeds or fails.[5] However, the states of the Middle East and the wider developing world are united by a common perception that they share a much greater vulnerability to external forces, both economic and political, than the developed states of the North. Born of the post-colonial predicament and heightened by the effects of the Cold War, this sense of vulnerability appears to have been heightened by the effects of globalization.

Increasingly, academics and commentators point up a division between the theoretical explanations of globalization and how it is experienced in the everyday lives of people in the Middle East, between the ideological promotion of globalization and its cultural, political and economic effects. Governments in the developing world blame their heightened feelings of insecurity under globalization in large part on the rise of neo-liberal economics. It is, they claim, the adoption of neo-liberal policy prescriptions by the Bretton Woods international funding institutions (IFIs), the World Bank and the International Monetary Fund (IMF), that has weakened

---

[5] See Mohammed Ayoob, 'Subaltern Realism: International Relations Theory Meets the Third World', in Stephanie G. Neuman (ed.), *International Relations Theory and the Third World* (New York: St Martin's Press, 1998), p. 37; and Caroline Thomas, 'Where is the Third World Now?', *Review of International Studies*, Special Issue, Vol. 25, December 1999, p. 227.

their sovereignty and reduced their ability to influence their own societies.[6] In the unipolar post-Cold War world where the bargaining power of the non-aligned movement has been greatly reduced, politicians in the developing countries see the rise in influence of neo-liberal policy prescriptions as a direct attack on their states' sovereignty and their own autonomy.

The division between the ideology and the effects of globalization is at the heart of divergent understandings of globalization. Explanations of it by Western-based academics tend to stress its impersonal and universal effects. The lack of authority within the international economy means that its negative effects tend to reach all states, if not equally. Interpretations of globalization that originate in the Middle East see it not as a universal and multi-causal process but as the rejuvenation of Western, specifically American, dominance in the post-Cold War world.[7]

It is possible to provide a framework within which to identify the main elements of globalization by asking six questions and highlighting six areas of research. First, there is the question of *definition*. Why is there no settled definition? What are the central arguments in favour of it and against it? Secondly, the *extent* of the phenomenon: how much globalization is there, and what are the meaningful indicators of its presence and effects? Thirdly, *timescale or evolution*: is globalization new? If so, when did it start, and where is it heading? Fourthly, *causation*: how do we explain the development of globalization? What are the main agents of change? Who and what are the principal actors and agencies involved in this new 'great game' of the late twentieth and the early twenty-first century? Fifthly, *consequences*: are we heading for convergence or divergence in the global economic and political order? How is globalization affecting the policy-making capabilities of nominally sovereign states? Finally, there is the question of *responses*. Are international governmental agencies the best organizations to control and direct the international economy? At a national level, what are the principal policy problems raised for governments in the Middle East? At a societal level, how should individuals, communities and groups across the world react to globalization? If state institutions are being redefined by globalization, can populations in the Middle East adopt a new relationship with their governments? Does globalization, as some of the more optimistic liberals claim, empower individuals at the expense of their states?

---

[6] See, for example, *The Constitutive Act of African Union: The Millennium Partnership for the African Recovery Programme*, launched by the member states of the Organization of African Unity in July 2001, especially p. 21.

[7] Tim Niblock, *'Pariah States' & Sanctions in the Middle East: Iraq, Libya, Sudan* (Boulder, CO: Lynne Rienner Publishers, 2001), p. 5.

Given the different experiences and understandings of globalization across the world, the growing feeling of vulnerability and the perception that the ideological promise of globalization is not being met, the framework within which to understand globalization – the questions of definition, extent, timescale or evolution, causation, consequences and responses – can give rise to very different answers.

Definition

There is no one settled or agreed definition of globalization, merely a range of more or less plausible understandings. Most common understandings equate globalization with internationalization. This, in turn, is a synonym for increased interdependence and exchanges across borders. Economic explanations of globalization stress the impact of the deregulation (the reduction of state-imposed barriers) of trade in goods, services and financial flows, growing economic integration and often the privatization of public assets. Along with the increased flow of ideas, knowledge, experiences and information, globalization is thus also seen as synonymous with 'liberalization'.

Those in the developing world and beyond who wish to challenge this definition highlight the fact that it largely underplays or ignores the power relations at work in the globalizing process. The deregulation and liberalization of trade have been forced upon weaker states by the Bretton Woods institutions and by international economic regulations. States in the developing world have often been the unwilling recipients of increased trade flows, and argue that the benefits of this process are far from universal or uncontested.

The second issue at the heart of the contested definition of globalization is the 'convergence' thesis or the effect of increasing transnational flows in information and culture on different communities around the world.[8] Typified by Francis Fukuyama's 'end of history' thesis, this argues that globalization is a normatively good thing and represents the triumph of capitalism and democracy.[9] On closer examination, the brand of democracy and capitalism being championed as universal is a very specific, Anglo-Saxon one. It is the liberal democracy of John Locke, not Jean-Jacques Rousseau, and the brand of capitalist relations favoured by Milton Friedman, not John Maynard Keynes.[10]

[8] For an example of this thesis see Richard Falk, 'Will Globalization Win Out?', *International Affairs*, Vol. 73, No. 1, 1997, p. 129.
[9] Francis Fukuyama, *The End of History and the Last Man* (Harmondsworth: Penguin, 1993).
[10] Richard Higgott, 'Globalisation and Regionalization: New Trends in World Politics', *Emirates Lecture 13* (Abu Dhabi: Emirates Centre for Strategic Studies and Research, 1998), p. 31.

The normative argument that convergence is good in and of itself is questionable. The communications revolution that has, through satellite and computer technology, spread Western liberal culture across the Middle East is proving to be a double-edged sword. The reaction to an alien and seemingly hegemonic culture has proved to be militant and often destabilizing to the ruling regimes of the area. The vehicle of new technology that has been used to spread Western culture has in turn been used to counter it. By using new media, previously disjointed Islamic communities have been able to spread their own message to a wider transnational community, citing the alleged negative effects of globalization as the centrepiece of an urgent call to defend existing identities.[11] The result is a resurgence of religious and communal identities mobilizing against what they see as the effects of globalization. 'Globalization … is a process consisting of, on the one hand, the "particularization of universalism", that is rendering the world a single place, and on the other the "universalization of particularism" or the globalized expectation that societies should have distinct identities.'[12]

The normative teleology of the 'convergence' thesis is greeted in the Middle East in two ways. First, it is pointed out that universalization often brings overly materialist and individualist economic and cultural creeds. It is argued that this process, Americanization for short, is 'disembedding' the cultural commonalities key to providing social harmony and community. The ills of modernity, selfishness, dislocation and the atomization of society are, it is also argued, sweeping across the Middle East in the wake of trade liberalization and economic interdependence.[13]

Secondly, the most abstract and difficult, but in the long run probably the most important, understanding of globalization sees it as progressive 'deterritorialization'. In this idea geography, space, place, distance and borders, affected by the revolution in technology, cease to be significant barriers to communication. This is not the same as saying that territory no longer matters. Clearly it does, especially with regard to the availability of resources or to feelings of identity. Rather, deterritorialization suggests that for many people there is an added dimension to their life above and beyond the geographic.[14]

---

[11] Jeff Haynes, 'Introduction', in Jeff Haynes (ed.), *Religion, Globalization and Political Culture in the Third World* (London: Macmillan Press, 1998), p. 4.

[12] Vicky Randall, 'The Media and Religion in Third World Politics', in Haynes (ed.), *Religion, Globalisation and Political Culture in the Third World*, p. 50.

[13] For a detailed discussion of this, see Farhang Rajaee, *Globalisation on Trial: The Human Condition and the Information Civilization* (West Hartford, CT: Kumarian Press, 2000), pp. 103–7.

[14] See for examples of this argument David Held, Anthony McGrew, David Goldblatt and Jonathan Perraton, *Global Transformations, Politics, Economics and Culture* (Cambridge: Polity Press, 1999); and J.A. Scholte, *Globalisation: A Critical Introduction* (Basingstoke: Palgrave, 2000). For a trenchant critique of this see Justin Rosenberg, *The Follies of Globalisation Theory. Polemical Essays* (London: Verso, 2000).

The posited end result of deterritorialization is the interaction of individuals and groups with global markets, with a much reduced role for states. But deterritorialization as a process without reference to the different histories of the states involved is problematic. And the danger of time–space compression, or the 'end' of geography, is that it will replace the traditional division within the world economy – that between a wealthy set of Northern states and a poor set of Southern states – with another, even more inequitable one: the divide between those individuals who can participate in the new global economy and those who are left behind or excluded from it.[15]

In the post-colonial Middle East the primary role of the state was to take the lead role in the economic development of society and to shield its population from the vagaries and instabilities of the market and provide a social safety net against market failure.[16] In spite of the very mixed record of Middle Eastern states in fulfilling this role, the fear is that if deterritorialization continues at an increasing rate, these states will have little or no role to play in development. Despite deterritorialization the great majority of the world's poor will still be in the post-colonial states of the South, and their governments will have little or no power to lead them away from the periphery of the world economy.

As Fukuyama's 'end of history' thesis represents the triumphant celebration of the victory of neo-liberal economics, so Samuel Huntington's 'clash of civilizations' thesis is an attempt to deal with the opposition to globalization and its rationalist liberal philosophy.[17] Huntington's thesis has been widely criticized for its pessimistic if not paranoid conclusions.[18] It is certainly simplistic and highly problematic, both in its use of evidence and in its understanding of the cause and effect of modernity. But his work offers an example of how those promoting globalization perceive Middle Eastern and Islamic culture.

Although Huntington lists five or possibly six non-Western civilizations that could come into conflict with the West, it is Islam that appears to pose

---

[15] Ankie Hoogvelt, *Globalization and the Postcolonial World: The New Political Economy of Development*, 2nd edn. (London: Palgrave, 2001), p. 143.

[16] See David Williams, 'Aid and sovereignty: quasi-states and the international financial institutions', *Review of International Studies*, Vol. 26, No. 4, October 2000, pp. 557–73; and Robert Cox, 'Global Restructuring: Making Sense of the Changing International Political Economy', in Richard Stubbs and Geoffrey R. Underhill (eds), *Political Economy and the Changing Global Order* (Basingstoke: Macmillan, 1994), pp. 45–55.

[17] The thesis was first set out in Samuel P. Huntington, 'The Clash of Civilizations?', *Foreign Affairs*, Vol. 72, No. 3, 1993, pp. 22–49 and then expanded in Samuel P. Huntington, *The Clash of Civilizations and the Remaking of the World Order* (New York: Simon and Schuster, 1996).

[18] See 'Responses to Huntington', *Foreign Affairs*, Vol. 72, No 4, 1993, pp. 2–26.

the immediate threat to Western interests.[19] That Huntington should select Islam generally and the Middle East specifically as the major post-Cold War adversary of the US and its Western allies should come as no surprise. The Middle East has long occupied the position of the negative 'other' to Western society, allowing the West to define its own identity by projecting onto the Middle East all that it does not want to be.[20] In this way it is easy to portray the Middle East as an unchanging and dangerous barrier to globalization.

Since the Iranian revolution of 1979 with its anti-Western rhetoric and Islamic radicalism, the Middle East has become the *bête noire* of those trying to gauge the spread of globalization by identifying economic integration, 'zones of peace' and the growth of rationalistic liberal sentiment. Ayatollah Khomeini's proclamation of a fatwa against the author Salman Rushdie for blasphemy was portrayed in Britain as a direct attack on the liberal traditions of humanism in the arts. Hizbullah's use of suicide bombing to expel Israel's army from southern Lebanon, the collapse of Algeria into civil war, attacks on tourists by Islamic radicals in Egypt, the rise of the Taliban in Afghanistan and, finally, the failure of the peace process between Israel and the Palestinians have all been cited as examples of a region constrained by the dominance of religion, untouched by the positive effects of globalization and the end of the Cold War.[21]

In spite of persuasive arguments that put the rise of Islamic radicalism in its sociological, historical and ultimately secular context,[22] it was easier to play to dominant stereotypes that portrayed the Middle East as unchanging, irrational and dominated by Islam. A closer look at the region over the past 30 years, and especially since the end of the Cold War, shows Middle Eastern states and societies struggling to deal with changing strategic, economic and political circumstances.

Although the political and economic changes since 1990 have not brought the wholesale transformation that some would have liked, the region's interaction with the processes of globalization is nonetheless producing

[19] Huntington lists 'Western, Confucian, Japanese, Islamic, Hindu, Slavic-Orthodox, Latin American and possibly African civilization'. See Huntington, 'Clash of Civilizations?', p. 29.
[20] See Edward W. Said, *Orientalism: Western Conceptions of the Orient* (London: Penguin Books, 1991). For a cogent examination and critique of Said's work, see James Clifford, *The Predicament of Culture: Twentieth-Century Ethnography, Literature, and Art* (Cambridge, MA: Harvard University Press, 1988), pp. 255–76.
[21] See Neil Smith, 'The Satanic Geographies of Globalisation: Uneven Development in the 1990s', *Public Culture*, Vol. 10, No. 1, p. 172. For an extended discussion of the link between modernization theory, secularism and Islam, see Ali M. Ansari, *Iran, Islam and Democracy: The Politics of Managing Change* (London: Royal Institute of International Affairs, 2000), pp. 11–18.
[22] See especially Charles Tripp, 'Islam and the Secular Logic of the State in the Middle East', in A. Ehteshami and A.S. Sidahmed (eds), *Islamic Fundamentalism* (Boulder, CO: Westview Press, 1996).

dynamic and far-reaching change. There has been a powerful interaction between states, societies and peoples in the region and the forces of globalization. This means that the Middle East provides a difficult but potentially productive case by which to judge the interaction of local and regional factors with international trends. However, in examining this interaction it is all too easy to get the balance wrong between the local and the international or between the political, the economic and the cultural. Globalization is certainly an international phenomenon, but its causal effects are mediated by the geographic and cultural specifics of the societies with which it interacts.

Extent

Throughout the 1990s the issue of scale evoked heated contention among analysts and practitioners alike. The debate ranged across the spectrum, from the 'hyper-globalists' such as Kenichi Ohmae, who see the world economy well on the way to integration, to the 'globalization sceptics', led by Paul Hirst and Graham Thompson.[23] The sceptics argued that globalization is little more than the ideology of the modern global corporate managerial elite. The global economy was barely more open at the end of the twentieth century than it was at the end of the nineteenth. Fortunately, we have moved beyond this polarization of argument.

Data refute the position of the 'globalization sceptics'. Over the past 20 years the level of capital flows across state borders has been the lead indicator of globalization.[24] Driven by a combination of technological advancement and deregulation, financial flows leaped from approximately $200 million per day in the mid-1980s to $1.5 trillion per day in the late 1990s. The power of the financial markets has now escaped the ability of any single state to control it.[25] In the wake of capital mobility, international trade, foreign direct investment (FDI) and other cross-border transfers across the range of human, economic, technological, cultural and social experience are now greater than ever.[26] On the other hand, the wilder

[23] Kenichi Ohmae, *The Borderless World* (London: Fontana, 1990) and Paul Hirst and Grahame Thompson, *Globalization in Question*, 2nd edn (Cambridge: Polity Press, 1999).
[24] Roger Tooze, 'International Political Economy in an Age of Globalisation', in John Baylis and Steve Smith (eds), *The Globalization of World Politics: An Introduction to International Relations* (Oxford: Oxford University Press, 1998), p. 223.
[25] Richard Higgott, 'Economic Globalisation and Global Governance: Towards a Post-Washington Consensus?', in V. Rittberger and A. Schnabel (eds), *The United Nations Global Governance System in the Twenty-first Century* (Tokyo: United Nations Press, 2000).
[26] 'Global production sharing now involves more than $800 billion in trade in manufactured produce annually, representing at least 30% of the world's trade in such products.' Rajaee, *Globalisation on Trial*, p. 82.

claims of the 'hyper-globalists' about the demise of the state as the principal seat of authority and sovereignty remain grossly overstated.

One of the essential issues concerning scale is the uneven spread of globalization and the degree to which the discrepancies between 'winners' and 'losers' have been exacerbated over the past 20 years. On the evidence from these two decades, globalization has delivered very mixed results, alleviating the worst degrees of poverty while exacerbating economic inequality in and among states. Of the conflicting evidence, the best data identify a clear growth in global income gaps since the end of the Second World War. And the income gap ratio between the 20 per cent of the world's population in the richest countries and the 20 per cent in the poorest countries grew from 30:1 in 1990 to 74:1 in 1995. The world's poorest 20 per cent account for only one per cent of total global GDP.

The undoubted growth of a transnational economy has not spread evenly across the globe. Transnational economic activity occurs largely in three areas: Europe, North America and East Asia. Within these areas 85 per cent of world trade and 90 per cent of technologically advanced production take place.[27] Other indicators point to the geographical stratification of the global economy. By 2000, for example, Internet populations by region were roughly as follows: North America, 160 million; Europe, 69 million; Asia–Oceania, 41.9 million; and Africa and Latin America combined, 8 million. The geographically divided scale of globalization highlights the weakness of the states and populations of the developing world. Under globalization, economies in the Middle East risk being further marginalized from the wealth-generating process as the needed education and technology move further away from their grasp.

If access to globalization depends on the openness of economies to international trade and hence economic development, then the Middle East is in danger of being left behind. After the growth of the economies of the Middle East and North Africa during the oil boom of the 1970s, the region faced an economic slump in the 1980s and experienced only very moderate growth in the 1990s.[28]

In a global economy the region's ability to attract foreign direct investment is crucial to its future development. During the past 20 years the developing

[27] Michael Mann, 'Has globalisation ended the rise and rise of the nation-state?', *Review of International Political Economy*, Vol. 4, No. 3, Autumn 1997, p. 480.

[28] According to Hassan Hakimian, real Gross National Product fell by about 2.4 per cent per annum during the 1980s. The 1990s witnessed only a moderate recovery, with growth estimated at about 0.5 per cent. See Hassan Hakimian, 'From MENA to East Asia and Back: Lessons of Globalisation, Crisis and Economic Reform', in Hassan Hakimian and Ziba Moshaver (eds), *The State and Global Change: The Political Economy of Transition in the Middle East and North Africa* (Richmond, Surrey: Curzon Press, 2001), pp. 82–3.

world's share of FDI has risen sharply, from 17.4 per cent from 1985 to 1990 to 36.4 per cent in 1994–6. The Middle East and North Africa's share of this is very small. Most FDI has flowed into the economies of Asia, leaving an average annual investment in the Middle East of only $2.5 billion. In 1994–6 this amounted to less than one per cent of global FDI.[29]

The low level of economic performance and of FDI in the Middle East results in part from regional governments' policies. Dependence on oil exports for foreign currency has led them to neglect other sectors of the economy: between 90 and 100 per cent of export earnings in oil-producing countries comes from oil.[30] But how these export revenues have been invested has shaped the region's economies too. It is estimated that for every $100 of oil revenues Middle Eastern states earn from the West, $40 is sent back in arms deals while another $40 is reinvested in Western banks and stock markets.[31] If Middle Eastern governments do not invest in their own economies, it is easy to understand why FDI is relatively scarce. The liberalizing and opening up of Middle Eastern economies has been slow too. The Middle East's position in indices of economic openness actually declined between the 1970s and the 1990s.[32] This was accompanied by very limited government moves to privatize state-owned industries.[33]

After the flow of investment and finance, it is the flow of ideas that is a key marker of globalization. The rise of anti-Western, anti-liberal Islamic radicalism would appear to indicate that Middle Eastern societies are somehow hostile to globalization. In fact, the rise of Islamic radicalism can be explained in part not by the rejection of modernity but by the failure of regimes to deliver on their promises of economic development. The modernizing policies of the post-independence regimes certainly produced rapid urbanization and an expansion in education and those directly employed by the state, but they also resulted in a decline in agricultural production and in urban poverty, unemployment and corruption. The result has been cynicism and resentment towards incumbent regimes and a rise in support for the Islamic opposition. To portray this as a movement against modernization itself is to misunderstand its genesis and motivation. It is the expression of an anger directed against what is seen as the failed policies and corruption of unrepresentative regimes. This is often combined with

[29] See ibid., pp. 88–9 and Yezid Sayigh, 'Globalisation Manqué, Regional Fragmentation and Authoritarian-Liberalism in the Middle East', in Louise Fawcett and Yezid Sayigh (eds), *The Third World Beyond the Cold War: Continuity and Change* (Oxford: Oxford University Press, 1999), p. 215.
[30] Massoud Karshenas, 'Structural Obstacles to Economic Adjustment in the MENA Region: The International Trade Aspects', in Hakimian and Moshaver (eds), *The State and Global Change*, p. 69.
[31] Ankie Hoogvelt, *Globalisation and the Postcolonial World*, p. 210.
[32] Hakimian, 'From MENA to East Asia and Back', p. 89.
[33] See Sayigh, 'Globalisation Manqué', p. 216.

arguments against the hypocrisy of the West in its dealings with Israel or against the perceived dominance of United States in the region.[34] To claim that the Middle East has somehow rejected modernity or is hostile to liberal ideals is to ignore the history of the region.

The final gauge of globalization concerns the arguments about deterritorialization, the idea that geography and borders are no longer barriers to communications and trade and thus partially lose their political prominence. This argument is often linked to the perceived demise of geopolitics and to the low utility of war in a post-Cold War world dominated by trade and the global market.[35] Evidence of deterritorialization (or lack of it) in the Middle East is linked in part to the nature of the regional economies and their integration in the world economy. The oil boom of the 1970s tended to integrate the economy of each oil-producing state into the world economy individually. The legacy of this development can be seen in the distinct lack of regional economic integration. Inter-Arab trade amounts to less than 10 per cent of the region's total trade.[36]

The lack of regional economic integration can also be explained by the historical fragility of state sovereignty in the Middle East. From independence until the mid-1970s the power of transnational and sub-state ideologies meant that states in the region had to fight very hard to maintain their political independence.[37] The division of the Arab 'nation' into sovereign states was seen as an unwelcome legacy of colonial intervention.[38] It is understandable in these circumstances that attempts at regional economic integration and policy coordination have foundered on the fears of each state for its national sovereignty.[39]

The link between deterritorialization, economic integration and the lack of sovereign legitimacy also offers a partial explanation as to why war continues to be so prevalent in the region. The dispute between Israel and its Arab neighbours and now between Israel and the Palestine National Authority is rooted in the lack of acceptance both of the norm of sovereign non-interference, and of borders themselves, across the region. Territorial

---

[34] See Niblock, *'Pariah States' & Sanctions*, pp. 8–10.

[35] Mark W. Zacher, 'The Decaying Pillars of the Westphalian Temple: Implications for International Order and Governance', in James N. Rosenau and Ernest-Otto Czemiel (eds), *Governance Without Government: Order and Change in World Politics* (Cambridge: Cambridge University Press, 1992), p. 67.

[36] Sayigh, 'Globalisation Manqué', p. 207.

[37] See Michael C. Hudson, *Arab Politics: The Search for Legitimacy* (New Haven, CT: Yale University Press, 1977).

[38] See Michael Barnett, 'Sovereignty, nationalism, and regional order in the Arab state system', in Thomas J. Biersteker and Cynthia Weber (eds), *State Sovereignty as a Social Construct* (Cambridge: Cambridge University Press, 1996).

[39] See Michael Hudson (ed.), *Middle East Dilemma: The Politics and Economics of Arab Integration* (London: I.B. Tauris, 1999); and Toby Dodge, 'Regional Issues Ten Years after the Gulf War', *The Middle East and North Africa 2002* (London: Europa Publications, forthcoming).

disputes between Israel and its neighbours, and also between states in the Arabian peninsula and on either side of the Gulf, all point to the continuous prominence of territory and military force in the region.

Evolution

We can, of course, go back to the beginnings of time to understand the development of interconnection in the known world. More sensibly, we can identify a range of important historical landmarks that have underpinned the basis of the globalized world as we know it today. The 'modern era' can be dated from the seventeenth-century development of the Westphalian state system, the eighteenth-century Enlightenment and the nineteenth-century development of telecommunications. But progress is not simply unilinear, inevitable or indeed irreversible. Some periods have seen greater advance than others. The late nineteenth and late twentieth centuries saw a much more dramatic advance than did other periods (notably 1914 to 1945).

It is in the current era that advances, especially in technology, have been the most dramatic. And the last three decades have been an era of unparalleled economic liberalization, mass air travel, telecommunications, ecological change and the development of transnational actors and international organizations in the state, market and non-state domains. By way of illustration: in 1966 there was the first photograph of planet Earth; in 1969 the first wide-body jet and the first multi-site computer network (ARPANET); in 1971 the first electronic stock exchange; in 1974 the first 'global issue' conference; in 1976 the launch of the first public broadcast satellite; in 1977 the first commercial use of fibre optic cable; in 1977 the creation of worldwide electronic inter-bank transfers; in 1987 the identification of the first complete 'ozone hole' over Antarctica; and in 1989 the invention of the World Wide Web.

In assessing the evolution of globalization in the Middle East, one could start with the forced integration of colonized economies into world markets under European imperialism in the nineteenth century. Key events would include the nationalist struggle for political independence from the end of the First World War, culminating in decolonization after the Second World War. In the 1960s and 1970s there were arguments about neo-colonialism, a new international economic order and demands for economic independence.[40]

---

[40] See, for example, Hedley Bull, 'The Revolt against the West', in Hedley Bull and Adam Watson (eds), *The Expansion of International Society* (Oxford: Clarendon Press, 1989), p. 220.

For Middle Eastern states, however, the rise of neo-liberal economics and their influence within the Bretton Woods institutions in the 1980s and the end of the Cold War in the early 1990s are the two principal events that mark the arrival of globalization. The latter removed a powerful bargaining chip in a once bipolar world and made the non-aligned movement a thing of the past. The relative autonomy from global economic forces afforded to regional governments by oil wealth or inter-Arab aid and worker remittances were drastically reduced by the collapse of the oil price in the mid-1980s. This triggered a recession in the oil-producing states and a much harsher economic downturn among the non-oil producers of the wider Middle East. As foreign aid shrank, workers' remittances declined and debt repayment began to increase sharply. Non-oil-producing states were forced to negotiate with IFIs and oil producers had to cut budget deficits and raise capital from commercial banks.[41] The end of the Cold War also marked a steep decline in the political autonomy of leading states in the region. Syria, Iraq and South Yemen had all relied to a certain degree on the Soviet Union for arms supplies, diplomatic support and technology transfer. With the end of their Soviet patron these states felt increasingly vulnerable to US and UN pressure.

Causation

A single explanation of what causes globalization is not possible. Globalization comes about in a number of ways, such as processes of two-way interaction, emulation, one-way telecommunications and institutional isomorphism (the tendency for institutions to converge on a common pattern of operation over time). But three explanations carry more weight than others. First is the ascendancy of a secular, rationalist and techno-scientific conception of knowledge, the dominance of a certain type of 'modern' knowledge and technology thought to be bringing a convergence of behaviour the world over. Second is the universalization of capitalism as a system of economic production, distribution and exchange. Were they alive today Adam Smith and Karl Marx would both agree on this. Both identified, albeit for different reasons, the way in which capital has an inbuilt propensity

---

[41] See, for example, Rex Brynen, 'The Politics of Monarchical Liberalism: Jordan', in Bahgat Korany, Rex Brynen and Paul Noble (eds), *Political Liberalisation and Democratisation in the Arab World, Volume 2, Comparative Experiences* (Boulder, CO: Lynne Rienner Publishers, 1998), p. 81; Raymond Hinnebusch, 'The Politics of Economic Liberalisation: Comparing Egypt and Syria', in Hakimian and Moshaver (eds), *The State and Global Change*, p. 115; and Robert Springborg, 'Egypt', in T. Niblock and E. Murphy (eds), *Economic and Political Liberalization in the Middle East* (London: British Academic Press, 1993) p. 148.

to expand beyond the borders of the nation-state. In so doing, capitalism has, over the last century, enhanced the mobility of capital, technology, production, sales and management practices and created a new global division of labour. Finally, and often overlooked in the burgeoning literature on globalization, there is the degree to which governments have developed the regulatory environment and structure of multilateral institutions, especially in the economic domain, that have fostered globalization.

Since 1945 institutions (of varying effectiveness, it has to be conceded) have been developed to oversee the international trading regime (the General Agreement on Tariffs and Trade and the World Trade Organization) and the international financial system (the Bretton Woods institutions noted above: the IMF and the World Bank Group). A panoply of public and private regimes has evolved too, such as the Organization for Economic Cooperation and Development (OECD), the International Labour Organization (ILO), the Bank for International Settlements (BIS) and the International Organization of Securities Commissions (IOSCO). There are as well quasi-formalized activities such as meetings of the G-7/8 and that whole array of bodies and specialized agencies in the UN system such as the UN Development Programme, the UN Environment Programme, the UN Conference on Trade and Development etc. These bodies act as *de facto* and, at times, *de jure* institutions at which standard-setting and policy harmonization is developed on international public policy issues.

States in the Middle East are rule-takers, as opposed to rule-makers. Over the past 20 years they have often experienced universalization of capitalism as the external imposition of rules and regulations that have systematically undermined their autonomy to make economic policy, not as the endogenous growth of liberalized domestic markets. This imposition has been driven by the increased policy coordination of international government organizations following the lead of IFIs. This process can be tracked in the rise of what became known as the Washington Consensus in the 1980s and the development of 'good governance' in the 1990s.

The Washington Consensus has its origins in the IMF's reaction to the Mexican debt crisis of 1982 and its transformation of the Mexican economy. Under IMF tutelage Mexico continued to repay its debts while exchange rates were reformed and its trade regime was liberalized. With the perceived success of its role in Mexico, the IMF, and also the World Bank, set about applying the 'wisdom of market reliance' to other developing countries in economic difficulty, advocating not only free trade but also the liberalization of their capital and financial markets.[42] By the

---

[42] Michael Mastanduno, 'Models, markets and power: political economy and the Asia-Pacific, 1989–1999', *Review of International Studies*, Vol. 26, No. 4, October 2000, p. 499.

middle of the 1980s structural adjustment loans accounted for more than 25 per cent of World Bank lending, and came to be seen by both the World Bank and the IMF as a precondition for further lending.[43] These loans had a large number of policy conditions attached that were designed to reduce drastically the state's role in the economy. The removal of import quotas, the cutting of tariffs and interest rate controls, the devaluation of currencies and the privatization of state industries were all imposed on governments.

As in much of the developing world before the rise of the Washington Consensus, the dominant economic model used by the republican states of the Middle East after independence relied heavily on socialist rhetoric and state intervention to drive development. Between the 1950s and 1973 regional oil-producing states managed to gain increasing control over the oil extracted from their territory. This gradually increased their autonomy from their own populations and within the international economy. This process was dramatically accelerated by the oil price rises of 1973–4. Oil-rich states could in effect demobilize the political aspirations of their societies by generous welfare spending, by not levying taxes and by imposing political quiescence. This autonomy from domestic and international society spread to the non-oil-producing states of the region as either recipients of aid from the Gulf states or as exporters of cheap labour. However, problems with this model propelled Tunisia from 1969 and Egypt from 1974 to reform their approach to economic development, describing it in Arabic as an opening to the world or infitah.[44]

In the late 1980s the collapse in oil prices opened up the economies of the Middle East to the forces of globalization. The non-oil-producing economies of the region were forced to submit to the market discipline of the IFIs, and the oil-rich states of the Gulf, faced with severe budget shortfalls, had to scale back the public services offered to their populations and seek commercial loans on the international financial markets. This, combined with the perceived failure of state-led development initiatives, increased political unrest and forced regional governments to delegate some of their previous roles to the private sector. More robust attempts to reform regional economies under the Washington Consensus started in the second half of the 1980s. Tunisia signed its first deal with the World Bank in 1986, followed by Egypt in 1987 and Jordan in 1990. Since then all three countries have had large loans from the World Bank and have seen substantial involvement of the Bretton Woods institutions in their economies.

---

[43] Williams, 'Aid and sovereignty', p. 568.
[44] Mustapha al-Sayyid, 'International and Regional Environments and State Transformation in Some Arab Countries', in Hakimian and Moshaver (eds), *The State and Global Change*, p. 160.

With the rise of the Washington Consensus in the 1980s and its overt extension into the political realm with 'good governance' in the 1990s, governments in the developing world perceived IFIs as the shock troops of globalization. Structurally adjusted states in the Middle East have seen their economies opened up to international markets and multinational companies in return for the provision of much-needed loans. This has caused globalization to be perceived as a Western imposition forced on countries that have very little alternative.

For the Middle East the end of the bipolar world magnified the effects of declining oil prices. This was dramatically emphasized in the conduct of the war against Iraq after its invasion of Kuwait in 1990. With the Soviet Union preoccupied with internal problems, the United States was free to use the UN to build a multinational coalition against Iraq. The superiority of American weapons and statecraft in the post-Cold War world was evident for all regimes in the region to see. Not only was Iraq ejected from Kuwait but it was also effectively placed in political and economic quarantine for more than a decade.

Consequences

As with questions of chronology and causation, the understanding of the consequences of globalization elicits widespread dispute across the spectrum of analysis and policy. This is hardly surprising. The contemporary era demonstrates continuity with the past in the patterns of human and state behaviour but also gives evidence of a massive and profound transformation. Many of the competing analyses are laced with large doses of ideology. Indeed, how we interpret globalization is perhaps the most important contextual influence on the development of the international debate for the coming decade and beyond.

Realist analysts of globalization (those scholars and policy-makers who ascribe the central role in international affairs to states) argue that changes notwithstanding, globalization has done nothing fundamental to undermine the sovereignty of the nation-state. Marxists and radical critics simply see globalization as capitalism by another name. 'Hyper-globalists', especially those technology-driven beneficiaries of the new 'wired world', believe we are witnessing a revolution that is transforming not only the relationship between the state and the economy but also relationships within civil society. For them, the meta-trends of technological change and a new ethos of openness will progressively open up national economies and continue the integration of world markets. By an invariably unexplained logic, these trends will have the happy effect of bringing about the beginnings of a global civilization. This view developed in the period of 'globophoria', in the 1980s and the first half of the 1990s.

The advocacy of globalization as a universal good dominated popular and academic debates throughout the 1980s and 1990s. The neo-liberal recipe of open markets and small states became the mantra of the parliamentary right and left across the Western world. However, the East Asian economic crisis of 1997, the 'battle of Seattle' in 1999 and the violent clashes at Genoa in summer 2001 have done much to raise doubt in the public mind about the whole concept of globalization. One side of the debate on globalization concentrates on the increased mobility of investment finance and production and on the intense competition among states in the periphery to attract inward investment. Comparative advantage, it is argued, will allow developing states with low wages, good infrastructure and wise government policy to escape poverty through astute interaction with the global economy. The other side of the argument presents globalization as 'aggravating socio-economic divisions within weak states'.[45] Globalization, it asserts, mirrors and exacerbates existing social and economic cleavages.

Whether the relationship between increased inequality and globalization is causally related or merely correlated is theoretically very important. But in the current context, theory matters less than perception. The correlation alone, which is not in doubt, is sufficient to make it an issue of the utmost political importance. It is the identification of the correlation that leads the dispossessed to believe that globalization is the cause of their plight. At the very least, there is clearly no inevitable relationship between globalization and emancipation. Globalization may be winning the economic argument now, but it has yet to gain political legitimacy. This is the key contest, and it will steer the agenda of global politics into the foreseeable future.

In these circumstances the example of the newly industrialized countries of East Asia becomes crucial to arguments about the effects of globalization on the developing world. The rise of the East Asian developmental state, and now the shock of the international instability caused by the 'Asian contagion', have both proved to be powerful correctives to the economic model championed by the neo-liberal explanation of globalization. The East Asian model highlighted the need to re-evaluate the state's central role in driving economic development among late industrializers. The East Asian economic crisis caused a major rethink of the Washington Consensus. As the problems of East Asia spread and affected Russia and

---

[45] Thomas, 'Where is the Third World Now?', p. 229.

Brazil,[46] the World Bank itself started to question the 'one size fits all' model of restructuring. The model developed to deal with the problems of Latin America and Africa had little utility for the starkly different economies of East Asia. In addition the international economy itself, previously the benign hand that was to deliver all the benefits of globalization, was seen to be part of the problem. It continues to grow in size and complexity while still being 'the only market that is not regulated by an overarching institution or authority'. The

> principle [*sic*] message of the crisis is that the costs of globalization may have been underestimated so far, resulting in an unduly upbeat view of its net benefits. But if East Asia's successes were instrumental in driving such optimism in the past, its recent financial woes can help provide a more balanced perspective on the net potential benefits of Globalisation.[47]

To analysts of the Middle East the failure of the statist model popularized a neo-liberal approach. In the post-Cold War euphoria of the early 1990s, economic and especially political transformation appeared imminent. The notion that a vibrant and assertive civil society could unseat dictatorship was enthusiastically imported from Eastern Europe. This sense of democratic possibility was enhanced by the claim (at least) that the war against Iraq was being fought in the name of democracy and human rights. The rhetoric of Arab nationalism, of state-delivered economic growth and even socialism, was looking jaded as the lack of economic development in the more populous Arab countries became apparent.

A decade latter the scale of transformation has been modest.

> The discourse of democracy and pluralism [has] ... become widespread, although Arab political scientists and commentators have been making a clear distinction between *dimuqratiyya* [democracy] and *ta'addudiya* (which can mean anything from multipartyism to pluralism) – concluding that while the latter has become more prevalent, the former is still some considerable way off.[48]

The reasons why the grand expectations of the early 1990s were not matched by the subsequent realities of Middle Eastern politics are to be found both in the shortcomings involved in exporting liberal theory and in

---

[46] Mastanduno, 'Models, markets and power', p. 500.
[47] Hakimian, 'From MENA to East Asia and Back', pp. 96–7.
[48] Gerd Nonneman, 'Rentiers and Autocrats, Monarchs and Democrats, State and Society: The Middle East between Globalization, Human "Agency", and Europe', review article, *International Affairs*, Vol. 77, No. 1, January 2001, p. 144.

regional states' surviving autonomy from their societies.[49] The legitimacy of Arab states had only recently been accepted by populations and states-people alike, military force was still used in regional as well as domestic politics and there were region-specific differences in state economies that made World Bank-sponsored liberalization less than straightforward.[50]

The purpose of this book is not to take a position on either side of the arguments about the pros and cons of globalization but rather to suggest that this debate is the academic terrain on which the future of globalization and its effects on the Middle East will be contested. And here globalization is not new. Neither 'public goods' nor 'public bads' are intrinsic to the contemporary global era. The conflict at the heart of the debate over globalization is as old as that about how societies are organized and governed. The perennial questions of 'who gets what, how and when' remain the very stuff of everyday Middle Eastern politics. The difference in the contemporary age is that these contests can no longer be conducted (if they ever were) within the borders of territorially defined states or culturally defined regions. They will increasingly be conducted where the global meets the local at a sub-state level in societies across the region.

Responses

The structures of globalization, arising from the impacts of modernity and technology on the Middle East, are strong, but they are not immutable. Actors in the region (states, institutions, individuals) are not powerless. Policy is important; and the persistence of state power, as opposed to growing limitations on states' sovereign capabilities, means that they remain the principal, but not the only, agent of policy change. Nowadays, governments have to accommodate not only the structural constraints imposed by globalization, especially the shifting balance in the relationship between state authority and market power, but also new actors. States, and their domains of activity (intergovernmental institutions and regimes at regional and multilateral levels), have now been joined by a range of non-governmental organizations. These NGOs are finding a voice, if not as yet too much influence, in the domestic and regional policy processes of the Middle East.

[49] On state autonomy from society see H. Beblawi, 'The Rentier State in the Arab World', in G. Luciani (ed.), *The Arab State* (London: Routledge, 1990), pp. 85–98; and F.G. Gause, *Oil Monarchies: Domestic and Security Challenges in the Arab Gulf States* (New York: Council on Foreign Relations Press, 1994).
[50] Barnett, 'Sovereignty, nationalism, and regional order', pp. 148–89; and Massoud Karshenas, 'Structural Obstacles to Economic Adjustment in the MENA Region', pp. 59–79.

The main non-state actors in the Middle East come mainly from the market but also from civil society, and include respectively multinational corporations (MNCs), NGOs and individuals too. They now interact in a more overlapping way under conditions of globalization than in the past. Although MNCs and NGOs have been with us for a long time, it is only in the past few decades that their number has grown dramatically. As of the late 1990s there were in excess of 45,000 transborder corporations (MNCs) and nearly 20,000 transborder NGOs. Moreover, many of these bodies, whether an MNC such as General Motors or Toyota, an international regime such as the WTO or the World Intellectual Property Organization or an NGO such as Amnesty International, consider that they have global terms of reference.

To a large extent, the basic tenets of neo-liberalism's understanding of globalization have become conventional wisdom, accepted if not welcomed by Middle Eastern states. The power of international markets for good or ill cannot be denied. MNCs, inward investment and international capital have to be courted by states in the region, whatever their previous ideological inclinations. The fate of the poorest states in Africa is graphic evidence to Middle Eastern states without oil that in the present international economy, exploitation by international capital may have widespread negative ramifications, but it is far worse to be ignored or bypassed by the market. However, the instabilities and inequities produced by an unregulated international economy have given rise to increasing calls for Keynesian policy prescriptions. The assertion of the political over the economic in the name of greater stability and equality now seems to be gaining the upper hand in debates on globalization. The role of the developing world in these debates could be crucial. Developing states were the unwilling testing ground throughout the 1980s for neo-liberal policy prescriptions. Having the most to gain and to lose from globalization, they bring no power to the negotiating table but a great deal of moral influence. As the anti-globalization movement develops, the states of the developing world can offer it leadership and evidence of the dangers of unrestrained liberalism.

Since 1990 regimes in the Middle East have undertaken a delicate balancing act in an attempt to deal with some of the pressures of globalization and the shortcomings of previous state-led development strategies without losing power. The result has been avoidance of a genuine process of democratization by the implementation of a policy of calculated economic and political 'decompression'.[51] Economically, this has meant a partial

---

[51] Raymond A. Hinnebusch, 'Calculated Decompression as a Substitute for Democratization: Syria', in Korany, Brynen and Noble (eds), *Political Liberalisation & Democratisation in the Arab World*, pp. 223–40.

retreat by the state from the economic sphere. In both rhetoric and policy Middle Eastern states have retreated from their role as providers of economic growth. The role of capital accumulation has slowly been devolved to those in the private or semi-private sector who have close links with the governing elite. Politically, however, hardly any progress has been made. Moves towards liberalization have been very tightly controlled, with any threat to the regime being met with violence. Viable opposition parties, especially Islamist ones, with an actual or potential mass following have been ruthlessly suppressed. Political liberalization, if indeed it can be called that, has been carried out within strict barriers enforced by the state's security services. The 'political manoeuvrings of the Middle Eastern regimes amount to a delicate balance between economic and political reforms, the guarantor of which is ultimately, and in the absence of democratic forms of accountability, the military.'[52]

Conclusions

Globalization reflects the development of structural forces in world affairs far stronger than at any previous time. The causal power of these international forces is now undeniable, and must be factored into any explanation of the political, economic and cultural dynamics of the Middle East. However, the example mentioned above of Sainsbury's short-lived supermarket chain in Egypt is instructive. In its attempt to export its economic logic, Sainsbury's, a representative of Western mass consumerism, ran up against different political and economic logics, those specific to Egypt and the wider region.

An accurate understanding of both the theory and the practice of globalization must pay due attention not only to the most visible and celebrated causes of globalization – the economic, cultural and political forces emanating from the international sphere – but also to the effects these causes have on the communities that they interact with around the world. Only by paying attention to the causes and effects of globalization can the crucial questions of the scale, consequences and reactions to globalization be properly answered in a truly global context.

The undoubted methodological and empirical shortcomings of the 'convergence' thesis and the neo-liberal policy prescriptions of the Washington Consensus appear to have sprung from a desire to impose on the whole world a 'one size fits all' approach to globalization. This imposition took

---

[52] Emma C. Murphy, 'Economic Reform and the State in Tunisia', in Hakimian and Moshaver (eds), *The State and Global Change*, p. 53.

little or no account of the specific historical or economic structures in the states that this approach was meant to describe or to reform. The grand predictions of economic and political transformation in the Middle East that greeted the end of the Cold War suffered from this same tendency to underplay or ignore local specificities. The Middle East is certainly not immune to liberalism in either its political or its economic form. But both forms of liberalism are imports, born and developed in the very different geo-historical surroundings of Europe. To expect that they can readily be used to interpret and predict change in the Middle East is a common mistake. The liberalization of Middle Eastern economies has to interact with the dominance of oil. It has take account too of failed polices of state-driven development. Predictions of liberal democratic transformation also have to take into account numerous states that have not had to depend on their populations for economic resources. On top of this a heritage of imperialism and Cold War interventionism has left populations very sceptical about the good intentions of outside bodies, especially Western governments which claim to be operating with the best intentions. By concentrating on the interaction between the global and the local, this study hopes to avoid these mistakes and over-optimistic assessments of globalization.

The states and societies of the Middle East are certainly subject to the influence of globalization, especially in the manner in which markets impose fiscal and monetary disciplines on governments and, as a consequence, limit their revenue-raising capabilities. But these same states and societies are not merely passive actors. The states have residual assets and can develop new ones; the societies have strong attachments to deeply held convictions that are not going to dissipate under pressure from a nascent global society. The challenge for all governments and peoples in the twenty-first century lies in how they will adapt to the evolving structural environment resulting from the changing relationship between global market power and state authority. Some states have better capabilities for turning these structural forces to their advantage than others. Some states must simply accommodate to them.

2 The Middle East and the politics of differential integration

Fred Halliday

Introduction

Globalization as a topic invites general speculation, but requires specification: broad-brush statements about modernity, markets and the post-Cold War age can get analysis only so far. What is needed in equal measure is precision, above all about two issues: definition – *what* is meant by the term? – and analytic focus. The purpose of this chapter is to contribute to the discussion of globalization by analysing the form of the Middle East's integration into global processes and particularly one response to this integration: political discourses in the region about globalization.[1]

Globalization is a process that involves markets and foreign direct investment (FDI), states and rights. But it also involves political discourses and values. The argument *for* globalization stresses a growing convergence of values and also of economic and political systems; that *against* it emphasizes the fragmentation of the world into different cultural, as well as economic and political, blocs. An examination of discourse is only one part of the study of globalization. However, it may serve to illuminate broader aspects of the globalization process and of the formation of the contemporary Middle East. It may also diminish the conflict between the two conventional approaches to globalization: homogenization or fragmentation. Hence, as regards values, the polarity between generalization in

[1] The debate on ideology and discourse in the Middle East falls along an analytic spectrum. At one end of this is the cultural, textual approach, which stresses the endurance of distinct religious and regional values; at the other end is the contextual, modernist approach, which sees the language and themes of discourse in contemporary terms. My own approach, much influenced by the work of Sami Zubaida, Ervand Abarahamian, Aziz al-Azmeh and others, is at the modernist end of the spectrum. See in particular my *Nation and Religion in the Middle East* (London: Saqi, 2000). The germ of the general argument on modernity and the world historical context of underdevelopment lies in the classic critique of development theory, 'The Development of Underdevelopment' by André Gunder Frank in *Monthly Review* (September 1966). While disagreeing with Frank's prescription for how to develop, namely to 'delink' from the world market and pursue an autarkic path, I share his emphasis on the international, and historical, forces that constitute contemporary interstate inequalities.

terms of globalization and that in terms of cultural clash or civilizational difference may not be as fixed as it is often presented. The point is not that the Middle East is like the rest of the world, particularly the countries of the Organization for Economic Cooperation and Development (OECD), nor that it is somehow outside the globalization process. Rather, it is precisely because it is, and has for a long time been, part of the broader international system that it is now so distinct in its major characteristics. It is not exclusion but inclusion, on unequal and conflictual terms, that has produced the Middle East of today. It is this historically located and contradictory perspective that is termed here 'differential integration'.

Study of the Middle East in terms of 'globalization' presents an immediate paradox. This is evident in the contrast between different general views of its place in the contemporary world – 'globalization' on one side, 'clash of civilizations' on the other. Each posits a general trend, but the former assumes integration and homogenization and the latter assumes historical separation and confrontation. In the first perspective, the Middle East appears in some ways to be relatively outside the set of processes that accelerated in the 1990s and that characterize globalization in its three main aspects: economic, political and socio-cultural.[2] In economic terms, it continues to display a high degree of state control of domestic economies, low levels of interregional trade, meagre exports of manufactured goods to OECD states and, above all, low indices of FDI. In many significant respects the Middle East, except Israel and, to some extent, Turkey and Tunisia, is outside the globalization process. There is, for example, little inclusion of this region in surveys by the *Economist* or the *Financial Times* of economic globalization and the changes associated with it. In comparative analyses of what is one of the most important dimensions of globalization, foreign investment in manufacturing, the region is almost wholly absent: neither the political security of good governance nor the quality of the labour force is present.

In political terms, in which globalization is associated with democratization at home and a broader pattern of regional cooperation, the region is also exceptional. A decade after the end of Soviet communism and democratization in much of Latin America, Middle Eastern political systems remain very much under authoritarian control, some stage-managed

---

[2] For discussion of the Middle East and globalization see Hassan Hakimian and Ziba Moshaver (eds), *The State and Global Change: The Political Economy of Transition in the Middle East and North Africa* (London: Curzon, 2001); Clement Henry and Robert Springborg, *Globalization and the Politics of Development in the Middle East* (Cambridge: Cambridge University Press, 2001). My own general approach to globalization is in Fred Halliday, *The World at 2000* (London: Palgrave, 2000), Chapter 5: 'Globalization and its Discontents'.

diversity in elections and civil society apart. Respect for human rights, by states and opposition movements alike, is deficient. Much use is made in this region, as in others, of the word 'transition' – the implication is that these states are moving towards democratic governance. But it may be that they are in transition to nothing and that what now exists, semi-authoritarian regimes at best, is what will remain. As for relations among states, the situation is no better: there is no growth of what is seen elsewhere, a 'Zone of Peace' in the region, be it in the Arab-Israeli context, the Gulf or relations between Turks and Arabs. In social and cultural terms, a similarly static picture seems to prevail. Authoritarian forms of social control continue to be strong, through family, community and religion, while in public discourse the region seems to have gone backwards: press and political statements, as well as much of the debate on social and cultural issues, are framed more in religious terms than they were two or three decades ago.

In contrast to this picture of Middle Eastern exclusion, one can make a case for 'differential integration'. In many respects the Middle East *is* integrated into the globalization process, and an analysis of this integration will contribute much to an understanding of how globalization itself works. This integration is evident in all three aspects of globalization. Politically, the Middle East is not a region shaped by atavistic forces but a product of the modern world. It is the international system that has in modern times shaped the state system, the political character and many of the interstate conflicts of the region. Economically, the region has been extensively integrated into the world economy, through the export of the most important global commodity of all, oil, and the provision to Middle Eastern states of large amounts of capital in the form of oil revenues. The whole argument about FDI misses the point. Large amounts of investment money *are* flowing between this region and the developed world, *in the opposite direction*: total GCC private investments in the capital markets of the West alone are reckoned to be well over $1,500 billion.[3] The trade linkage is equally dramatic: the economies of the OECD countries would seize up in a few weeks if they did not receive energy supplies from the Gulf. In terms of culture and discourse, a similar level of integration prevails: it is not the Middle East's isolation from the modern world but its antagonism to it that informs its response to globalization.

The Middle East suggests a corrective to prevailing liberal views of globalization, in two respects. First, it suggests that analysis of globalization and its impact is crucially determined by the time-frame of the analysis. As the editors of this book point out in Chapter 1, a starting point

---

[3] *Middle East Economic Digest*, 11 January 2002. This figure omits assets held by GCC governments.

in the early 1990s may miss precisely those factors that determine what has happened since. This is not to say that there was nothing new about globalization in the 1990s but rather that the 1990s were a chapter in a longer, already structured, process. Second, the Middle East demonstrates in dramatic form the fact that globalization, far from producing a more homogeneous world in which politics, economics and society in each country converge more and more, is itself an unequal process and one that generates increasing difference. This recognition of unequal globalization is widespread among analysts of the world economy and, in some measure, in analyses of politics. Culture, however, remains a redoubt of apparently essential, and enduring, differences. Yet here too there is as much integration, historical and differential, as in investment or state organization.

Historical context: formative and discursive

Discussions of globalization conventionally begin with the changes of the 1990s, and for good reason: the end of the Cold War and the collapse of the Soviet model on the one hand, the spread of neo-liberal policies in trade, investment, financial markets and macro-economic regulation on the other. Something important, and global, did occur in the 1990s, and it affected all societies, including those of the Middle East.[4] The collapse of the USSR had important strategic and ideological consequences for the region: the bipolar system collapsed and its states came under increasing pressure to democratize and privatize. The Internet and satellite TV spread to much of the region.[5]

Yet in some respects, this is a misleading starting point for an analysis of globalization: the 1990s may be seen as one chapter in the process, but the broader context of global integration already existed. The shadow of that earlier history, prior to 1990, continues to hang over much of the region. Each of the three main components of globalization has a history long before 1990. The impact of a more powerful European state system on the Middle East began in the seventeenth century and gathered pace from the early nineteenth century. Throughout the period from 1774, the first major Russian defeat of Ottoman Turkey, Napoleon's occupation of Egypt and the successive wars involving the Ottomans and Persia that followed to the aftermath of the First World War and the collapse of the

---

[4] Fred Halliday, 'The Third World and the End of the Cold War: An Interim Assessment', in William Hale and Eberhard Kienle (eds), *After the Cold War: Security and Democracy in Africa and Asia* (London: I.B. Tauris, 1997), pp. 15–42.
[5] See *Middle East Journal*, vol. 54, no. 3 (Summer 2000), Special Issue: The Information Revolution.

Ottoman and Qajar empires, the political, economic and social systems of the region were under pressure from outside. They sought, as did the Manchu in China, to resist, to imitate, to reform. The terms of the relationship with the European state system, integrated and unequal, were already established by that time.

The twentieth century took this process of differential integration much further: all of its major phases, colonialism, world war and Cold War, affected the Middle East and left legacies that shaped the later process of globalization. In political terms these legacies involved three major elements: the creation of a state system, carved out of earlier empires, with about 25 distinct components; the promotion of nationalism, an ideology that served two functions: legitimizing the state and resisting external domination; and the formation of interstate rivalries that made up the regional political system. The wars that have ravaged the Middle East were a product of this contemporary formation, not of ancestral or cultural conflict. Economically, the region's integration was less than that of many other parts of the Third World. But Egypt was integrated via the cotton industry, the Suez Canal and finance from the 1860s, and the development of the oil industry from the First World War provided a mechanism for funding states and associated local elites.[6] Socially and culturally, Middle Eastern societies were profoundly affected by this integration. Economic change led to urbanization and mass migration, especially after the oil boom of the 1970s; new states were established in order to control their respective societies and to build alliances with external powers; and communications, the family and education were all affected. In sum, the Middle East of the late 1980s was a product of its incorporation into the external world and of the impact, integrative and differential, of that incorporation.[7]

This general perspective can be applied to each of the three main facets of globalization. The state system, and also the pattern of interstate relations, are the product not of an ancient legacy, such as that of 'Asiatic despotism', but of the impact of the modern world on the Middle East. The economic system is equally a product of that impact. In this chapter the

---

[6] Roger Owen, *The Middle East in the World Economy, 1800–1914* (London: I.B. Tauris, 1993); Roger Owen and Sevket Pamuk, *A History of Middle East Economies in the Twentieth Century* (London: I.B.Tauris, 1998).

[7] This point is especially well made in Reinhard Schulze, *A Modern History of the Islamic World* (London: I.B. Tauris, 2000), in which he examines how the Islamic world has been part of world history in economic, cultural and political terms. For general overviews of this relationship, see Albert Hourani, *A History of the Arab Peoples* (London: Faber and Faber, 1991), Part Four: 'The Age of European Empires'; and Bernard Lewis, *The Middle East* (London: Weidenfeld and Nicolson, 1995), Part V: 'The Challenge of Modernity'.

focus is on ideology and discourse, an area notoriously traversed by rigid positions, as the argument about cultural differences stresses alternative value systems and perceptions in the contemporary world. More recently, there has been a call for the study of what are termed 'non-Western' voices on the assumption that ideologies opposed to the West are conceptually distinct. An alternative, historical but integrative, approach suggests that what appear as distinct, 'non-Western' voices outside the broader process of globalization are indeed both product and part of that process seen in its wider context. This is quite clear in areas outside the Middle East: the greatest opponents of Western domination in the twentieth century – Mao Zedong and Ho Chi Minh, Mahatma Gandhi and Gamal Abd al-Nasser, Kwame Nkrumah and Amilcar Cabral, Fidel Castro and Che Guevara – all invoked universal but originally Western concepts of independence, freedom and equality against their imperial opponents. The same applies to the Middle East: Islamist opponents of Western domination, be they Ruhallah Khomeini or Mu'ammar al-Qadhdhafi, have spoken in an Islamic idiom, but their denunciations of imperialism and their calls for independence are part of this modern discourse.[8]

Three more specific comments on the modernity of discourse in the Middle East are in order here. First, contemporary public discourse there has been shaped by one ideology above all – nationalism, and two central components of the nationalist world-view – the state and imperialism. Thus, forms of Islamist discourse, ostensibly alternatives to nationalism, are on closer study cognate with nationalism in theme and programme and replicate much of what nationalism has said already. The post-1990 Middle Eastern debate on globalization reproduces much of what was said in earlier times about Western imperialism. Second, for all the specificity of regional and religious idiom, the major themes embodied in the debate on globalization are not specifically regional at all: they embody broader ideas common to much of the Third World and, indeed, to Western critiques of globalization. Although Khomeini spoke a different language, his denunciations of Western domination, corrupt regional rulers and economic exploitation and his appeal to the virtuous mass of the oppressed to rise up would have been understood across the non-European world, from Beijing to Buenos Aires. Third, discourse and political ideas are not free-floating, autonomous entities: no discussion of discourse can ignore the role within it of interest, whether of states, which seek to mould public discourse to further their ends, or of opposition movements, which seek to

---

[8] On Khomeini, see Sami Zubaida, *Islam, the People and the State* (London: Routledge, 1989); Ervand Abrahamian, *Khomeinism* (London: I.B.Tauris, 1993); and Daniel Brumberg, *Reinventing Khomeini* (London: University of Chicago Press, 2001).

challenge states in their pursuit of power. All of this leads to something evident enough from within the region but rather obscure from without, namely the diversity of views on globalization. This diversity reflects not uncertainty about what is an 'authentic' response to global processes but differences of interpretation, and interest – in other words, differences that are themselves a product of the modern world.

The debate on globalization in the Middle East

The contemporary debate on globalization has found many echoes in the Islamic world in general and in the Middle East in particular. However the term is understood, the issues debated in the developed West or in other parts of the developing world, whether China or Latin America, are also debated in Islamic states. Through this debate a range of political and ideological approaches to politics and society becomes evident, as does the degree to which, whatever the specific Islamic idiom, these debates overlap with discussions elsewhere. Although language, political vocabulary and symbol may be specific, we are not looking at an insulated discursive and ideological world. Indeed the debate on globalization is reflected in the discussion that has taken place in Middle Eastern states about how to translate the word 'globalization'. In Arabic there were initially two options. One was *al-koukaba*, based on *koukab*, 'star' or 'cosmos'. This easily lent itself to the pejorative variant *al-koukala*, 'Coca-cola-ization'. The rival, and ultimately prevailing, candidate was *al-'awlama*, from *'alam*, the world, a rendering more of French 'mondialisation' than of English 'globalization'. In Persian there was a dispute between those who favoured the more neutral *jahani-shodan*, 'world-becoming', and those who advocated *jahani-giri*, 'world-taking'. For the moment at least, *jahani-shodan* appears to have won.

Anyone surveying the debate on globalization in Middle Eastern states will find a combination of themes that are specific to the region and ones that are more general. Much of this debate, be it in the press or in academic writing, is secular in character, relating to the working issues encapsulated by globalization, such as trade, education or satellite TV. A good example of this is the work of the Iranian writer Farhang Rajaee, *Globalization on Trial*.[9] Rajaee, a former member of the Iranian delegation to the UN and a professor at Tehran University, provides an astute and wide-ranging engagement with Western and Middle Eastern concerns. He sees in globalization

[9] Farhang Rajaee, *Globalization on Trial: The Human Condition and the Information Civilization* (Ottawa: International Development Research Centre, 2000).

both opportunities and dangers: his favoured stance, 'prudent vigilance' (p. 106), reflects a middle position shared with some Western writers. The most common Middle Eastern response, however, has been one of opposition, but this reflects not so much cultural differences as differences of structural position within the global distribution of economic, military and political power. In large measure this replicates the same critiques that are made elsewhere in the world and draws on many of the same, nationalist and left-wing, themes; indeed, the enduring influence of the Leninist theory of imperialism is evident. In a country such as Egypt or Kuwait, conferences denouncing globalization replicate anti-globalization themes echoed elsewhere.

In regard to culture, for example, two contrasting Islamic arguments can be heard. The first is that globalization threatens the Muslim world as a form of corruption of Muslim societies. The second, drawing on the universalist appeal of Islam and on specific cosmopolitan themes in the Koran itself, argues that Islam is itself a global, indeed *the* global, religion and should respond positively to the new context. Politically, there is concern with specific causes or conflicts in which Muslims are involved – Palestine, Kashmir, Chechnya, Kosovo – and, more broadly, with the threat, real or imagined, which the non-Muslim world poses to Muslim states. Here again there is no single discourse: Arabs in the Gulf, including many Iraqis, do not support Palestine; Iran has remained notably silent on 'Islamic' causes that might undermine its state interest: Xinjiang, Chechnya, Kashmir and, above all, Nagorno-Karabagh. In the run-up to the crisis of September 2001, Osama bin Laden denounced the West for waging a 'crusader war', *al-harb al-salibia*, against the Islamic world. This was presented, and widely interpreted, as a pan-Islamic theme, but it was only in the previous few years that the issue of the Crusades, a military conflict on the eastern shore of the Mediterranean, had come to have popular resonance among Muslims elsewhere. Many of the issues being debated are secular, broad international ones that reflect the specific concerns of Muslim countries but are not in any sense Islamic: pressures for trade liberalization, signing intellectual copyright conventions, WTO membership, IMF conditions for liberalization of economies. The debate in the Muslim world about the Internet replicates that taking place elsewhere – concern at its effects on society countered by enthusiasm for what it can provide. Where there is resistance to the Internet from states, the reasons are similar to those encountered in other non-democratic societies, such as China, where the state wishes to control the flow of information.

An examination of how globalization is viewed serves several functions. First, it provides access to a range of opinions from states that are on the receiving end of globalization and thus are part of the broader, non-hegemonic world that today confronts this process. If the central experience of globalization for many is growing inequality, it is particularly important to address what these countries are saying. Second, an examination of this debate in the Islamic world draws attention, as do other non-hegemonic voices, to critical questions within the analysis of globalization itself. One question clearly is that of the time-frame of analysis: those on the receiving end tend to see today's globalization as a continuation of earlier forms of domination, in particular imperialism. The question of when and how globalization has taken over from other forms of Western domination is of general relevance. Pertinent here is Immanuel Wallerstein's argument that the formation of a single world system, in effect globalization, began in 1500.[10] Another issue to which this Islamic debate draws attention is that of culture – of cultural penetration or hegemony as part of globalization, but also of how an alternative form of cultural globalization, based on diversity and dialogue between different cultures, may be possible. Third, an examination of the way in which globalization is viewed within Islamic societies can contribute to our understanding of political ideology and discourse in those societies themselves. It will contribute to, if by no means resolve, the debate that has been taking place in recent years about the analysis of 'Islamist' discourse. As noted, this debate is broadly between those who have a cultural or essentialist view of Islamist ideas and see them as specific to the Muslim world and those who have a modernist view, which sees the variety and choice of discourses as reflecting contemporary, often secular, concerns. One can, for example, apply to the debate on globalization the kinds of argument applied to Islamist writings in general or to the work of Ayatollah Khomeini. Fourth, an analysis of the discussion of globalization in the Islamic world should serve to correct the impression, propagated in the Muslim world as well as in the West, of a single Islamic discourse.

What emerges is that, for all the shared historical context and cultural references, there are multiple voices on globalization, as on all other contemporary issues, in Muslim states. It is also evident that many of these voices are in large measure or wholly secular in tone and reference: debates on, say, WTO membership or the environment or tariffs reflect differences of interest, not of culture. Recognition of this may serve not only to correct a simplistic view of discussion in the Muslim world but also to question how far it is religion, in the sense of faith or holy text, that determines ideology or practice in these societies. We are looking

[10] Immanuel Wallerstein, *Historical Capitalism* (London: Verso, 1984).

essentially at states and societies which exist in the modern world, a world both globalizing and unequal, and whose reaction to this process may be shaped only partially by religion, if at all.

Contemporary Islamic responses: a general overview

Within political contexts and discourses that are specifically Islamic, one can identify at least three major positions on globalization: accommodation, denunciation and participation. These do not cover the whole range of options and opinions but they illustrate the diversity of views and provide a way into a broader understanding of the Middle East's response to globalization. Statist accommodation is the stance adopted by, for example, President Khatami of Iran. As will be discussed below, Khatami has argued most extensively in philosophical terms that the Islamic world has nothing to fear from the West and should learn from the writings of Western philosophers while itself promoting its particular view. His view of this is statist, however, and therefore resistant to the transnational character of globalization. He is proposing a policy for states, Iran in particular, and also wishes states to be in control of this process. His 'Dialogue of Civilizations', which the UN adopted as an official programme for 2001–2, does not give a legitimate place to individual, dissident or 'non-state' views. A contrasting view is that of the religious leader of Iran, Ayatollah Khamene'i. He has denounced globalization, certainly in Islamic terms, but also in terms that would be understandable in any developing country or context of protest. An even more striking example is that of the Moroccan Islamist thinker Abdessalam Yassine, for whom globalization is a major threat to the Islamic world, its culture and its faith. By contrast, the diaspora intellectual Ali Mazrui calls for the Islamic world to make a contribution to globalization in the spirit of its own universalism and of cultural diversity.

Accommodation

One of the most evident forms of statist accommodation is found in the widespread debate in Iran on globalization and many other international issues. The quarterly *Siasat-i Khareji*, 'Foreign Policy', published by the Institute for Political and International Studies (attached to the Foreign Ministry), produced a special issue on globalization in summer 2000. In addition to numerous articles by Iranian writers on themes such as globalization and MNCs, America's promotion of a single culture, cultural rights, international law and regional security, it included translations of articles by Joseph Nye and Robert Keohane and by Susan Strange. The quarterly *Discourse*, published by the Center for Scientific Research and Middle East Strategic Studies, led its fall 2000 issue with a roundtable on 'The Effects of Globalization on the Islamic Republic of Iran', in which four Iranian academics discuss how Iran can best respond to globalization. The shared assumptions of this discussion are that globalization is occurring and that it provides opportunities as well as dangers for Iran. One participant points out that in Iran as elsewhere there is an Islamic response that welcomes the process: 'For example, if you speak to a student of theology about your concerns over the ideal society, he might say "I have heard about globalization from one of my friends. It is a prelude to the reappearance of Imam Mahdi (May God hasten his reappearance). Therefore we must welcome this development".'[11] It is relevant here to recall the earlier debate in Iran on how to translate this term into Persian. Khomeini had denounced Western 'arrogance', *istikbar*, as 'world-devouring', 'Man-devouring', 'energy-devouring' and much else besides. Hence the attraction of the pejorative term *jahani-giri*, 'world-taking'. That the more neutral term *jahani-shodan*, 'world-becoming', prevailed reflects a more cautious inflection.

Khatami's starting point on globalization is, as already noted, a philosophical one. This is laid out in his two major works, *Fear of the Wave* and *From the City-World to the World-City*. They argue for a dialogue between different philosophical traditions and seek to enrich Islamic thinking, and politics, by drawing on Western ideas of tolerance and freedom. In a comparison with much relevance to contemporary Iran, Khatami alludes to the collapse of Soviet communism in order to argue that in a conflict between dogma and freedom the latter will always prevail. In political pronouncements this comes through as the basis for an engagement by Iran with globalization:

We cannot afford to remain heedless of the political, economic and cultural origins, impacts and mechanisms of the consequential phenomenon of globalization. Against this background, do we have any option but to look for new prospects relying on our collective will and capabilities, and making an intelligent and timely utilization of our historical opportunities? ... Instead of looking at globalization from the viewpoint of hegemony and domination, we ought to foster partnership

[11] *Discourse, An Iranian Quarterly*, vol. 2, no. 1 (fall 2000), p. 13.

and co-operation, recognizing the essential contribution to be made by every community and region. Indeed, the attempt by self-centred powers to commandeer this process (while neglecting the rightful share and cultural, political and economic contribution to be made by other regions and nations) can only jeopardise world peace and stability. Against this peril, it is necessary to think of ways of enabling economies of all nations and regions, raising the level of their spirituality and cultural productivity, and respecting their sovereignty and independence. The dialogue of civilisations and cultures as intended by us and now put on the international agenda is supportive of the logic of common heritage and upholds the existing culture, economic and political diversity and plurality throughout the world. ... It is in this way that we shall be able to counter the credo of domination and imposition of uniformity on a world devoid of spirituality, morality and faith.[12]

A similar approach, of critical, statist accommodation, was evident in a speech on Iranian foreign policy given by Dr Said Kamal Kharrazi, the foreign minister of Iran, to the Royal Institute of International Affairs in London in January 2000. This was the first official visit by a minister of the Islamic Republic of Iran to London since the revolution of 1979. The majority of the audience may have wanted to get down to current issues – Afghanistan, Nagorno-Karabagh, Palestine, terrorism, oil prices – and this they got, apparently to their general satisfaction, in a lively question and answer session. But Dr Kharrazi's formal speech was of much greater interest, as it laid out the general philosophy of the Islamic Republic on foreign policy.

Kharrazi began by appearing to give support to those such as Samuel Huntington or post-modernist theorists or Islamists who see the world as governed by culture. 'The fundamental and challenging question relates to the cultural foundation on which this new world order will rest,' he said. But what he then went on to say had a quite different import. The world is divided into two cultures: one of exclusion and one of inclusion – in Persian, *farhang-i shumul, farhang-i inhisar.* The culture of exclusion is marked by centralization, authoritarianism and the evasion of law, discrimination and injustice, accumulation of wealth and militarism. That of inclusion is marked by cultural pluralism and diversity, democracy, freedom and participation, justice, tolerance and collective security. He continued:

[12] British Broadcasting Corporation, *Summary of World Broadcasts*, ME/3864 MED/18, 12 June 2000. (Referred to below as BBC *SWB*.)

> The culture of inclusion is the culture of free-minded, justice-seeking and peaceful person[s]. The new world order must be based on inclusion so that our world will manage to pass through the remaining traces of culture of obscurantism (*farhang-i tarik andishi*) and move towards the culture of a new enlightenment (*farhang-i rushangiri andishi*), and put our global house in order on the basis of the rule of law and equity.

The culture of inclusion rested on political, cultural, economic and security bases. In his speech, in which he quoted John Locke as well as President Khatami, were many of the most contemporary political terms – civil society, human rights, good governance, confidence-building, globalization. He recognized the diversity of human rules and religions. There was only one reference to Islam, in his call for the need to promote 'good governance on the basis of Islamic teachings'.[13]

The significance of this speech is evident: Iran remains a country committed to challenging the West's domination of the international system, and identifies this system as having multiple dimensions – political, economic, military, cultural. It sees challenging this form of domination, the culture of exclusion, as central to the building of a stable and just world. Herein lies, twenty years on, one international message of the Iranian revolution. Yet the philosophical basis of this policy is not specific to, or dogmatically derived from, Islam. It is compatible with a modern rendering of Islam – note Dr Kharrazi's use of the flexible term 'Islamic teachings' – but this is part of a broader, global, anti-hegemonic and human vision. This is a voice that is non-Western in practical import, but not in its terms of reference, nor in the proposals it offers. It is, rather, a rendering, in a universal language and terminology that all peoples of the world can understand, of a critical, anti-hegemonic message.

Denunciation

Iran's statist accommodation is, in some measure, replicated by others, writers and politicians, in the Islamic world. It is not, however, the predominant response in a political climate where denunciation of the West, or at least suspicion of it, is prevalent. The rhetoric of denunciation is often diffuse and repetitive, but there is a recurrent range of themes, ones that in their own way reflect both the appropriation of specific Islamic themes and the contemporary, modernist context within which Muslim states find

[13] English and Persian texts provided by the Islamic Republic News Agency, London.

themselves. Two examples will suffice – one from a political leader in power, Ayatollah Khamene'i of Iran, the other from an Islamic leader in opposition, Abdessalam Yassine, leader of the organization *al-'adl wa al-ihsan* (Justice and Spirituality) in Morocco.

The conservative right in Iran has been concerned ever since the revolution of 1979 to label its opponents as agents of Western imperialism. Globalization has provided a new means of achieving this: external goals and the resisting of foreign criticism and pressure are linked to, and in large measure subordinated to, domestic politics. The weekly *Ya Lesarat ol-Hossein* is the mouthpiece of the militant right-wing vigilante group Ansar-i Hizbullah. In attacking liberals in Iran as 'American reformers' it seeks to make this link:

> On the surface, the meaning of globalization is that due to technological, cultural, economic and political changes that have taken place in the modern world, especially after the collapse of the bipolar system, all economic and cultural and even political boundaries are naturally collapsing. In other words, national cultures will be gradually absorbed in the global culture. However, the truth is quite different. Technological, economic and cultural developments came about simultaneously with the creation of huge economic and communications monopolies and empires. As for the rest of the great volume of information, not [only] do they possess greater ability for production and distribution, they even strongly control the ability of their weaker rivals from access to technology and to mass media.[14]

Hence the need to resist 'American' reforms even more.

The clearest exponent of this view is Ayatollah Khamene'i. Since his assumption of the position of spiritual leader of Iran on the death of Khomeini in 1989, he has positioned himself as a militant defender of the Islamic revolution and of Islam. He has repeatedly linked his opposition to secular or liberal trends within Iran to his opposition to the West and in particular the United States. Recently, he has come to intervene more directly in Iranian politics in order to crush the liberal press. His views on globalization contrast markedly with those of Khatami:

> A nation like the Iranian nation that is alert, alive, wise, young and revolutionary must be able to overcome all of the said threats. When I talk about external threat, I mean the centres of world power. ... Today, not only Iran but all countries that are not on the same level of the

---

[14] *Ya Lesarat ol-Hossein*, no. 82, 14 June 2000, translated by Farhang Jahanpour.

advanced European and American countries are faced with a dual threat
… It is on the one hand, the direct influence of super powers, headed by
America, and on the other, the wave of globalization. It is what you have
seen recently in America where demonstrations have been staged
against this wave by a section of the American people. What is
globalization? It means that a group of world powers, a number of
countries – mainly those who have influence over the UN and mainly
those countries which have been colonialists in the past – want to expand
their culture, economy and traditions throughout the world. They want
to set up a share-holding company in which they should hold 95 per cent
of its share while the rest of world countries should have 5 per cent.
They want to have authority. They want to make decisions. That is what
globalization means. You see that so much pressure has been exerted on
the fact that Iran does not pay any attention to America. Americans use
all pressure in order to crush this grim face that the Iranian nation has
shown towards America – a grim face and no attention. The reason for
this is they have made every effort in all corners of the world aimed at
persuading world politicians to flatter, to show humility, to bow down
and to surrender. There is only one country, one nation and one
government in the world which has not submitted to this pressure. We
have nothing to do with America. However, we are not prepared to
surrender to bullying, to pressure and to imposition of policies. We are
not prepared to surrender. That country is the Islamic Republic of Iran.[15]

The enemy, Khamene'i continued, aims to create chaos in Iran by infil-
trating the young people.

The people should know what the enemy is doing in the country in the
field of cultural issues. They should know what objectives the enemy is
pursuing. The enemies' objectives are to take away the people's faith,
and to create a chasm between this generation and their elders … Separating the young generation from the previous generation and from its
historic achievements, separating people from the officials, separating
people from religious beliefs can only be pursued by the enemy.[16]

The general impression given by the Arab world suggests that this view
of globalization is widespread there too, but articulated not so much by
politicians in power, as in Iran, as by the intelligentsia, whether secular or
Islamist. A survey of attitudes to globalization among Arab intellectuals by

[15] BBC *SWB*, ME/3822 MED/2, 24 April 2000.
[16] BBC *SWB*, ME/3822 MED/6, 24 April 2000.

François Zabbal, editor of *Qantara*, the journal of the Institut du Monde Arabe in Paris, quotes from the plea by the Lebanese writer George Tarabishi for a more informed and open discussion of globalization in the Arab world without immediate labelling of those who participate.[17] According to Tarabishi, globalization has become the mental demon of the Arab intelligentsia, hostile to change while its own societies are largely insulated from this process. The main themes involved are recycled Leninist and nationalist ones about global capitalism and imperialism. Yumna Tarif al-Kholi, an Egyptian writer, sees globalization as a linguistic plot 'which aims to destroy the Arabic language. This is because we are the only nation in the world which speaks a holy language.' The Gulf intellectual Mohammad Abed al-Jabiri sees globalization as a frontal attack on the three pillars of Arab existence: state, nation and fatherland. Muta al-Safadi, a Syrian nationalist, sees 'globalization' as a seductive term, designed to subordinate all countries to the power of big capital. The Palestinian writer Feisal Darraj sees globalization as a form of cultural subjugation: hamburgers, jeans, Marlboro and Pepsi-Cola are all instruments of homogenization designed to destroy cultural pluralism.

These are views of members of the secular, that is nationalist and Marxist, intelligentsia in Islamic societies, many of whom replicate conventional anti-globalization arguments from elsewhere. The Moroccan thinker and Islamist politician Abdessalam Yassine echoes similar themes in Islamist form in his book *Islamiser la Modernité*.[18] These emphasize the relevance of Islam, and the Koran in particular, to modern life and the need for all people, in North and South, to return to their spiritual values. Yassine ranges far and wide, from discussions of Moses, Abraham, Nimrod and classical figures in Islam to reflections on the Internet, Bill Clinton, Samuel Huntington and much else. The starting point of the book is the refusal of the modern West, particularly Europe, to listen to the South. The Internet is both opportunity and danger. The great enemy is secularism, the secular crusade that threatens Europe and the Muslim world. Modern man is 'hyper-informed' but ignorant of himself, corrupted by consumerism and neo-Darwinian nihilism (p. 138). Modernity drowns indigenous peoples in 'its libertine and homogenising culture. Even in the Western world, nations jealous of their cultural identity and of their independence are crying out that they are being robbed' (p. 177). Yassine's inspiration (p. 88) comes

---

[17] François Zabbal, 'Die arabische Intelligenz und das Gespenst der Globalisierung', *Neue Zürcher Zeitung*, 24 January 2001.
[18] All quotations in this and the next two paragraphs are from Abdessalam Yassine, *Islamiser la Modernité* (n.p.: Al Ofok Impressions, 1998). For general background see François Burgat, *L'islamisme au Maghreb* (Paris: Karthala, 1988).

from the more rigorous trends within Islam, from Ibn Taimiya (1263–1328), a mediaeval opponent of liberal interpretations of the tradition; Sayyed Qutb, a leader of the Egyptian Muslim Brotherhood executed by Nasser in 1966; and the contemporary Algerian Islamist Malik ibn Bani. Repeated use is made of the Koran in justifying revolt against injustice as well as in denouncing Jews (pp. 122–5). The solution is a return to faith, the holy book and prayer, a call Yassine supports by reference to Western sociologists, such as Edgar Morin, who themselves call for a return to moral values within modern society.

Not surprisingly, a section of Yassine's book is concerned with 'globalization'. The first paragraph is clear enough: 'The menacing character of the new political order and of economic globalization proclaim the offensive launched in all directions by the great hegemonic power against the underdeveloped countries who suffer from it more than the rich countries. This politico-economic aggression forces us to mobilise all our forces to confront it' (p. 245). The negative impact of globalization is placed in the historical context of the struggle for independence and of the failure of the post-independence leadership, whose two components, atheistic socialists and the corrupt elite, he denounces as secular forces opposed to the values of Islam. 'The fate that is now knocking on our doors is globalization. Countries such as ours, underdeveloped and exposed to the wrangling and hesitations of politicians pre-occupied with fighting over power and the privileges of powers, always ready to change allegiance, will be indicated as the first victims' (p. 246). The new colonialism struggles not through direct occupation but through proclaiming such anti-Islamic goals as freedom of thought, democratic pluralism removed from any Islamic norms and the 'right to difference, understood as the right to proclaim oneself a Muslim without any conviction' (p. 289).

When it comes to globalization, however, Yassine does not advance a distinct or indigenous Islamic analysis. In order to substantiate his arguments he turns to *The Globalization Trap*, a critical work on globalization by two German writers, Hans-Peter Martin and Harald Schuman. 'I always prefer to let the sons of the West speak about their own modernity in the hope of not being accused of exaggeration. Our Islamic point of view will rest therefore on objective statements and direct observation.' Yassine also invokes the environmental critique of US hegemony, responsible in his view for global warming, the flooding of Bangladesh and El Niño. The Koran (Surat al Ra'ad, Verse 25 and, Yassine says, 50 other relevant verses) is invoked to support the view that God condemns those who violate the pact between man and nature. The two strands of critique, of the secular and destructive character of modernity and of globalization as a hegemonic project, are thereby joined into one sustained appeal for the 'remoralization' of society along Islamic lines. An Islamic state should be established and wealth should be distributed through charity or *zakat*, leading to more effective cooperation and ultimately to unity among all Muslims (p. 301). Corrupt, imported democracy should be replaced by Islamic consultative processes, *shura*.

This is the voice not of those in power, as in the case of the Iranian figures discussed above, but of the leader of an important and influential Islamist opposition movement. This text, although phrased in general terms, reflects a challenge both to the monarchical state and to the secular parties who have dominated Moroccan life since the 1950s. It is, therefore, intended to present an alternative to these secular political forces and their ideologies. But even in this rejection of the international system, and in his characterization of it, Yassine, like Khomeini and his followers, reflects a modern context. This is shown, first, by the very context of his writing, one of reflection upon and contestation of the political history of Morocco since the time of French colonialism; and, second, in the interweaving of recognizable, and often very generic, Muslim themes with what are prevalent elements of the radical critique of globalization: North–South inequality, the destruction of national culture, MNCs, the environment. The very extent to which Yassine cites, indeed relies on, 'Northern' authors to make his points underlines this interrelationship.

Participation

Accommodation and denunciation may well cover most of what is argued for and against in the Muslim world about international relations and globalization. If they do, however, it is as much because they provide, in an Islamic idiom, a response to the inequalities of colonialism and globalization shared by other developing states as because of any specifically Islamic explanation they use. This contingency may also be evident in the third response to globalization, that of participation. The argument for participation is much more positive about globalization, and it too draws on appropriate elements in the Islamic tradition.

One forceful if atypical variant of this approach is that of Mu'ammar al-Qadhdhafi, the leader of Libya, when he speaks of the new regional context of states:

Libya ... is merely a drop in the ocean in the face of the nature of today's world. The mindless and ignorant must wake up and try to understand the nature of today's world. It is regrettable that the era of nationalism and religious beliefs which bring people together as well as the era of languages and cultures have retreated. These are replaced by the new globalization, the era of territorial space. You can no longer say that a particular people belong to my religion, to my country, language or culture. I myself saw that those who belong to the same space are those with whom I share interests... The Comoros Island or Libya cannot survive alone but they cannot also rescue each other despite the fact they belong to the same nation and religion... Mediterranean basin countries form the Mediterranean territory. France and Libya are closer to each other than Libya to Syria or Libya to Kuwait.[19]

Qadhdhafi has in recent years come to stress the difficulties of Arab nationalism and to call for Libya's participation in a wider world context: this may be connected to the problems Libya has had with other Arab states, from which it is relatively isolated. This isolation has led him to emphasize the radical nature of contemporary international change.

From a very different perspective, the writer on international relations Ali Mazrui has offered a similar argument on the relation of Islam as a civilization to globalization.[20] Civilization, he argues, is born of creative synthesis – Islam was a synthesis of Judaism, Christianity and the message of the Prophet Mohammad, and between the ninth and fourteenth centuries Islamic thinkers such as Ibn Rushd and Ibn Sina fused classical Greek thinking with Islam. Heeding divine injunction, Islam emphasizes the importance of reading and learning from diverse traditions. The Islamic world, in its strongest era, learnt extensively from other civilizations, and in all four of the main dimensions of globalization: religion, technology, economy and empire. It can, and should, do so today, but by the same token it should also offer what it values to others. Here perhaps a conflict of discourse and of external context becomes visible. This is because the message of Islamic universalism and synthesis is arguably the one closest to the doctrinal traditions of the religion, one that knows no political or ethnic boundaries and that celebrates in Koranic text as in historical practice a diversity of languages, cultures and economic and political forms. Here Islamic reality administers a rebuttal to any claims of a single reading or implementation of Muslim culture and to any suggestion of an Islamic world shut off from the non-Islamic world. Yet it is these latter themes that have, to a considerable degree, prevailed as a result of the real

[19] BBC, *SWB*, ME/3781 MED/18, 6 March 2000.
[20] Ali Mazrui 'Globalization and the Future of Islamic Civilisation', lecture, Westminster University, 3 September 2000; text on *http://Islam21.org*.

subordination of Islamic societies to hegemonic forces from the West. It is the issues raised by this latter experience rather than a textual interpretation that most confront Muslim states today.

Conclusion

The debate on globalization is itself global, in the elementary sense that it is a topic which is discussed in all societies and to which all states have to articulate a response. But it is also global in two other senses: many of the themes encompassed by this debate are shared between all societies, and many of the ideas, terms and lines of dispute are reproduced within each society and discursive context. The responses found in the Islamic world illustrate this, just as they illustrate the degree to which the differences that do exist, between states, societies and cultures, reflect differences of structural power, above all in economic and technological terms, rather than differences of value. The problems faced by Arab states or Iran with regard to the Internet, trade liberalization or narcotics are faced in broadly similar ways by other societies too. We can thus identify Islamic responses to globalization, but even in the realm of discourse we see that these are not monolithic or insulated.

The recognition of this discursive variety is not the end of the story, however. Equally important is the relating of the ideologies and positions in these debates to practice in the real world. Here the divide between textualists and modernists recurs, for although the former, including many Islamists, might argue that the behaviour of Muslim societies and individuals is explicable in Islamic religious or cultural terms, modernists treat this as an open question. An examination of structures of political power, of educational practice, of international security policy and, above all, of the economy might show very little specifically 'Muslim' content. This question is of considerable relevance for the debate on globalization because, rhetoric and symbol apart, it is contestable how far the 'Islamic' discussion of globalization affects the practices of Muslim states in the areas central to the globalization debate. Islamic oil-producers determine their output and pricing in terms of the opportunities of the world market. As already noted, the discussion of the absence of FDI *into* the region distracts attention from the massive flow of FDI *out of* the Middle East and into OECD capital and property markets. Statist elites with access to 'rent', i.e. unearned income, resist liberalization because their material interests will be threatened. States, and patriarchs, resist the Internet because they fear it will undermine their power. Gulf Cooperation Council states and private investors have invested over $2,000 billion in Western capital markets, and very little at home, because of the comparative advantages of security and return. Despite much talk of a specifically 'Islamic' approach to economics – to interest, banking or redistribution of wealth – the practices of Islamic states, companies and economies are determined by other considerations. Therefore, apart from the recognition of the diversity and transnational character of 'Islamic' discourses on international relations and on the inequalities involved in the global economy, it is questionable how far these discourses affect the practices of those concerned. In this context, discourse may obscure as much as it explains.

The Middle East may be different, but this difference is constituted and reproduced by the patterns of integration into the modern world. And this integration does not necessarily produce the consequences in politics, economics or culture that are seen in the region today. To assume that this is the case, that everything in the region is determined by external factors, is to deny the room for manoeuvre, the autonomy that Middle Eastern states and their opponents have in the international system. Here again a discursive legacy from pre-1990 times plays a negative role, for in the period of colonialism and Cold War, Middle Eastern states and other actors had a margin of manoeuvre, and used it. The Middle East was never so controlled, or manipulated, by external forces as it claimed. This applies even more in the period of globalization. Differential integration does not entail passivity or subordination. That it is interpreted in this way is a matter of choice. Like all ideology, it serves to obscure the very real choices and options that these states and their opponents confront.

3 The end of historical attachments: Britain's changing policy towards the Middle East

Rosemary Hollis

Globalization is transforming the shape of interstate relations, and the responses of the US and other governments to the events of 11 September do not signal a reversal in this trend so much as a reordering of priorities. Terrorism is now seen to have a global reach, with alienated fanatics angry about US power projection in the Middle East and venting their spleen on unsuspecting civilians in the US heartland. The reaction of the United States has been to declare a war on terrorism, starting in Afghanistan, and to re-examine its alliances and policies across the Middle East too.

For Britain the unfolding crisis has demonstrated just how much its influence has declined in the Middle East, a region where once it was a key player. In the wake of 11 September, British Prime Minister Tony Blair swept to the forefront of international diplomacy, positioning Britain 'shoulder to shoulder' with the United States and providing stirring rhetoric to elevate the war on terrorism to a more noble quest to eliminate poverty, prejudice and human rights abuses too. However, when Tony Blair ventured to the Middle East in autumn 2001 his personal style of diplomacy was hampered by his lack of first-hand connections with his counterparts in the region. Hitherto he had focused on building ties with the most prominent global power brokers, Presidents Clinton and Bush of the United States, as well as Russian President Putin and the leading statesmen of Europe. Blair's sense of priorities would seem to reflect the dictates of globalization, which require the British government to maximize Britain's leverage in the most important power arenas – namely, Washington, Brussels, the United Nations Security Council, the G-8, the World Trade Organization (WTO) and the North Atlantic Treaty Organization (NATO) – at the expense of bilateral and regional relations *per se*.

Globalization and foreign policy

Even though Blair's leadership style is presidential rather than collegial and his tendency is to use personal intervention to circumvent bureaucratic procedures when possible, he is nonetheless operating within an international environment characterized by globalization. This requires governments to deal with one another in the context of multilateral or supra-territorial fora and organizations, as well as through the traditional mechanisms of bilateral diplomacy. The external relations of states are as much about negotiating regional and global financial, environmental and trade regulations as about the pursuit of conventional foreign policy goals. The jury is still out on whether the United States, by virtue of its sole superpower status, can ignore the imperatives pushing other states to agree on common rules of conduct or will simply use its power to set the rules. In any case, the point to be emphasized here is that states in general are reorienting their foreign policy goals around issues as opposed to geographical regions and it is to be expected, therefore, that changes are taking place in the way states external to the Middle East deal with those in the region, and vice versa.

An examination of British policy-making with respect to the Middle East at the turn of the century reveals more change than continuity in comparison with previous decades. It is not that the British have set out deliberately to reformulate their policies towards the region but rather that British policy priorities increasingly lie elsewhere. Consequently, issues arising in the entire Middle East (from Morocco to Iran and Iraq to the Sudan) are by default addressed piecemeal and often through multilateral fora such as the European Union (EU), the UN Security Council and the WTO.

This development has been most apparent in the decade since the end of the Cold War. Also apparent has been the perplexity with which most governments in the Middle East have responded to the trend. An expectation has persisted that Britain will honour its perceived historical responsibilities dating from imperial times and help to resolve some of the region's enduring territorial, security and economic problems. Even if US involvement in the region draws the most attention today, the British are still held to blame for continuing problems over Palestine, Iraq and the islands dispute between the United Arab Emirates and Iran. British foreign policy may be moving away from traditional preoccupations with territorial security, but for the Middle East, disputes over territorial sovereignty are still at the forefront of government concerns.

The case of Britain and the Middle East (as broadly defined above) offers some interesting insights on the general subject of this volume.

Britain qualifies as a 'major European power with global interests and responsibilities',[1] and is therefore comparable with a number of other significant state actors. More importantly for present purposes, under its New Labour leadership Britain can be considered a strong advocate of the benefits of globalization. Its government bureaucracy has been reorganized in order to respond to the new policy imperatives attributed to globalization. By its own enthusiastic embrace of globalization, therefore, Britain suggests itself as a suitable case study for examining how the phenomenon may transform traditional foreign policy-making.

With respect to the Middle East, Britain ranks alongside France at the forefront of European states with leverage on policy-making towards the region in the principal supra-territorial arenas of the EU and the UN Security Council. Britain can also boast greater access to and potential leverage with the United States, the predominant external actor in the Middle East. Given Britain's voice in key circles and its historical legacy in the region, players there have greater expectations of the British than of most other external powers. This raises the question of how far Britain's response to the imperatives of globalization can explain its perceived failure to live up to those expectations.

The opposite side of this question, touched upon here, has to do with the impact of globalization on the states of the Middle East. As discussed in other chapters, the region has been globalized in terms of its extra-regional relations or interdependence with the global economy, but far less so in terms of intra-regional linkages and the progress of internal liberalization.[2] Add to this a sense of disappointment with what outside players can and will do for those who live in the region, and it could be that the experience of globalization is a predominantly negative one for the Middle East so far.

Britain in contemporary context

Before turning to British policy positions on Middle Eastern issues and how best to explain them, a few words are in order about Britain's standing and orientation in the context of globalization. As is discussed elsewhere in this volume, globalization has reduced the autonomy previously enjoyed by state actors, but it does not herald the demise of the state as a player on the global stage. Britain ranks among the privileged few countries which

[1] John Coles, *Making Foreign Policy* (London: John Murray, 2000), p. 180.
[2] Louise Fawcett and Yezid Sayigh, *The Third World Beyond the Cold War: Continuity and Change* (Oxford: Oxford University Press, 1999), pp. 207–8.

hold a seat at all the top tables where collective responses to the imperatives of globalization are devised. Its economy places it among not only the OECD countries but also the G-8. It is the largest overseas investor after the United States and, according to KPMG, it spent about $130 billion in 1998 on acquiring foreign companies.[3]

Britain is one of the five permanent members (P-5) of the UN Security Council. Although still outside the Euro zone, it is a member of the EU and in the forefront of efforts to develop a European defence capability. A founder member of NATO, Britain has nuclear weapons in its arsenal, and its armed forces are unrivalled in western Europe. The British contingent in the Gulf War coalition that ousted Iraq from Kuwait in 1991 was second only to that of the United States. The United Kingdom is also one of the top three or four global arms exporters; and it is a net exporter of oil.

These assets are useful only in the context of the multilateral bodies that are determining the rules of the game in the new, post-Cold War global order. By itself Britain has limited power to act decisively in any arena. Even in conjunction with France and Italy, Britain could not mount the operations 'Poised Hammer' or 'Provide Comfort' in northern Iraq in 1991 without US engagement. Its submarine-based nuclear capability was put under review in 2000 after problems were detected with the missile platforms. At the end of 2001, as Britain prepared to send a contingent to Afghanistan as part of the International Security Assistance Force (Isaf), Chief of the Defence Staff Admiral Sir Michael Boyce warned against the dangers of over-committing British troops to more missions and theatres than they could handle simultaneously.[4] Some of Britain's major companies, including those in the defence sector, are in the process of merging with their US and European counterparts. The success of British efforts to attract inward investment has brought with it the vulnerability of exposure to developments in the world economy, with many foreign companies that operate in the UK pressing for Britain to join the Euro and maximize their market access. Britain is the largest foreign investor in the United States, and hence its economic well-being is exposed to the fortunes of the US economy. The leading British companies today are themselves global operations.

Yet, judging by the pronouncements of ministers in the first and second New Labour governments, Britain's presence in various international fora is counted among its strengths, not its limitations. In his keynote foreign policy speech during the 2001 election campaign, Tony Blair said: 'Britain

[3] *The Economist*, 23 January 1999, quoted in Coles, *Making Foreign Policy*, p. 112.
[4] 'UK Strategic Choices Following the Strategic Defence Review and the 11th September', Annual Chief of Defence Staff Lecture by Admiral Sir Michael Boyce at the Royal United Services Institute, 10 December 2001.

still has enormous diplomatic assets in the world to bring to play... With our seat in the UN Security Council, our role in the G-7, our closeness to the US, our membership of the EU, our position in the Commonwealth, our trade links with Asia ... we still have huge diplomatic strengths.'[5] Indeed, the prime minister has been one of the most enthusiastic advocates of globalization as the new panacea, full of promise and opportunity. On a trip to Latin America shortly after his re-election in 2001, Tony Blair devoted most of his speeches to singing the praises of economic liberalization and free trade. In other words he chose to focus on broad global concerns, not narrow issues of national interest. A new note entered his rhetoric after 11 September. Thereafter, Blair tempered his enthusiasm for economic liberalization with calls for more aid to the poorest countries and multilateral intervention to avert conflicts around the world, but if anything his theme became literally visionary on a global scale.

Peter Hain, Minister of State at the Foreign Office, has articulated his views on the implications of globalization for traditional foreign policy-making in a pamphlet entitled *The End of Foreign Policy?*[6] In this he argues that new global imperatives require the current generation of world leaders to realign the way their own countries see their interests and to act collectively to combat climate change, poverty, social exclusion, disease, drug abuse and terrorism. Hain greets the increased influence of non-governmental organizations (NGOs) such as Oxfam, Save the Children, Greenpeace and Amnesty International as a signal for national governments to respond creatively and, where possible, by forming partnerships with these new actors.[7]

Bearing in mind that the British population's membership of NGOs far exceeds its membership of the traditional political parties, there is reason to believe that expectations of government are changing in Britain, as in other developed economies. According to one commentator writing in the American press about the 2001 British election:

Politics has become the business of managing government, and elections are increasingly like the annual general meetings of a big utility company. Some people saw this coming a while back. As early as July 1997 Mr Blair offered insight into his own thinking when justifying the use of focus groups to sample public opinion on specific policies: 'Suppose you're running a business like Marks and Spencer or Sainsbury's,' he

[5] Andrew Parker, 'Blair set to give higher priority to foreign policy', *Financial Times*, 20 June 2001.
[6] Peter Hain, *The End of Foreign Policy? British Interests, Global Linkages and Natural Limits* (London: Fabian Society, Green Alliance and RIIA, 2001).
[7] Ibid., p. 15.

told *The Independent*, 'you will be constantly trying to work out whether your customers are satisfied with the product they are getting.'[8]

Prior to the events of 11 September, there was little reason to expect Britain's New Labour governments to pay much attention to the Middle East in the name of maintaining voter confidence. Focus groups and polls have consistently shown that the electorate cares most about economic well-being, services and education. Beyond the domestic sphere, the imperatives of globalization have obliged the British government to concentrate on maximizing its leverage in key global fora that affect the economy, and these do not include the Middle East *per se*. By 2000 less than four per cent of total British exports were destined for the Middle East, against some eight per cent in the boom period of high oil revenues and capital expenditure. Defence sales remained an important component, with Saudi Arabia accounting for perhaps 15 per cent of UK defence sales and related work, or about £1.2 billion worth of business each year. Of the estimated £4.23 billion invested overseas by the British, only 0.3 per cent went to the Middle East, although Britain was the recipient of £2.27 billion of inward investment from the region.

After 11 September the requirement to protect the population from potential terrorist attacks has led the British government to introduce new measures to apprehend and detain terrorist suspects in coordination with other EU members, the United States and any other countries willing to cooperate. The fact that the attacks of 11 September were perpetrated by Arabs with grievances against the United States for its policies in the Middle East has prompted greater interest in that region as such. However, as Tony Blair discovered on his forays into the Arab world after 11 September, British diplomacy cannot by itself deliver very much in isolation from the United States. This being so, the British government is unlikely to see much political capital to be gained from seeking to raise its profile in the region and can be expected to continue focusing above all on trying to influence Washington's policies. Meanwhile, the imperatives of globalization have already left their mark on the British policy-making machinery.

[8] Niall Ferguson, 'Now Comes (Yawn) a Big Conservative Victory in Britain', *International Herald Tribune*, 31 May 2001.

Reorientation of the policy-making machinery

Not only must the British Foreign Office work more closely than ever with other departments, as the lines are so blurred between what is domestic and what is foreign, but also the internal organization of the Foreign Office has had to change. According to John Cole, a former Permanent Under Secretary at the Foreign and Commonwealth Office:

> In Whitehall the evolution has been considerable. When I became a diplomat in 1960, the most prestigious departments in the Foreign Office were the so-called geographical departments, those that dealt with specific areas of the world such as the Middle East or the Soviet Union. The great men (and they were nearly all men) were those who advised during the Arab-Israeli wars of 1967 and 1973 or who developed policy towards the Soviet world in the 1970s or who analysed events in China and their possible impact on Hong Kong. Today, reflecting interdependence and multilateralism, the largest departments, where the most ambitious and able want to work, are the 'functional' departments, those that deal not with a geographical area but with a subject or group of subjects, such as the two European Union departments dealing with external and internal EU affairs, the International Security Department, dealing among other things with NATO, and the United Nations Department.[9]

Notwithstanding this reorientation, Peter Hain has gone further and suggested that as informational links to overseas posts improve, 'there will be a case for dismantling the geographically oriented departments' in the Foreign Office.[10] Instead the focus will be on strengthening the centre in order to use those posts 'to support cross-cutting objectives in areas such as the environment, conflict prevention and human rights'.

Under the first New Labour government there was reorganization at the Department of Trade and Industry (DTI) too. A body called British Trade International (BTI) was set up within the department in order to coordinate the trade promotion activities of the Foreign Office and the DTI. In line with the shift in foreign policy as outlined by Hain, less emphasis is being given commercially to regional markets than to sectoral opportunities. This is reflected in the reduction in the number of regional boards of leading business people appointed worldwide to advise on export policy and resource allocations. Under this system, the Middle East and Africa

[9] Coles, *Making Foreign Policy*, p. 118.
[10] Hain, *The End of Foreign Policy?*, p. 47.

have been lumped together as the responsibility of a single board, much to the consternation of some in the business sector who feel that the two regions do not have enough in common to benefit from a common strategy.

When Tony Blair formed his new cabinet after the June 2001 election, he appointed Baroness Symons as trade minister, with offices, staff and responsibilities at both the DTI and the Foreign Office. This was intended to end confusion and conflict between the two ministries over responsibility for trade.[11] The ability of the prime minister's office to deal with foreign policy issues was also enhanced: two senior diplomats were appointed as advisers instead of just one, as previously.[12] At the Foreign Office the replacement of Robin Cook by Jack Straw as foreign secretary was taken as a signal that Straw would be a more convincing advocate of joining the Euro zone, which was considered the major foreign policy issue facing Labour in its second term. Peter Hain was given the number two job, with responsibility for Europe, while the rest of the world was split between three parliamentary secretaries instead of being the responsibility of another junior minister. The changes were interpreted in the press as signalling greater priority for the trade and investment aspects of foreign policy, for special provision for handling the expected Euro debate and for enhancing the prime minister's leadership on foreign policy delivery.

End of an era

As implied by the changes described, the trend has been for British dealings with the Middle East to be filtered through the prism of multilateral organizations and take second place to the government's preoccupations with responding to global economic, security and environmental agendas. To emphasize the point being made here, it could even be argued that the end of the 1990s was the end of an era in British policy towards the Middle East.

During the twentieth century, it became the norm to define British policy towards different parts of the world by first enumerating British interests in the region concerned and then examining how these were being pursued through diplomacy, commerce, finance and military strategy. It also became the norm, certainly in the Middle East, to have a British government view on which developments in the region should be encouraged, and which discouraged or counteracted. In other words there was a British view on what was 'good' for the region and what was definitely not.

[11] Robert Shrimsley and Rosemary Bennett, 'Symons' appointment ends battle over trade brief', *Financial Times*, 13 June 2001.
[12] Andrew Parker, *Financial Times,* 20 June 2001.

Two documents reveal how British thinking about the Middle East was to take shape during the last century. One was the address made by Lord Curzon, Viceroy of India, at Sharjah in 1903, which was described by the India Office in 1905 as follows: 'He [Curzon] had evolved a new and original conception of the Gulf as forming in itself a complete and distinct political entity; this idea, latent rather than expressed, dominated his own policy in the Gulf region and may now be regarded as having entered the domain of established political principle.'[13]

The second document was the de Bunsen Committee Report,[14] drawn up by an interdepartmental committee created in 1915 to formulate objectives for the aftermath of the First World War and the anticipated collapse of the Ottoman Empire. In summary, the committee designated the following goals for British policy:

1. Recognition and consolidation of Britain's position in the Gulf;
2. Prevention of discrimination against Britain's trade by Turkey, the continuance of trading links with the area and/or acquisition of compensation for discontinuation of such trade;
3. Fulfilment of pledges given to the rulers of Kuwait and Najd and the maintenance of assurances given to other Arab leaders;
4. Protection of projects in which Britain held an interest, including oil and water developments;
5. Consideration of Mesopotamia as a possible area for Indian colonization;
6. Security of communications in the Mediterranean, with minimum increase in naval and military expenditure;
7. Maintenance of the independence of and freedom of worship in religious shrines;
8. A satisfactory solution to the Armenian problem; and
9. A satisfactory solution to the question of Palestine (i.e. one in which Britain would retain control of the Suez approaches).

Obviously, by the end of the twentieth century not only was the vision much less grand, but the terms of discourse had changed fundamentally too. Foreign Office ministers are now more likely to talk about Britain's position on events and issues arising in the region than to itemize Britain's interests in the region as a whole as a prelude to articulating policy. It is more common as well to find a defence minister approaching the issues

[13] India Office, 'Summary of the Principal Events and Measures of the Viceroyalty of Lord Curzon' (1905), Part I, Chapter 4.
[14] See FCO, Foreign Policy Document No. 36, 'Jordan and Palestine 1914–1920'.

that way. Even so, the emphasis is likely to be on Britain's contribution to multilateral endeavours. As John Reid, then the armed forces minister, said in a speech at the Royal United Services Institute in 1998:

> Of course our interests do not extend equally everywhere. Europe and NATO must be a priority. Beyond Europe, we believe that our interests are most likely to be directly affected by events in the Gulf, the Near East and North Africa. This does not mean that the [Strategic Defence] Review will lead to our re-creating a military capability 'East of Suez'. That would be a retrograde step. But it does mean that the Review has confirmed the importance of the Gulf region in British economic interests, the value of our bilateral ties with Gulf states and the importance of our wider UN responsibilities in the Gulf area. We must therefore be ready to respond, in combination with others, to support stability when it is threatened in the Gulf.[15]

More tellingly, George Robertson, then the defence secretary, said on the same occasion: 'The United States is of course central, both to underpinning Gulf security and to reinvigorating the Middle East Peace Process. But I believe that the United Kingdom also has a worthwhile role to play, both in its own right and as a trusted ally of the United States, an ally that is able to make a distinctive contribution to the formulation of policy in Washington.'[16] In other words, if the crucial decisions are being made in Washington, better to concentrate on developing leverage there than on trying to go it alone. A case can easily be made for including Washington in the list of supra-territorial arenas in which Britain seeks to exercise leverage today. As the sole superpower, and therefore almost by definition the biggest winner from globalization, the United States is more than just another state actor. Access and leverage in Washington is a necessary foreign policy goal for most other governments, not least those in the Middle East. And Britain has worked harder than most to preserve what influence it has there.

Since 11 September the ramifications of Britain's focus on Washington have become more apparent. The British prime minister excelled in the competition to demonstrate solidarity with the United States in the face of the terrorist attacks, winning him the unique honour of addressing a joint session of both Houses of the US Congress, which accorded him a standing ovation.

---

[15] John Reid, 'Gulf Security: UK Policy and Implications for the Strategic Defence Review', in Emirates Center for Strategic Studies and Research, *The Gulf: Future Security and British Policy* (Abu Dhabi: ECSSR, 2000), p. 10.
[16] George Robertson, *Welcome Address* in ibid, p. 7.

However, when it came to influencing the prosecution of the war in Afghanistan, the United States heard but did not necessarily heed British and other allied entreaties to use allied troops to help bring in humanitarian aid, and US commanders preferred to do without even British military assistance in the interests of maintaining full control of the operation.[17] By December 2001 British Chief of the Defence Staff Admiral Boyce was warning:

> Both the UK and United States wish to promote regional stability, but our perspectives of global and regional stability have been distorted by the focus on fighting terrorism. *We* have to consider whether we wish to follow the United States' single minded aim to finish Osama Bin Laden and Al-Qaeda; and/or to involve ourselves in creating the conditions for nation-building or reconstruction as well... Altogether, that there will be some slight difference in emphasis in the approach between the United States and UK is clear – but with a previously isolated single super power background and a global capability, the United States has less need of consensus than we do.[18]

In the 1990s Britain moved away from pursuing a coherent regional strategy in the Middle East simply because globalization dictated new foreign policy imperatives which took precedence. After 11 September the imperative of keeping on-side with Washington looked destined to draw Britain into dealing with the Middle East more and more through the prism of its alliance with the United States.

The Middle East and Britain's historical baggage

Britain's 'moment in the Middle East' is long since over.[19] That 'moment' had its beginnings in the nineteenth century when ties were forged with Iran, the Arab sheikhdoms of the Gulf and Aden, took off in 1914 and concluded in 1971 when British forces were withdrawn from 'East of Suez'. In between, of course, Britain exercised imperial dominance in Egypt and Sudan for several decades; made conflicting promises to Sherif Hussein of Mecca (the Hussein–McMahon correspondence), to the Jewish community seeking to establish a 'homeland' in Palestine (the Balfour Declaration)

---

[17] Ewen MacAskill, Richard Norton-Taylor, Julian Borger and Ian Black, 'Clouds hang over special relationship', *Guardian*, 9 November 2001.
[18] Admiral Sir Michael Boyce, *UK Strategic Choices*.
[19] As described in Elizabeth Monroe's book of that name, *Britain's Moment in the Middle East: 1914–71* (London: Chatto & Windus, 1981).

and to the French (the Sykes-Picot Agreement); established and relinquished the League of Nations mandates in Palestine and Iraq; suffered the débâcle at Suez in 1956; retreated from Aden; and finally negotiated its way out of the sheikhdoms of the Gulf.

Given this record it is perhaps surprising that governments in the Middle East still seek British engagement in the region. In fact, Britain's history there is relevant to today in two important respects: first, in terms of regional perceptions of Britain's responsibility for sowing the seeds of land and border disputes which endure to this day, most notably in Palestine but also with respect to the Iraq–Kuwait border and the islands dispute between the UAE and Iran; and, second, in terms of personal relationships, sustained over generations, between British individuals and members of the elite across the region. It is these factors that underlie expectations in the Middle East that Britain could and should do more about the region. Meanwhile, given Britain's role in key global organizations such as the UN Security Council and the EU, and its assumed influence in Washington, it is expected to use this access to highlight Middle Eastern concerns, if not to lobby for those who count themselves among its friends and allies in the region.

As it is, with some notable exceptions Britain under New Labour has been less visible than France in international diplomacy concerning the Middle East. British diplomats will argue that it is more effective through quiet diplomacy, behind the scenes. Even if that is true with respect to the Arab-Israeli conflict, Britain's diplomacy in the Gulf has been so quiet as to be near invisible at times, except for its contentious stance on Iraq. Arab governments in the Gulf have expressed disappointment with what they see as British sycophancy towards Washington and a failure to show more unilateral interest in their individual concerns. For example, for the duration of the first New Labour government, a number of Arab Gulf governments sought in vain to encourage British ministers to visit their countries and include the region more often in their travel itineraries. When Tony Blair did go to the region in the aftermath of 11 September, his initial attempt to include Saudi Arabia in his itinerary failed on the grounds that more diplomatic preparation was needed.

During the first Labour term Iran received no visit at foreign minister level, Robin Cook having postponed plans to go to the Islamic Republic twice before losing office. Cook's successor Jack Straw, however, did make the journey to Tehran twice in rapid succession, in the wake of 11 September and the war in Afghanistan. In North Africa, the governments would have liked to see Britain and other northern Europeans take more interest in the implications for them of the EU–Mediterranean Partnership Initiative, or Barcelona process. Cook's efforts to resolve the issue of

Libya's role in the Lockerbie bombing was considered a breakthrough, although serious problems remained because of the conviction of one of the Libyans accused in the case. Meanwhile, the Libyans continued to live in hope of a British ministerial visit to boost business relations.

Robin Cook did make a couple of well-publicized trips to Israel and its neighbours, but on the first occasion he had the thankless task of conveying EU disapproval of Israel's settlement policy to the government of Binyamin Netanyahu. He suffered the indignity of having the Israeli prime minister cancel dinner with him for his pains. He subsequently made light of the episode as beneficial for his waistline, but he was reportedly sufficiently bruised not to want to rush back into the cauldron of Arab-Israeli relations. On the second occasion the foreign secretary tried to mediate between the Palestinians and the Israelis shortly after the outbreak of the intifada in autumn 2000, but he arrived on the heels of several other international figures and met with no greater success. The visit of Jack Straw to Israel, straight after his first trip to Iran in October 2001, was almost as ill-fated at Cook's first foray there. Israeli Prime Minister Ariel Sharon had to be persuaded by a phone call from Tony Blair not to shun the foreign secretary for remarks he had made about Palestine during his time in Iran.

In trying to piece together Britain's stance at the United Nations and in the European Union on the unfolding Israeli-Palestinian conflict, its posture on Iraq and its engagements with both Iran and Libya, many are at a loss to discern a coherent region-wide policy towards the Middle East. That, however, is precisely the point at issue. At the highest level, policy is organized around not regions but issues that come up in multilateral fora or have a bearing on Britain's relations with Washington and the EU.

Britain and the Middle East peace process

Britain does not approach peace-making in the Arab-Israeli context as another chapter in its historical involvement in the region. Rather, it seeks to bolster and support whatever process seems most likely to resolve the conflict. Since the mid-1990s, that has meant supporting the Oslo process and accepting US custodianship of that process, and thereafter calling for implementation of the Mitchell Report, again under Washington's tutelage. The approach has not meant promoting the role of the United Nations and UN resolutions, except possibly in the case of Lebanon. Until Israel's unilateral withdrawal from Lebanon in 2000, Britain adhered to the European position that Israel was obliged to leave, with or without negotiations, as stipulated under UN Resolution 425.

As of the Madrid Conference of 1991, Europe was given a strictly limited role in Middle Eastern peace-making by the United States. Britain enjoyed no better access than other Europeans to what was going on in the early days of the Washington negotiations. For a time this was cause for irritation in Europe, and attempts were made to forge a key role for the Regional Economic Development Working Group (REDWG), the multilateral working group under EU stewardship, to circumvent Europe's exclusion from the bilateral talks. However, having gained some momentum after the Oslo accords of 1993, the multilateral track begun at Madrid ran out of steam in the face of subsequent stalemate in the bilateral negotiations.

Meanwhile, in 1995 the EU launched its Mediterranean Partnership Initiative, to build a free market in the Mediterranean, and for a time this operated almost in competition with the US-sponsored MENA (Middle East–North Africa) initiative to convene regional economic summits. The Euro-Mediterranean process proved the more enduring, because of its detachment from the peace process, but, as was demonstrated at a tempestuous meeting in Marseilles in 2000, it too can become caught up in the Arab-Israeli confrontation. In any case, not even the Egyptian and Jordanian governments, which are supposed to be at peace with Israel, have been willing to meet Israelis in official fora if they can avoid it since the intensification of the Israeli-Palestinian conflict.

The pattern that emerged in the 1990s in EU policy towards the peace process was for Brussels to support the US-brokered negotiations when these were going well and to make noises and political gestures from the sidelines when they faltered. There was a particularly interesting episode in US–European diplomacy in the Middle East over the 4 May issue of 1999, when the Palestinians were threatening to declare statehood unilaterally. The EU went further than the United States felt able to then in supporting the goal of a Palestinian state, in order to dissuade the Palestinian leadership from making the declaration at that time. But in doing so Brussels had Washington's blessing and encouragement.

By 1999, in fact, the EU was working in close coordination with the United States on promoting the Oslo formula for peace. The prevailing logic was that Washington was best placed to influence Israel and that without such influence no deal could be done. Europe therefore accepted the primary role of funding the Palestinian Authority and encouraging it to embrace the principles of good governance, confident in the view that with the victory of Ehud Barak in the Israeli election of 1999, the Oslo process would eventually produce a final status agreement between the parties. Britain operated comfortably within this EU–US coordinated approach; so, basically, did France.

Britain's policy may best be characterized as balancing its role in the EU with its 'special relationship' with the United States. It contributed to EU policy-making on the Middle East in such a way as it calculated would mesh best with US efforts at peace-making. However, under Tony Blair's premiership Britain has occasionally gone further and tried to contribute from the sidelines unilaterally. In some respects this is no different from the policies of a number of other European states, including Norway, as well as Canada and Japan, which have each chosen to reinforce a specific aspect of the peace process. In Britain's case, funds from the Department of International Development have been channelled into efforts to improve accountability and efficiency within the Palestinian Authority, and the Adam Smith Institute was brought in to advise on financial matters.

More curious, however, has been the role of Tony Blair's special envoy Lord Levy in regional diplomacy. The most plausible explanation for this could be pure serendipity. Lord Levy has generated funds for both the British and the Israeli Labour parties. He is a personal friend of the British prime minister, and his son worked for the Labour government of Ehud Barak in Israel. Consequently, he could be a trusted emissary; and if he could contribute to peace, so much the better. His principal contribution seems to have been in trying to promote negotiations between Israel and Syria. But although he may retain the ear of the British prime minister, he has had less access in Israel since the replacement of Ehud Barak by Ariel Sharon as leader.

According to Peter Hain when he was briefly in charge of the Middle East at the Foreign Office, British policy on the Arab-Israeli conflict aimed to take account of the situation on the ground and work pragmatically for a solution, as opposed to pronouncing on what should or should not happen. This sounds like traditional British pragmatism rather than the pursuit of high principle, but it also sounds more like the American position than the French one. Since the outbreak of the Palestinian intifada Britain has echoed the concerns of its European and American allies on Israel's use of force, but has never taken the lead in criticizing Israel.

Certainly, the British have sought to improve their access in Israel and to overcome Israeli perceptions of the Foreign Office as pro-Arab. According to Arab diplomats, that strategy has worked, and the British are now perceived as more sympathetic to Israel than ever before. Meanwhile, according to Brussels bureaucrats, Britain has shifted its position within the EU. It had, until autumn 2000, played the role of bridge-maker between the positions of Israel's staunchest supporters, Germany and the Netherlands, on the one hand, and the pro-Arab camp, frequently championed by the French, on the other. Of late, however, it has been more likely to side with the former and/or echo the US position.

In October 2001 Tony Blair tried his hand at direct intervention in the Arab-Israeli maelstrom and was left rather bruised for his pains. While making the first visit of a British prime minister to Syria he received a public rebuke from the Syrian President who criticized the war in Afghanistan, lamented the loss of civilian life there and refused to equate Palestinians and others resisting Israeli occupation with terrorists.[20] He did make it to Saudi Arabia on this occasion, but little was said publicly about his conversations there, except that he had failed to win Saudi backing for the Afghan campaign. He also visited Israel and the Palestinians, and reportedly took the message to Washington thereafter that more had to be done to quell the Israeli-Palestinian conflict. It was shortly after this, and following calls from Secretary of State Colin Powell for the establishment of a Palestinian state alongside Israel as the formula for peace, that Tony Blair himself pronounced on the need for 'a viable Palestinian state'.[21] This marked a significant development in Britain's public position; however, nothing was to come of it. The US initiative to push more vigorously for a ceasefire, led by retired General Anthony Zinni, crumbled in a spate of Palestinian suicide bombings in Jerusalem and Haifa, followed by Israeli military retaliation which trapped Palestinian leader Yasser Arafat in Ramallah. Thereafter attention shifted to the survivability of the Palestinian leader and Britain was instrumental in pushing for an EU statement requiring Arafat to rein in the military wings of Hamas and Islamic Jihad, as called for by Washington.[22]

Overall, British policy of late looks designed to make sure that London has the ear of Israelis as well as Arabs, in the name of being even-handed. The potential drawback in this strategy is that in the Arab world generally, Britain is increasingly perceived as a lackey of the United States – a perception fuelled by its policy on Iraq. In fact, when it comes to the Gulf Britain is not in Washington's pocket, even on Iraq, but it could be paying a price for that perception while gaining little benefit from the support it has given the United States.

Britain and Iran

Britain's assessment of Iran, in common with other European states, is that it is too important to ignore. The Islamic Republic has the potential to be a

[20] Andrew Parker, 'Assad tells Blair that Arab anger is growing', *Financial Times*, 1 November 2001.
[21] Brian Groom, 'Blair says the time is right to tackle global problems', *Financial Times*, 13 November 2001.
[22] Judy Dempsey, 'US pressure on EU over Mideast resolution', *Financial Times*, 17 December 2001.

very important and sizeable market, and could become integrated into the global economy. Obviously, Iran is energy-rich and has sought to attract inward investment from foreign energy companies. The fact that Britain's view of Iran is at one with other European countries has facilitated policy coordination within the EU towards Tehran. For their part the Iranians have courted the Europeans, partly in order to counteract US efforts to isolate the Islamic Republic.

During the pre-Khatami period, as the United States hardened its position by way of 'dual containment', it was highly critical of European dealings with Iran. Up to a point the EU, and Britain in particular, had to keep demonstrating to Washington that its 'critical dialogue' was a better approach than 'containment' and isolation. Its efforts evoked criticism from Iran that it was simply pushing the US agenda by other means.

However, America's Iran-Libya Sanctions Act (ILSA) of 1996 caused a furore in Europe, with Britain its most outspoken critic. This act set out to punish foreign companies for pursuing their own interests in Iran; it was unacceptable on principle as far as the British were concerned. Britain was at the forefront of lobbying efforts in Washington against ILSA. The act contravened the free trade philosophy that Britain advocates and upholds and that it counts as one of its shared interests with the United States. In the end, the act could not be implemented, because of European resistance and defiance. Even so, British companies with significant investments, partners and subsidiaries in the United States were for a time deterred from openly defying ILSA. No doubt this was one of the reasons why the British government was so opposed to the act and saw it as a dangerous precedent.

In terms of bilateral British–Iranian relations, it was Robin Cook who oversaw resolution of the problem of the fatwa issued against British author Salman Rushdie in 1989 for his book *The Satanic Verses*. The breakthrough came during the visit of President Khatami of Iran to New York for the opening of the UN General Assembly in September 1998. After talks with the British delegation, President Khatami declared that Iran regarded the affair as 'completely finished', and Foreign Minister Kharrazi told his British counterpart that 'Iran has no intention, nor is it going to take any action whatsoever to threaten the life of the author of *The Satanic Verses*, or anybody associated with his work, nor will it encourage or assist anybody to do so.'[23] Britain could now restore full diplomatic relations with Iran, and in April 1999 London and Tehran agreed on an exchange of ambassadors.

[23] Adam Tarock, 'Iran–Western Europe: Relations on the Mend', *British Journal of Middle Eastern Studies*, Vol. 26, No. 1, May 1999, p. 60.

Even so, British–Iranian relations remain troubled from time to time by residual Iranian suspicions, dating from imperial times, of British intentions. Thus in autumn 1999, media reports in Iran claimed that the British were so jealous of Iran's improved ties with other European countries that they were determined to give a negative spin to domestic events in Iran. The object of Iranian concern was the BBC's Persian Service, which had given less than favourable coverage to the handling of student unrest by members of the Iranian security forces in summer 1999. Subsequently, plans for Kharrazi to visit London in January 2000 were nearly derailed when the new year's issue of the London *Times* republished the obituaries of famous people of the twentieth century. An extract from the one on Ayatollah Khomeini was deeply offensive, and it took a formal statement of regret from the British ambassador in Tehran to defuse the crisis.

As mentioned previously, Robin Cook never returned Kharrazi's visit to London. It was Cook who first postponed his trip to Tehran, perhaps because it would have coincided with the trial verdict on 13 Iranian Jews accused of spying for Israel (this was denied as a reason by the Foreign Office). Then, when the trip was rescheduled for autumn 2000, it was the Iranians who asked for a postponement, and thereafter both British and Iranian elections have been cited as the causes for further delays.

In any case, British policy on Iran under the first New Labour government may best be explained as the outcome of Foreign Secretary Robin Cook's interest in making a mark where he could. As noted, it is to him personally that the breakthroughs with Libya and Iran are attributed. Meanwhile, in both cases there were strong commercial reasons for improving relations, not least in the energy sector. In both cases, too, British policy was depicted as smoothing the way for Washington to overcome its antipathy to at least two of the various countries it had labelled as 'rogue states' in the mid-1990s. That said, the British government was apparently happy to give British business a chance to get in ahead of the Americans, in the expectation that they would follow in due course.

British attention to Iran, for its own sake and irrespective of US policy, could be considered to have proved its worth in the wake of 11 September. The visits of Jack Straw to Tehran were clearly designed to sound out Iranian views on Afghanistan, the Taliban regime there and the war which was to topple them. It is to be assumed that this line of communication contributed to gaining Iranian acquiescence if not cooperation in the campaign.

However, Britain has become tainted by association with the United States, at least in Iranian eyes. At the beginning of 2002 Tehran delayed approval of Britain's nominee for its new ambassador to Iran, David Reddaway, and in February he was turned down. Iran's claims about his unsuitability could not be substantiated, fuelling the view that Britain was being punished for new accusations directed at Iran by the Bush administration in Washington.

Relations with the Gulf Arab states

Commercial competition between Britain, other Europeans and the United States in the Gulf Cooperation Council (GCC) states has been fierce since the oil boom of the 1970s. In fact, it is not unusual for US and British defence companies to talk of each other as 'the enemy' when it comes to their dealings with the GCC states, especially in the lower Gulf. At the beginning of the twenty-first century, however, the Gulf states feature less prominently in the British government's export promotion policy. This may be attributed to perceptions that the defence market has peaked, and in general the perception prevails that opportunities are more limited than they were. The exception, of course, is in the energy sector, where British companies are as eager as their competitors to invest where they can, but it is for the Gulf oil producers to decide what is on offer to the companies.

Meanwhile, when it comes to British security cooperation with the Gulf states the driver of British policy has been the Ministry of Defence rather than the Foreign Office or the DTI. As indicated in the statements of defence ministers quoted above, care is taken to honour commitments made to Gulf governments. As a demonstration of this, British forces conducted a major joint forces exercise with their Omani counterparts in the sultanate in autumn 2001. That exercise was planned well in advance of 11 September and went ahead irrespective of the build-up of US forces that ensued in the Indian Ocean in preparation for the war in Afghanistan. However, British forces were on hand in the region, as a result of the exercise, to assist with the US war in so far as they were called upon.

As has been mentioned, the British prime minister was to make his first visit to Saudi Arabia in the wake of 11 September, in a mission designed to sound out Saudi reactions to the crisis. It was further assumed at the time that he wanted to solicit the Saudis' support for the war in Afghanistan and learned of their reluctance. Since then, however, the US–Saudi relationship has taken on a new complexion, as the US administration pressures the Saudi government to pursue local funders and supporters of Osama Bin Laden. It is to be expected that British companies, not least in the defence sector, will seek to distance themselves from such US pressure and this may raise some interesting dilemmas at the political level, where British policy has become more closely aligned with that of Washington.

The vexed question of Iraq

Because sanctions on Iraq were imposed by the UN Security Council, this body comes into play in a way that is not mirrored in Britain's relations with Iran or the GCC. Following on from this, it is those European powers, Britain and France, which are permanent members of the UNSC along with Russia that have made the running in debates with the United States about policy towards Iraq. The EU has not featured. Also, Britain and France were at the forefront of European contributions to the military alliance that fought Iraq over Kuwait and that, together with the United States, established the no-fly zones (which France subsequently abandoned).

To understand US, British, French and Russian differences over Iraq before 11 September 2001, the following factors need to be taken into account:

1. France and Russia have debts outstanding in Iraq, unlike Britain and the United States.
2. France, unlike Britain, is dependent on oil imports for domestic use, and obviously wants to spread the risk to supplies. The US security arrangements in the Gulf and Clinton's 'dual containment' policy therefore posed more of a threat to French than to British energy security.
3. Britain has always had a closer relationship with the United States in the defence arena than has France. Shared intelligence assessments led the British and American defence establishments to similar readings of Iraq's capabilities in weapons of mass destruction.
4. Maintenance of a close relationship with the US government, including policy coordination where possible, has been more important to Britain than to France. In contrast, for France it is sometimes a matter of honour to demonstrate the independence of its foreign policy. For Britain, especially given its divergent line on Iran and competition with American contractors for business in the GCC, there has been a greater urge to demonstrate alignment with Washington, where possible.

Although these factors may explain Britain's closer proximity to the United States than to other members of the UN Security Council when it comes to the question of Iraq, there were also differences between London and Washington on how to proceed. Whatever led Britain to join the United States in 'Operation Desert Fox' – the bombing of Iraq in December 1998 – from the British perspective the outcome posed more problems than it solved. It brought to an end weapons inspections in Iraq and thereby cut off the possibility, on which UNSC policy had rested, that once these inspectors declared the 'all clear', sanctions could be lifted. Technically, air surveillance can substitute for weapons inspections, which suggests an open-ended commitment to overflying Iraq and therefore an open-ended commitment to keeping British air forces alongside American air forces on operation in the Gulf. Meanwhile, as was evident by the end of the 1990s, tolerance in the Middle East for the continuation of sanctions on Iraq was dissipating fast, while resentment of US force predominance was growing.

The British clearly wanted a diplomatic way out of the impasse, and it was they who worked determinedly within the UN Security Council to devise and win support for Security Council Resolution 1284 as a solution. (Even before 11 September and a new determination in Washington to change the regime in Baghdad, Britain apparently deemed the objective to be unrealistic. Indeed, had it been implemented, Resolution 1284 would in effect have meant dealing directly with the Iraqi government in charting a path to formal suspension of sanctions.) In the end the United States did support the resolution, although France abstained, seemingly because the Russians did and because it did not want to be at a disadvantage in its dealings with Baghdad. However, the new formula embodied in the resolution, for new inspections by a new team as the prelude to suspending sanctions, could not be implemented. Baghdad declined to cooperate, and Washington shelved it.

Britain is much more concerned than Washington to retrieve and uphold the credibility of the United Nations. In this respect Britain has been at one with France and Russia. Washington has far less interest in upholding the UN's credibility, especially given the prevalence of hostility to the United Nations in certain quarters of the Congress. More importantly, the administration of George W. Bush, determined to distance itself from the perceived faults of the Clinton approach to the Middle East in general, has reinvigorated the idea of supporting the Iraqi opposition and instigating moves to overthrow the government of Saddam Hussein.

By spring 2001 it was apparent that there was a serious battle in the Bush administration over policy towards Iraq. The State Department cautioned against adventurism, especially in view of the rise of anti-American sentiment across the Arab world. This was fuelled by the sense that Washington had supported Israel uncritically and would do nothing to rein in effectively Israel's strategy for suppressing the Palestinian intifada. Voices at the Pentagon, meanwhile, were much more bullish about confronting Iraq.

It was in the midst of this debate that Britain set about devising a new UN resolution that would realize the proposals of Colin Powell, the US Secretary of State, for 'smart sanctions'. The thinking was that if sanctions could be tightened on the Iraqi regime, principally by controlling its access to cash, then the general trade in civilian goods could be resumed. France supported the initiative, much to the irritation of the Iraqi government. The first attempt to gain agreement at the UNSC on the implementation of this scheme failed in June 2001. A resumed effort was expected in the autumn but was overtaken by events. The principal stumbling block was Russian opposition, which, it was speculated, inducements might overcome. What is of interest here is the intensity of diplomacy, with the British in the forefront, within the UN Security Council. This suggests that Britain's anxiety not to be dragged along with any foolhardy American initiative drove it to seek a way out through the Security Council that would simultaneously rescue that institution from appearing utterly ineffectual. However, the greater the effort put in to closing the gaps among members of the UNSC, the further away the initiative veered from what was apparently practicable.

Three of Iraq's neighbours, Turkey, Syria and Jordan, had become tightly enmeshed in Iraq's smuggling activities and its circumvention of sanctions. Their governments could not be expected to go along with the new measures unless they were financially compensated and protected from the ire of both Baghdad and their own populations. Jordan's position looked particularly precarious, as it was locked between the Israeli-Palestinian maelstrom, on the one hand, and Iraq, on the other.

After 11 September and more particularly after the overthrow of the Taliban in Afghanistan, the debate in Washington over what to do about Iraq heated up dramatically. Hawks in the Pentagon and other circles began to advocate transposing the strategy used in Afghanistan to Iraq. British diplomacy sided with the more cautious voices coming from the State Department, who warned against assuming that what worked in Afghanistan could do so in Iraq on the grounds that the two contexts were not sufficiently comparable. Even so, analysts in the British press had begun to warn that the British government would find it difficult to dissociate Britain totally if the United States were to go ahead with a military operation aimed at unseating Saddam Hussein.

Conclusions

Britain's policy on Iraq in the 1990s can best be explained as a juggling act, which neglected the regional implications, between the UN Security Council and the United States. British policy on the Arab-Israeli conflict can be seen as a separate juggling act between the European Union and Washington, intermixed with an attempt to retain access with both Israel and the Palestinians. In both these 'issue areas' the British prime minister has taken a personal interest, which may at times override the instincts of the regional specialists in the Foreign Office. The result has been no regional policy as such but a set of responses to specific problems dealt with not only in isolation from one another but also through diplomacy at a distance, in the arenas of the EU, the UN and Washington.

Meanwhile, the highest priorities of the British government have lain elsewhere. Its primary concern has been the domestic economy and its standing with the British public. There are few votes to be won from heavy engagement in the Middle East. When oil prices soared in 2000, instead of blaming OPEC the first reaction of the British public was to criticize the government for the level of domestic fuel taxes. Human rights activists and pressure groups have paid attention to the Middle East, but sporadically and usually not in ways that enhance British relations with most governments in the region.

Yet, since 11 September there has been a change in both government and popular perceptions of the Middle East. At the popular level, some have found new sympathy for the Israelis on the receiving end of suicide attacks. British Muslims, however, are more conscious of how US policy, with seeming British acquiescence, has perpetuated the occupation of Palestinian land. Confrontation between India and Pakistan over Kashmir is a matter of real concern for the many Britons whose origins are in the subcontinent. Arabs in Britain have been affected by new measures to freeze the assets of those allegedly funding terrorist organizations. British Muslims in general are caught up in a new campaign to identify and apprehend those supporting violence in the name of Islam.

At the government level there is a desire to dissociate the war on terrorism from any notion of a clash between the West and Islam, yet to achieve this the importance of resolving the Israeli-Palestinian conflict is seen as more pressing. There is fear, too, that Britain's historical alignment with Washington on Iraq policy could lead it into a new adventure which will alienate Arab and Muslim opinion both at home and abroad. Meanwhile, the government's assessment of British strategic interests, whether before 11 September or thereafter, has led it into ever closer alignment with Washington.

Surely the interweaving of issues, perceptions and interests, both domestic and foreign, is a testimony to the impact of globalization. And Britain's initial response to the imperatives of globalization since the end of the Cold War has led it to eschew a regional policy for the Middle East. There is no going back, however, and the course set for going forward binds Britain more closely to the United States. This will affect British relations with the Middle East in unintended ways. The only question remaining is how to distinguish the emerging era of US hegemony from the onset of globalization. If the former is a defining feature of the latter, Britain is set to lose more friends and influence in the Middle East, while the region can no longer be considered to be on the periphery of the process of globalization.

PART II
Globalization and the Gulf

4 The economic implications of globalization for the GCC countries

Ali Tawfik Sadik*

Introduction

Globalization is a multidimensional concept that is widely used by economists, policy-makers, politicians, journalists and others, and it has economic,
political, cultural and environmental connotations. Economic globalization is manifested in the growing integration of national economies through
trade in goods and services, investment and financial flows. The realization
of this integration is reflected, first, in the rising share of economic activity
in the world taking place among economic agents who reside in different
countries, and, second, in the extension of national markets to global markets
and their exposure to international competition. There is, however, no
consensus on the meaning of globalization and the issues it covers, nor on
the implications of its different dimensions; in addition, there is controversy about its impact on both developed and developing countries. This
paper is concerned mainly with the possible economic and financial
implications of globalization for the Arab Gulf Cooperation Council
countries (GCC).[1]

This analysis of the possible economic and financial implications of
globalization for the GCC will discuss briefly the concept of globalization
and the forces that shape and promote it as a phenomenon. The chapter will
then examine the economic features of the GCC and identify the global
links of its economies. Finally, it will outline the issues and challenges of
globalization that the GCC states face.

* Dr Ali Tawfik Sadik is Director, Economic Policy Institute, Arab Monetary Fund (AMF), Abu
Dhabi, United Arab Emirates (UAE). The views expressed in this paper are those of the author and do
not reflect those of the AMF.
[1] The members of the GCC are Bahrain, Kuwait, Oman, Qatar, Saudi Arabia and the UAE.

The globalization discussion: which way to go?

Globalization can be looked at in two different ways, with different policy implications. One way is to discuss it in the context of the multilateralism encompassing the global trading system, the liberalization of multilateral trade, and countries' trade policies and membership of the World Trade Organization (WTO). The other way is to view globalization as a micro-economic phenomenon generated by the strategies and behaviour of corporations. Here the focus of policy analysis is on the dynamics of global competition and international competitiveness among firms, countries and regions.

Globalization as multilateralism

Globalization as a multilateral phenomenon refers to the lowering of policy barriers to the movement of goods and services across borders that was initiated in 1947, at the first round of multilateral trade negotiations. This process was formalized by establishing the General Agreement on Tariffs and Trade (GATT) at its conclusion.[2] The prolonged difficulties in concluding the eighth round (the Uruguay Round) of multilateral trade negotiations, launched under GATT's auspices in 1986, and the proliferation of regional integration in Europe, North America and Pacific Asia before the Uruguay Round was concluded with the establishment of the WTO in 1995, have generated debate about the relationship between multilateralism and regionalism. In the context of globalization the question arises: are regional blocs building blocks or stumbling blocks for a more open global trading system? The debate on this issue is not settled yet. However, many OECD-based multinational firms have set up regionally integrated operations and support the lowering of intraregional trade barriers, especially non-tariff barriers (NTBs), and they are indifferent to interregional trade barriers.[3] These firms' investments are market-seeking and tariff-jumping. They are driven by larger markets or regional trading areas.[4] In contrast to this

---

[2] The first round of multilateral trade negotiations convened in Geneva in 1947. Twenty-three countries participated, of which 10 were industrial countries, led by the United States, and 13 were developing countries, including Syria and Lebanon. See Atif Ajwa, 'Economic Impact of GATT and World Trade Organisation Agreements', *Economic Affairs*, No. 12, April 1998, p. 42.

[3] Charles Oman, *Globalisation and Regionalisation: The Challenge for Developing Countries* (OECD Development Centre Studies, 1994), p. 28.

[4] A. Sadik and A. Bolbol, 'Mobilizing International Capital for Arab Economic Development: With Special Reference to the Role of FDI', paper prepared for the Regional Meeting on Finance for Development, organized by the United Nations Economic and Social Commission for Western Asia, Beirut, 23–24 November 2000, p. 29.

attitude, the increase of GATT membership from 23 in 1947 to 133 in 1995 reflects a global interest in an open and free trade system promoting the opportunity to share the benefits of globalization.

In the light of the equating of globalization with multilateralism, what are the policy implications of this understanding of the two phenomena? The situation requires policy-makers to be vigilant and to ensure that trends towards the *de jure* and the *de facto* establishment of regional blocs do not become instruments for protectionism at the regional level. Equating globalization with multilateralism highlights the importance for developing countries in general, and the GCC in particular, of maintaining an open and liberalized trading system. This stand on the issue reflects the fact that many developing countries changed their development strategies from inward to outward ones, a move accompanied by important unilateral trade liberalization, at a time when OECD countries were increasing their use of NTBs. In fact, GATT reported that 63 developing countries lowered their import barriers in 1987–92, and since the end of the 1970s, 20 of the 24 OECD countries have raised barriers to imports, especially NTBs.[5]

Globalization as microeconomic phenomenon

Globalization as a microeconomic phenomenon can be understood by looking at the growth of economic transactions among residents of different countries. This is reflected by the increased movement of goods and services across national boundaries through trade and investment and, to some extent, the increased movement of people. Globalization is thus a manifestation of a process of economic outreach beyond the confines of national territory; it is driven by corporate strategies and behaviour and is facilitated by legal and institutional arrangements emanating mostly from states.

The interaction between government deregulation and the spread of new information and communication technologies has been an important factor in facilitating and supporting globalization since the early 1980s. However, capitalist flexible production is a cornerstone of globalization. Flexible organizations are characterized by integrated thinking and action at all levels of operation. This generates inefficiency-reduction and productivity increases relative to organizations of mass production. According to a Massachusetts Institute of Technology study of the motor car industry, the flexible system, relative to mass production, increases productivity by almost 100 per cent. It is so superior to other systems of organization that

---

[5] General Agreement on Tariffs and Trade, *Annual Report* (1992).

ultimately it will drive out of the market any entrepreneurial competitor that does not shift to the new system, whether in the motor car industry or in other industries.[6] Further research is needed to gauge the applicability of the flexible production approach to the countries of the GCC and their development efforts.

Two microeconomic aspects of globalization have significant implications for countries trying to attract foreign direct investment (FDI) on the basis of cheaper labour costs. One is the decline in the share of variable, low-skilled labour in total production costs in many globally competitive industries, from about 25 per cent in the 1970s to 5–10 per cent in the 1990s.[7] The other aspect is the increased importance of the physical proximity between producers and their customers (global localization) and between producers and their suppliers of parts, components and services.

These microeconomic aspects of globalization are reflected in a deceleration in the 'offshore' production of OECD-based firms in low-wage sites in developing countries. This process emerged in the 1970s, with most of the output destined for the United States and Europe. The new trend is to build production networks in each of the three regional markets: Europe, North America and Pacific Asia. These three regions accounted for approximately 77 per cent of world GDP; 47 per cent and 50 per cent of world exports of merchandise and services respectively; 73.2 per cent of world FDI; and about 17.2 per cent of the world population in 1998 (see Table 4.1).

Having described briefly the two phenomena associated with the economics of globalization, namely multilateralism and microeconomics, we can now investigate their implications for the economies of the GCC. But first we must look at the GCC's economic features, its links with the global economy and its integration within it.

Economic features of the GCC

The relative size of the GCC economy

World GDP and world population amounted to $28,862 billion and nearly 5.9 billion people respectively in 1998, of which the high-income countries' share was 78.3 per cent and 15 per cent respectively. The corresponding

[6] Flexible production entails changes all along the value-adding chain, from product design and engineering to marketing and distribution, as well as the organization of work within the firm and with suppliers. The following features characterize the system: simultaneous engineering; continuous incremental innovation; team work; just-in-time production and the zero buffer principle; and integrating the supply chain.

[7] Oman, *Globalisation and Regionalisation*, p. 17.

Table 4.1: The three major regional blocs' percentage share of world population, GDP, exports and FDI, 1998

Region	Population (millions)	GDP (US$m)	Merchandise exports (US$m)	Service exports (US$m)	FDI ($m) (US$m)
World	5,896.6	28,736,978	5,397,430	1,316,688	619,258
% of world					
North America*	6.72	32.03	18.66	21.43	35.55
The EU*	6.35	29.54	12.30	17.02	33.93
Pacific Asia*	4.14	15.54	15.62	11.48	3.69
The three regions	17.21	77.11	46.58	49.93	73.17

* North America includes the United States, Canada and Mexico; the EU comprises the 15 members of the European Union; and Pacific Asia consists of Japan, South Korea, Singapore, Hong Kong and Thailand.
World in millions and regions in % of world.
Sources: World Bank, *World Development Indicators* (Washington, DC: World Bank, 2000), tables 2.1, 4.2, and 4.7, pp. 38, 186 and 206 respectively.

share for low- and middle-income countries was 21.7 per cent and 85 per cent respectively. In comparison the GCC had less than one per cent (0.8 per cent) of the world's income and half of one per cent of its population.

The average world per capita income amounted to $4,890, and the per capita income of the high-income countries was $25,510. The per capita income of the low- and middle-income countries was $520 and $2,950 respectively. In contrast, the GCC's per capita income was $7,900, and that of all the Arab countries was $2,225 (see Table 4.2).

Characteristics of the GCC economies

The economies of the GCC are relatively open; there are small populations and a heavy dependence on the oil sector and expatriate labour on the production side, and large government expenditures and oil exports on the demand side. The economy of Saudi Arabia dominates the GCC economies: Saudi GDP and population accounted, on average, for about 56 per cent of GCC GDP and 60 per cent of GCC population respectively in 1988–98 (see Table 4.3). The heavy dependence on the oil sector is not reflected properly by the direct contribution of the oil sector to income as measured by GDP. The indirect impact on GDP can be traced through government

Table 4.2: Relative size of the GCC economy in the global economy, 1998

Income groups	Population (m)	GNP/GDP ($bn)	Per capita income ($)
World	5,897	28,862	4,890
% of total	100	100	100
Low-income*	3,515	1,844	520
% of world	59.6	6.39	10.63
(excluding China and India)	1,296	494	380
% of world	21.98	1.71	7.77
Middle-income*	1,496	4,420	2,950
% of world	25.37	15.31	60.32
High-income*	885	22,599	25,510
% of world	15.01	78.3	522.
GCC	29.4	232.26	7,900
% of world	0.50	0.804	162.00
Arab countries	263	585	2,225
% of world	4.46	2.03	45.50
GCC % of Arab countries	11.18	39.7	355.06

* Low income: <$760; middle-income: $761–9,360; high-income: >$9,361.
Sources: World Bank, *World Development Report 1999–2000* (Washington, DC: World Bank, 2000), table 1, p. 230; and Arab Monetary Fund, *Joint Arab Economic Report* (Abu Dhabi: AMF, September 1999), tables 1/8 and 2/8, pp. 219 and 220 respectively.

Table 4.3: GCC economic indicators, 1988–98 (%)

Year	Trade ratio	Oil GDP/ GDP	Oil revenue/total revenue	Govt expen-diture/ GDP	Oil exports/ total exports	Saudi GDP/GCC GDP	Saudi pop./GCC pop
1988	71.75	27.27	67.54	52.02	n.a.	56.31	71.83
1990	76.34	38.37	78.39	53.00	85.44	57.87	69.72
1995	80.27	34.33	75.12	39.47	74.99	56.69	71.96
1996	81.00	37.68	76.06	39.30	74.90	56.23	71.29
1997	79.58	36.03	77.55	39.73	72.78	56.41	71.42
1998	76.73	n.a.	n.a.	n.a.	62.68	n.a.	71.45

Source: Calculated on the basis of GCC, *Economic Bulletin*, No. 14, 1999, table 8, p. 76; tables1/2–6/2, pp. 103–8; tables 1/3-6/3, pp.131–6; and table1/4, p. 199.

Table 4.4: GCC growth rates of GDP and oil GDP (1986–97) (%)

Year	GCC-GDP	GDP growth rate (%)	Oil GDP	Oil GDP growth rate (%)
1986	128,382	n.a.	35,010	n.a.
1987	135,795	5.77	40,399	15.39
1988	136,945	0.85	37,427	-7.36
1989	154,213	12.61	49,364	31.89
1990	174,175	12.94	66,831	35.38
1991	178,123	2.27	64,160	-4.00
1992	201,076	12.89	73,614	14.74
1993	205,115	2.01	73,205	-0.56
1994	203,993	-0.55	68,317	-6.68
1995	224,788	10.19	77,170	12.96
1996	251,001	11.66	94,577	22.56
1997	259,361	3.33	93,448	-1.19
St. Dev.		5.38		15.34
Average		6.60		12.95

Source: GCC, *Economic Bulletin*, No. 14, 1999, table 8, p. 12.

expenditure financed by oil revenue and by the share of oil exports in total exports. These characteristics of the GCC economies reveal their vulnerability to external shocks generated by developments in the international economy in general, and in the oil market in particular.

GCC GDP growth rates fluctuated between -0.55 per cent and 13 per cent during the period 1986–97, with an average annual rate of 6.6 per cent and a standard deviation of 5.38 per cent. In contrast, oil GDP fluctuated within a wider range: between -7.36 per cent and 35 per cent, with an average annual growth rate of 12.95 per cent and a standard deviation of 15.34 per cent (see Table 4.4).

Fluctuations in the growth rate of the GCC's GDP create uncertainties that cause difficulties for its members in managing their economies, and thus hamper and retard their development strategies. This does not imply that they have had a resource gap constraint. In fact, their savings rates were higher than those of the developing countries and the wider world. Their domestic investment rates were lower than those of the developing countries and the wider world and lower than their own savings rates by 4–12 per cent. Thus, the GCC countries enjoyed a resource surplus that ranged between 6 and 14 per cent in 1987–97 (see Tables 4.5, 4.6 and 4.7).

The oil sector is the main source of revenue for the GCC governments' budgets. Between 1986 and 1997 the fluctuations in the oil sector were paralleled by both the revenue and the expenditure sides of the budget. The

Table 4.5: Domestic savings and per capital GDP of Arab countries, GCC, Non-GCC, developing countries and the world (US$)

	1987–92[1]	1993	1994	1995	1996	1997	1998
Savings ratio (%)							
Arab countries[2]	15.1	17.4	19.5	20.1	20.0	21.8	18.6
GCC[3]	30.6	28.8	31.3	32.2	33.6	33.7	27.2
Non-GCC[4]	8.9	12.0	13.3	14.1	14.8	15.9	15.2
Developing countries	23.4	25.5	26.9	27.4	26.9	27.3	26.4
World	22.6	22.2	23.1	23.6	23.5	23.9	23.3
Per capita GDP ($US)							
Arab countries[2]	2,253	2,312	2,301	2,399	2,570	2,589	2,470
GCC[3]	10,820	11,545	11,400	11,675	12,257	12,154	10,920
Non-GCC[4]	1,138	1,108	1,100	1,166	1,272	1,296	1,323
Developing countries	1,031	1,093	1,090	1,090	1,190	1,250	1,250
World	3,884	4,420	4,470	4,880	5,130	5,180	4,890

[1] Annual average.
[2] Arab countries include both GCC and non-GCC.
[3] GCC includes: Bahrain, Kuwait, Oman, Qatar, Saudi Arabia, and UAE.
[4] Non-GCC includes: Algeria, Egypt, Jordan, Lebanon, Libya, Mauritania, Morocco, Sudan, Syria, Tunis, and Yemen.
Source: As for Table 4.4.

Table 4.6: Domestic investment of Arab countries, GCC, non-GCC, developing countries and the world (% ratios)[1]

	1987–92[1]	1993	1994	1995	1996	1997	1998
Arab countries	21.8	23.0	23.4	22.9	20.6	21.8	23.4
GCC	20.9	22.2	22.1	21.1	19.8	21.0	23.4
Non-GCC	23.2	23.9	24.4	23.5	22.3	21.8	23.1
Developing countries	25.2	28.6	28.2	28.9	28.0	27.8	26.6
World	23.7	23.7	23.8	24.1	23.9	23.9	23.2

[1] Annual average.
Source: As for Table 4.4.

growth rates of total GCC expenditures ranged between -14 per cent and 36 per cent, with an average of 4.88 per cent and a standard deviation of 15.29 per cent. In contrast, the growth rates of total GCC revenues ranged between -15.89 per cent and 34.32 per cent, with an average growth rate of

Table 4.7: Resource gap of Arab countries, GCC, non-GCC, developing countries and the world (% ratios)[1]

	1987–92[1]	1993	1994	1995	1996	1997	1998
Arab countries	−6.7	−5.6	−3.9	−2.8	-0.6	0.0	−4.8
GCC	9.7	6.7	9.2	11.1	13.8	12.7	3.8
Non-GCC	−14.3	−11.9	−11.1	−9.4	−7.5	−5.9	−7.9
Developing countries	−1.8	−3.1	−1.3	−1.5	−1.1	−0.5	−0.2
World	−1.1	−1.5	−0.7	−0.5	−0.4	0.0	0.1

[1] Annual average.
Source: As for Table 4.4.

Table 4. 8: GCC Total public expenditure and revenue ($m), 1986–97

Year	Total expenditure	Total revenue	Growth rate of expenditure (%)	Growth rate of revenue (%)
1986	66,785	37,434	n.a.	n.a.
1987	76,844	45,664	15.06	21.98
1988	66,451	42,945	−13.52	−5.95
1989	67,911	50,659	2.20	17.96
1990	92,362	68,045	36.00	34.32
1991	103,361	63,728	11.91	−6.34
1992	88,667	64,822	−14.22	1.72
1993	92,308	71,014	4.11	9.55
1994	84,802	59,727	−8.13	−15.89
1995	88,727	69,118	4.63	15.72
1996	98,651	84,683	11.18	22.52
1997	103,038	90,776	4.45	7.20
Average			4.88	9.34
St. dev.			15.29	15.00

Source: GCC, *Economic Bulletin*, No. 14, 1999, tables 1/2–6/2, pp. 103–8.

9.34 per cent and a standard deviation of 15 per cent during the same period, as shown in Table 4.8.

The preceding discussion indicates that although the GCC economies did not experience a resource gap constraint, but rather a resource surplus, the GCC governments' budgets experienced significant deficits, ranging between 2.41 per cent and 32.75 per cent of the GCC's GDP in 1986–97, with an average deficit of 11.65 per cent and a standard deviation of 8.07 per cent. By any standard these fluctuations are a cause for concern for the overall macroeconomic stability of the GCC economies.

Global links of the GCC economies

An economy is linked with the rest of the world's economies through three markets: the market for traded goods, the factors market, and the money and credit markets (the assets market). The rest of the world influences these markets, and consequently it impacts on the home economy.

The goods market linkages

The trade in goods is the first basic link with the rest of the world, and it is the most obvious manifestation of trans-world economic connections promoted and supported by capitalism. A country exports a part of its GDP goods and imports consumption goods, intermediary goods and capital goods. This trade implies that the rest of the world influences the prices and volumes of the traded goods. The influence of the rest of the world on domestic goods markets can be traced through prices and volumes for exports and imports. Revenue derived from export sales is income for residents, and import spending is income for the rest of the world. The terms of trade (TOT, the ratio of export to import prices) and the purchasing power of exports are a manifestation of the interdependence of goods markets. Table 4.9 presents the price indexes of petroleum, the G-5 unit value of manufactures and the calculated TOT. The TOT index is an important variable that focuses on the impact of external shocks on the economy and indicates the gain/loss from foreign trading. The deterioration of TOT by 37.08 per cent ((62.92–100)/100) x 100 in 1990–95 could have cost the GCC countries about 11.5 per cent of their GDP (0.3708 x (imports/GDP) = 0.3708 x 31).[8]

Measuring GCC globalization

The extent of globalization is measured by the trade ratio (the ratio of exports and imports to GDP). International trade grew rapidly in the aftermath of the Second World War as a result of the lowering of tariffs and quantitative restrictions within the framework of GATT. Global exports of goods and services grew by 5.2 per cent and 6.4 per cent in 1980–90 and

[8] Rudiger Dornbusch and F. Leslie Helmers (eds), *The Open Economy: Tools for Policy Makers in Developing Countries* (Washington, DC: World Bank EDI series in Economic Development, 1993), p. 39.

Table 4.9: Commodity price indexes (current dollar terms, 1990 = 100)

Year	Petroleum	G-5* unit value index of manufactures	Terms of trade (%)
1965	6	21.6	27.78
1970	5	25.1	19.92
1975	46	45.2	101.77
1976	51	45.8	111.35
1977	55	50.4	109.13
1978	57	59.7	95.48
1979	135	65.6	205.79
1980	161	72	223.61
1981	155	72.3	214.38
1982	143	71.2	200.84
1983	130	69.5	187.05
1984	125	68.1	183.55
1985	119	68.6	173.47
1986	63	80.9	77.87
1987	79	88.8	88.96
1988	64	95.3	67.16
1989	78	94.7	82.37
1990	100	100.0	100.00
1991	85	102.2	83.17
1992	83	106.6	77.86
1993	74	106.3	69.61
1994	69	110.2	62.61
1995	75	119.2	62.92
1996	89	114	78.07
1997	84	108.2	77.63

*The G-5 comprises France, Germany, Japan, the United Kingdom and the United States.
Source: World Bank, *Global Economic Prospects and the Developing Countries 1998/1999* (Washington, DC: World Bank, 1999), Tables A2–11, p. 208.

1990–98 respectively, while world GDP grew by 3.2 per cent and 2.4 per cent in the same periods.[9] The global trade ratio of goods and services increased from 41.5 per cent to about 46.4 per cent between 1980 and 1998. The trade ratio in high-income countries increased from 42.4 per cent to 45.1 per cent, while the corresponding ratio for low- and middle-income countries surged from 37.7 per cent to 51.1 per cent between those two years (see Table 4.10).

Trade ratios in all regions increased between 1980 and 1998, except in the Middle East and North Africa and in Sub-Saharan Africa, where the ratio declined by about 36 per cent and 3.6 per cent respectively. Trade in goods

[9] World Bank, *World Development Report* (Washington, DC: World Bank, 2000), Table 11, p. 251.

Table 4.10: World and regional trade ratios* (%), 1980 and 1998

Year		World	High income	Low & middle income	East Asia & Pacific	Europe & Central Asia	Latin America & Carib.	Middle East & N. Africa	Sub-Saharan Africa
1980	41.47	42.39	37.65	36.53	n.a.	30.53	71.57	19.91	61.58
1998	46.36	45.05	51.13	66.15	68.79	36.09	46.27	27.77	59.27

* Ratio of the sum of exports and imports of goods and services to GDP.
Source: World Bank, *World Development Indicators* (Washington, DC: World Bank, 2000), tables 4.2 and 4.5–4.8, p. 186 and pp. 200–10 respectively.

as a percentage of goods GDP increased from 72 per cent to 92 per cent in high-income countries between 1988 and 1998. The corresponding figures for the developing countries were 57.8 per cent and 88.8 per cent.[10] The relatively larger shares of international trade in goods GDP are a consequence of the structural change in that sector's contributions to GDP. In both developed and developing countries the services sector has taken the lead.

Increasing global economic integration through trade has been driven by two fundamental factors. First, regulation, emanating from public policy, has resulted in the progressive reduction in artificial barriers to international trade. Secondly, there has been a continuous improvement in the technology of transportation and communication. It is estimated that protection levels for domestic manufacturing in industrial countries have fallen by as much as 80–90 per cent since the end of the Second World War. This takes account of the fact that tariffs have been eliminated within the European Union and within the North American Free Trade Area (NAFTA). The remaining import protection is concentrated in agriculture, textiles and a few other manufactured goods.[11]

The levels of protection in developing countries are generally still higher than those in developed countries. However, the past two decades have witnessed significant liberalization of developing country trade regimes. The GCC members' trade regimes are relatively liberalized: NTBs are not significant, and tariffs range from 0 to 20 per cent, with the actual average tariff ranges between 2.1 per cent and 5.3 per cent.[12]

Trade ratios for the GCC averaged 77.5 per cent, with a standard deviation of 3.01 per cent during the period 1988–98 (see Table 4.11). Thus, as

[10] World Bank, *World Development Indicators* (Washington, DC: World Bank, 2000), Table 6.1, p. 316.
[11] Michael Mussa, 'Factors Driving Global Economic Integration', paper presented at a symposium sponsored by the Federal Reserve Bank of Kansas City on 'Global Opportunities and Challenges', 25 August 2000, p. 11.
[12] Ali Sadik (ed.), *Competitiveness of Arab Economies in Global Markets* (Abu Dhabi: Arab Monetary Fund, 1999), tables 8 and 9.

Table 4.11: GCC globalization – trade ratios, 1988–98

Year	Exports/GDP (%)	Imports/GDP (%)	Trade ratio (%)
1988	39.42	32.34	71.75
1989	43.67	30.21	73.87
1990	48.78	27.56	76.34
1991	45.84	31.63	77.47
1992	47.19	34.43	81.62
1993	44.63	32.85	77.48
1994	45.70	30.76	76.46
1995	47.95	32.32	80.27
1996	50.77	30.22	81.00
1997	49.29	30.29	79.58
1998	41.54	35.19	76.73
Average	45.89	31.62	77.51
St. dev.	3.42	2.15	3.01

Source: Calculated on the basis of Arab Monetary Fund, *National Accounts of Arab Countries: 1988–98*, No. 19 (Abu Dhabi: AMF, 1999).

Table 4.12: The GCC – Hirschmann export concentration indices*

Countries	1980		1994	
	Number of commodities exported	Concentration index	Number of commodities exported	Concentration index
Bahrain	58	0.790	117	0.597
Kuwait	189	0.732	140	0.932
Oman	101	0.922	128	0.747
Saudi Arabia	183	0.942	199	0.728
UAE	197	0.870	205	0.683

* The concentration index ranges between 0 and 1; and the higher the figure, the higher the concentration.
Source: UNCTAD, *Handbook of International Trade Development Statistics* (1995), Table 4.5, p. 203.

measured by the trade ratio, the GCC economies are highly globalized relative to the world economy and to the high-, low- and middle-income economies.

The relatively high trade ratios for the GCC states indicate the high dependence of their economies on the policies and performance of their major trade partners. Moreover, the high dependence of their exports on one commodity, namely mineral fuels and related materials (82–88 per cent of total exports of goods in 1990–97), reflects the vulnerability of

Table 4.13: Exports within regional blocs, 1970–98 (% of total exports)

Regional blocs	1970	1980	1985	1990	1995	1996	1997	1998
APEC	57.8	57.9	67.7	68.3	71.9	72.1	71.8	69.7
European Union	59.5	60.8	59.2	65.9	62.4	61.4	53.8	55.2
NAFTA	36.0	33.6	43.9	41.4	46.2	47.6	49.1	51.7
CACM	26.0	24.4	14.4	15.4	17	18.9	15.5	14.5
AMU	1.4	0.3	1.0	2.9	3.7	3.4	2.6	2.6
GCC	4.6	3.0	4.9	8.0	6.6	5.6	4.6	4.5

Source: World Bank, *World Development Indicators* (Washington, DC: World Bank, 1999), Table 6.5, p. 327.

their economies to developments in the international energy sector and the international oil market.[13] The Hirschmann export concentration index for the GCC improved between 1980 and 1994, but it continued to reveal a relatively high export concentration, as shown in Table 4.12.

The GCC's major trade partners

Trade within the GCC, as measured by its percentage of the total exports of the GCC bloc, is relatively low by comparison with most other blocs. It was 4.5 per cent, compared with about 70 per cent for the APEC bloc, 55 per cent for the European Union and 52 per cent for NAFTA in 1998 (see Table 4.13).[14]

GCC exports go mainly to Japan, the European Union and the United States. The share of these regions in total GCC exports ranged from 44 per cent to 60 per cent in 1986–97. GCC imports from them ranged from 59 per cent to 72 per cent during this time (see Table 4.14). The trade policies of these regions are very important to the GCC. Any negative trade policies implemented in them will have a significant impact on the GCC economies in the short run.

[13] Gulf Cooperation Council, *Economic Bulletin,* No. 14 (1999), p. 38.
[14] Asia Pacific Economic Cooperation (APEC, 22 members): Australia, Brunei, Darussalam, Canada, Chile, China, Hong Kong, Indonesia, Japan, the Republic of Korea, Malaysia, Mexico, New Zealand, Papua New Guinea, Peru, the Philippines, the Russian Federation, Singapore, Taiwan, Thailand, the United States and Vietnam; European Union (15 members): Austria, Belgium, Denmark, Finland, France, Germany, Greece, Ireland, Italy, Luxembourg, the Netherlands, Portugal, Spain, Sweden and the United Kingdom; North American Free Trade Association (NAFTA): Canada, Mexico and the United States; Central American Common Market (CACM, 5 members): Costa Rica, El Salvador, Guatemala, Honduras and Nicaragua; Arab Maghreb Union (AMU, 5 members): Algeria, Libya, Mauritania, Morocco and Tunisia.

Table 4.14: Major GCC trade partners

Year	Total GCC exports ($m)	% of exports			Total GCC imports ($m)	% of imports		
		EU	United States	Japan		EU	United States	Japan
1986	47,119	21	9	28	35,639	40	14	18
1987	55,188	18	11	26	38,693	36	12	17
1988	54,908	17	12	24	43,480	34	13	15
1989	63,742	17	15	25	44,963	34	14	13
1990	85,967	15	14	27	48,701	38	14	14
1991	81,777	16	15	26	58,535	35	17	14
1992	79,889	18	15	27	71,049	35	17	15
1993	80,706	15	12	23	68,797	33	14	13
1994	86,017	14	12	23	62,261	34	14	12
1995	63,078	17	14	17	70,760	37	14	9
1996	75,273	16	15	16	70,765	35	15	9
1997	78,679	15	12	17	73,649	34	16	9

Source: GCC, *Economic Bulletin*, No. 14, 1999, tables 19 and 20, pp. 33–4.

Factor markets linkages

The factor markets of a country are linked to those of other countries through the mobility of labour and capital.

Labour movement   Individual and family decisions to move from one country to another are affected by economic and non-economic factors. However, economic incentives are the main inducement for migration to the industrial countries and to the GCC countries from developing countries (including other Arab countries). Expatriates account for most of the labour in the GCC. For example, in the UAE they accounted for 91 per cent and 92 per cent of employment in the public and private sectors respectively in 1998.[15]

Financial capital mobility   The mobility of capital occurs in three ways: by borrowing from abroad by issuing debt; by foreign portfolio investment (FPI); and by foreign direct investment (FDI). Table 4.15 displays the stock of debt for all developing countries, its share of their GDP in 1992 and 1997 and the distribution of long-term debt among multilateral, bilateral and private shares. The developing countries' stock of debt increased by

[15] Matar Ahmed Abdallah, *Disequilibrium in the Structure of Population in the United Arab Emirates and Approaches of its Treatment* (Sharja, UAE: Al-Khaleej, 1999), p. 57.

Table 4.15: Developing countries' debt stock, 1992 and 1997

| | | | | | | Distribution of long-term debt (% of total) | | | | | |
| Total (US$m) | | As % of GDP | | Long-term % of total | | Multilateral | | Bilateral | | Private | |
1992	1997	1992	1997	1992	1997	1992	1997	1992	1997	1992	1997
1,635,061	2,316,601	37	35	79	77	18	16	35	28	47	55

Source: World Bank, *Global Development Finance, Country Tables* (Washington, DC: World Bank, 1999), p. 11.

Table 4.16: GCC External debt ($m)

| Country | Total debt stock | | Medium- and long-term debt | | % of GDP | | |
	1994	1997	1994	1997	1994	1997	1998
Bahrain	2,776	2,371	2,358	1,719	52.2	37.3	41.5
Kuwait	9,915	9,406	5,243	3,987	40	31	31.3
Oman	3,087	3,602	2,608	2,567	9.4	5.9	n.a.
Qatar	2,166	9,027	1,420	7,608	6.9	81.8	84.3
S.A.	19,951	21,357	6,710	7,793	n.a.	n.a.	n.a.
UAE	12,215	12,328	2,248	2,693	33.3	26.6	n.a.
Total	50,110	58,091	n.a.	n.a.	n.a.	n.a.	n.a.

Source: The Economist Intelligence Unit, *Country Profile, 1999–2000* (London: EIU, 2000).

more than 41 per cent between 1992 and 1997. The long-term share in the stock of debt declined from 79 per cent to 77 per cent, and the private share of long-term stock increased from 47 per cent to 55 per cent between 1992 and 1997. Both multilateral and bilateral shares in the debt declined. The GCC states' external debt stock amounted to $58,091 million in 1997, equivalent to about 22 per cent of their GDP (see Table 4.16).

The figure for total world FPI is not available. However, inflows of FPI to the low- and middle-income countries amounted to $3,935 million in 1990 and $55,225 million in 1998, comprising both bonds and equities.[16] The corresponding figures are not available for the GCC.

FDI flows surged in the 1990s, especially those to developing countries. World total FDI increased from an average of $173.5 billion in 1987–92 to $643.9 billion in 1998, an annual increase of more than 24 per cent. Table

[16] World Bank, *World Development Report* (Washington, DC: World Bank, 2000), p. 334.

Table 4.17: World and regional distribution of FDI inflows (% shares)

	1987-92[1]	1993	1994	1995	1996	1997	1998
Total FDI inflows ($bn)	173.5	219.4	253.5	328.9	358.9	464.3	643.9
Developed countries	78.7	60.1	57.7	63.3	58.8	58.8	71.5
EU	41.9	35	30.6	35.1	30.4	27.2	35.7
USA	26.6	19.8	17.8	17.9	21.3	23.5	30
Other	10.2	5.3	9.3	10.3	7.1	8.1	5.8
Developing countries	21.3	39.9	42.3	36.7	41.2	41.2	28.5
East Asia and Pacific	10.6	22.3	23.7	19.7	21.2	17.9	10.7
Europe and Central Asia	1.0	4.6	2.8	4.9	4.2	4.6	4.0
Latin America and Caribbean	7.2	9.2	12.4	10	12.8	14.7	11.6
South Asia	0.2	0.5	0.6	0.9	1.0	1.0	0.6
Sub-Saharan Africa	1.0	0.9	1.3	1.2	1.3	1.4	0.7
Arab countries	1.3	2.4	1.5	0	0.7	1.6	0.9

[1] Annual average.
Source: UNCTAD, *World Investment Report* (New York: United Nations, 1999).

Table 4.18: Arab countries – FDI inflows ($m)

	1987–1992	1993	1994	1995	1996	1997	1998	1998 Stock of FDI inflows	1998 Stock of FDI infl./GDP (%)
Algeria	n.a.	−59	22	−24	447	630	500	2,799	5.9
Egypt	806	493	1,256	598	636	891	1,076	16,700	20.2
Libya	52	31	69	9	209	10	150	n.a.	n.a.
Morocco	203	491	551	332	354	1,079	258	4,724	13.06
Sudan	−6	n.a.	n.a.	n.a.	n.a.	98	10	100	1
Tunisia	160	562	432	264	238	339	650	5,330	26.6
Djibouti	n.a.	1	1	3	20	25	25	84	12.03
Mauritania	4	16	2	7	4	n.a.	6	97	10
Bahrain	58	−5	−31	−27	47	26	10	642	10.4
Jordan	21	−34	3	13	16	361	223	1,226	16.53
Kuwait	7	13	n.a.	7	347	20	-10	439	1.75
Lebanon	2	7	23	22	64	150	230	554	3.45
Oman	103	142	76	46	75	49	50	2,395	16.9
Qatar	10	72	132	94	35	55	70	595	5.7
Saudi Arabia	−35	1,369	350	−1,877	−1,129	2,575	2,400	26,270	20.4
Syria	67	176	251	100	89	80	100	1,299	7.96
UAE	52	401	62	399	130	100	100	2,099	4.5
Yemen	198	897	11	−218	-60	−138	100	1,941	37.3

Source: As for Table 4.17.

4.17 presents the world and regional distribution of FDI inflows. FDI, for the most part, remains developed countries' business: their share averaged 78.7 per cent in 1987–92 and ranged between 60 per cent and 57 per cent in 1993–7, surging to 71.5 per cent in 1998. The Arab countries, including the GCC countries, received less than one per cent of the world total in 1998. FDI in the Arab countries is concentrated in six economies: Egypt, Jordan, Morocco, Oman, Saudi Arabia and Tunisia (see Table 4.18).

The relatively low level of FDI in the GCC countries denied them the opportunity to benefit from the efficiency gains that are generally associated with technology transfer and the competition that FDI generates. Such efficiency gains have been observed in East Asia. Moreover, FDI is always associated with increased trade. Exports expand because the foreign affiliates of multinationals are better placed than local firms in serving foreign markets, and imports expand because of FDI-induced growth of income. The impact of FDI on the current account, and consequently on international reserves, is ambiguous as a result of the expansion of both exports and imports in addition to the repatriation of profits.

FDI determinants

The importance of FDI warrants an investigation into its determinants. There are three sets of variables that are important determinants of FDI. The first set is related to investors and comprises ownership-specific advantages such as brand name, patent, technology and marketing. The second one is related to the host country and covers locational advantages such as large markets, lower costs of resources and superior infrastructure. The third set of determinants is related to internationalization advantages such as commercial benefits accruing from FDI or intra-firm activity.[17]

The second, host country set of variables is important for any state that seeks to attract FDI. Host country determinants can be classified into policy variables, such as tax, tariff and social policies; investment facilities, such as incentives, administrative efficiency and after-investment services; and economic variables, such as market size and cost of resources. FDI can be classified into two broad categories on the basis of its host country economic determinants: market-seeking FDI, which is attracted by larger markets or regional trading areas, and efficiency-seeking FDI, in the form of export-platform investment and investment in internationally integrated industries, in components and in intermediate goods. These host country

---

[17] Sadik and Bolbol, 'Mobilizing International Capital for Arab Economic Development', p. 15.

The 'deterritorialization' of communications and the challenge to territorially based social relations

The challenge posed by the example of the intifada to the states of the Gulf is to their capacity for cultural and political leadership. The Arab states of the Gulf are engaged in a struggle over the terms of political and cultural leadership in three areas: the domestic, the regional and the international. Domestically, all political leaders seek to use their power and influence to control the political agenda and to impose limits on political debate. In cultural terms, they seek to ensure that they exemplify national cultural norms. Part of the reason for this is that in order to join in the competition at regional and international levels, leaders have to be seen as legitimate representatives of nation-states. At both the regional and the international level, each state is involved in the mutual rivalry of alliance-building and in shaping the terms on which alliances are built. In this context there is a widespread interest among governments to develop the means to influence broadcasting of all kinds and shape political and cultural agendas in their own and their neighbours' territories and also in the regional and international spheres.

The development of transactional communications and the resultant growth of transnational communities appear to be making it harder for states to reconcile domestic and regional competition. This is largely because the terms of competition for influence within the transnational sphere has changed and because globalization has introduced new factors into domestic competition that are less controllable by the state. The difficulties facing states domestically are not simply those of regulating the new electronic media. The 'deterritorialized' media have contributed to a significant reorientation of the terms of public debate in matters of popular concern. This transformation has been driven by a more commercial impetus towards competition for audiences (as opposed to political competition for allegiance), which has in turn led to a greater convergence of programming in the transnational sphere than has occurred domestically so far.

The reawakening of the 'Arab street'

The problems of this kind confronting Arab states are typical of the tensions generated by the processes of globalization. The messages of transborder satellite channels are carried by high-impact visual images drawn from across the globe; they are received by a young population which is saturated with Western-style patterns of consumption and which is facing great uncertainty about its future. The young people of the Gulf states face a world that appears to put so much on offer while simultaneously denying them access to it. Their problems of exclusion or marginalization are compounded by domestic education systems that have produced a generation lacking the knowledge of technological advances and the problem-solving skills required for economic participation and progress. States confront deep-seated dilemmas when they try to address these problems. Attempts to use the education system to adapt to the social changes fostered by forms of globalization risk conflict with traditional institutions. Like the domestic media, political institutions, legal systems and national educational institutions remain under the influence of existing social and familial standards.[6]

Despite these constraints, as the example of Saudi Arabia shows, the new generation is very conscious of a world beyond national boundaries in ways its parents could not have been. In Saudi Arabia (and the other GCC states) the majority of the population are under twenty years old. During their lifetime there has been a steady increase in access to television broadcasting, first terrestrial and then satellite. The testimony of many of the new generation reveals that television has become a 'natural' aspect of daily life, with electronic images preferred to verbal or written material.[7] The development of satellite communications has increased the significance of television. Not only is there instantaneous live coverage of many vital events across the world; these new media increasingly set the agenda for the older forms of communication.

One result of this kind of exposure to news and information is globalization. Members of the new generation in the Arab Gulf states are more aware of themselves as distinctly Arab in a world context. Of course, like many communities, Arab youth can define itself as much by what sets it against others as by what its members have in common with one another. Being against Israel, the US or the West in general is one important way of clarifying what it means to be a member of the 'Arab street' today. More positively, however, globalization has produced a new identity within which members of the new generation can imagine 'their' Arab community. Young people in Saudi Arabia, for instance, conceive of their national community as becoming increasingly integrated into wider cultural groups at the level of the GCC countries and the wider Arab world.[8]

---

[6] Mai Yamani, *Changed Identities: The Challenge of the New Generation in Saudi Arabia* (London: Royal Institute of International Affairs, 2000), pp. 49–69.
[7] Ibid., pp. 15–22.
[8] Ibid., pp. 36–7.

The ideological use of the media in earlier periods of pan-Arab identity

Different phases in the history of Arab nationalism have been affected by the tides of modernization. Across the past century we can see how different moments of Arab nationalism, of the imagined community of Arabs, were related to the development of new forms of media. The development of Arab nationalist ideas in the 1920s was supported by the availability of newspapers. The radio became important as a means for spreading Arab nationalist ideas in the 1950s and 1960s. With Um Kalthum's Thursday night broadcasting and Gamal Abdul Nasser's powerful speeches the Sawt al-Arab radio station reached the four corners of the Arab world.[9]

During earlier phases of pan-Arab nationalism a language of collective renewal expressed a sense of communal 'moral stagnation' and 'unrest, dissatisfaction and growing impatience with [the] corruption' of the established authorities.[10] In common with many nationalisms, the associated cultural movements encompassed music and poetry giving voice to a self-sacrificing love of the homeland.[11] During the postwar period these themes remained to the fore, with the sense of political and cultural renewal being articulated in an increasingly secular idiom. The period since the 1967 war saw a shift towards nation-state-building, which has often been closely associated with the decisive move towards a more popular and Islamic idiom of collective and political belonging. The 1979 Islamic revolution in Iran was perhaps the most striking indication of this shift. The predominantly secular character of pan-Arab nationalism has now been successfully challenged as a part of the process of popular Islamization. Contemporary songs and poetry, widely and repeatedly broadcast through the new media, have taken up the deeply resonant themes of self-sacrifice for the nation. Popular singing of 'Ya Quds' calls for a sacrifice to match that made by the Palestinian youth confronting Israeli forces. Although few respond to a call to arms, many others recognize the importance of targeting US-based brands by boycotting McDonald's and Coca-Cola.[12]

---

[9] The importance of the spatial and temporal aspects of both print and broadcast media for the development of national identities has been well documented by Benedict Anderson, *Imagined Communities: Reflections on the Origin and Spread of Nationalism* (London: Verso, 1983).

[10] See, for instance, G. Antonius, *The Arab Awakening* (London: Hamish Hamilton, 1945).

[11] See Anderson, *Imagined Communities*, p. 16.

[12] Young Arab women, interviewed in London, recently described using this method of protest. See also the effects of the General Egyptian Committee for the Boycott of Zionist and American Products set up in the aftermath of the al-Aqsa Intifada. See Chapter 1 by Toby Dodge and Richard Higgott in this volume.

A new stage of contemporary pan-Arabism

In the past decade, Arab satellite TV has become a force for Arab cultural unification. Earlier, Western-produced programmes were heavily censored by local governments. The advent of satellite broadcasting has inadvertently prepared the way for the ideational unification of the 'Arab street' based on homogeneity of cultural consumption. This is a less overtly political process than previous periods of Arab nationalism. In contrast to Nasser's Sawt al-Arab state-controlled radio broadcasts promoting Egyptian views on Arab unity, contemporary broadcasting is self-consciously less ideological. In general, the language is quite different from that used during Nasser's era. It has instead made a concerted effort to develop the Arab cultural dimension.

Satellite broadcasts in the Middle East are significantly, if slowly, changing the meaning of what it is to be an Arab. They are helping to strengthen the bonds of the imagined Arab community by developing a broader and deeper sense of a common Arab and Muslim cultural inheritance. This in turn is breaking down some of the cultural boundaries between different Arab populations, making diverse and local cultural practices accessible across previously existing barriers. For example, shared cultural roots are vividly portrayed through the televising of common rituals from around the Arab world, showing that many traditional practices transcend regional and state boundaries. Alternatively, locally distinctive music and poetry are put before a much wider audience, so that today, thanks to developments in independent Arab television programming, a youth in Kuwait can readily recognize Moroccan or Tunisian songs, while his Syrian counterpart can see a Yemeni wedding ritual.

A similar change is taking place with respect to language. Partly as a result of Sawt al-Arab, Egyptian Arabic was unusual in being a national dialect familiar to an audience far beyond Egypt. Today, through satellite broadcasting, dialects from all parts of North Africa are regularly heard across the entire region. All in all, the relationships between differing Arab cultures and territories are being refashioned within an increasingly shared sense of a united Arab culture that is both broad and diverse. The result of the development of regional web-based print and satellite television communications is a rapid increase the number of young Arabs who can think of themselves or relate to others as being Arab in a new and more culturally inclusive way. For the current generation the 'deterritorialization' of cultural consumption is fashioning a transformation in Arab identity and unity.

The proliferation and development of satellite channels and independent programming

The first Arab satellite channel was launched by Egypt in 1990, but the Egyptians were unable to turn their quick start into an established leading position for their broadcasts. It was quickly followed by a host of other transnational Arab channels such as Orbit (al-Mawarid Group – Saudi); MBC (Saudi); al-Mustaqbal of Rafiq Hariri; al-Jazira, based in Qatar; al-Manar of Hizbullah; Abu Dhabi Satellite Television; ART (Sheikh Saleh Kamel – Saudi); LBC (Lebanese Broadcasting Corporation); ANN (Arab News Network, owned by the son of Rifat al-Assad, the estranged brother of the late Syrian president Hafez al-Assad); NBN (National Broadcasting Network – Lebanon); and MTV (Murr Television – Lebanon).

The first channel to achieve prominence was MBC, the London-based Saudi-owned private satellite channel. MBC came to fill the gap between national television and CNN coverage. Its slogan is '*al-'alam bi-'iyoon arabiyyah*', 'The world though Arab eyes', although it is actually the world perceived from a more narrowly Saudi perspective. The BBC World Service started a rival Arabic television channel in 1994, but this was closed down in 1996. When the BBC channel folded, many of its staff were recruited by the newly established Qatari station al-Jazira. Having been trained by the BBC, they showed a greater understanding of standards of objectivity and balance, and al-Jazira productions tended to show respect rather than deference towards the region's political leaders. More important, perhaps, was the attention that al-Jazira paid to programme development. As a result of these efforts, it has grown into the most watched channel in the region. Its output includes live talk shows that have presented controversial debates, and it has addressed a wide range of topics not usually given so open a public airing in the region. As a consequence of these developments there have been significant changes to the boundaries of public debate and to the ability of local political authorities to police them.

The new competition for cultural influence

States in the Middle East are now having to contend with the 'al-Jazira syndrome': the formation by satellite television of new public spaces and/or the reworking of the limits of public discussion that has spread through a plethora of new Arab news channels. The 1990s witnessed a surge in the number of Arab satellite channels. They have engaged in concerted competition with one another for sensational news coverage and debates and also entertainment. This kind of cultural competition has entered a new phase. Until now, governments have been able to regulate the domestic cultural field to a large extent, and they have frequently been the most powerful player on that field. Across the region, governments have shown themselves willing and able to use a variety of means, both regulatory and repressive, to control the availability of information and to restrict the scope of the issues and language of public debate.[13] In addition to establishing domestic broadcasting monopolies, they have sought to restrict public debate by the control of newspapers and journalists in various ways. In addition to legal regulation and enforcement, political and financial weight has been used to sustain formal and informal limits on what could receive public airing. Within states, individual journalists have been vulnerable to direct and indirect pressures; they have had to be keenly aware of where the lines of the permissible were drawn and when it was safe to cross them.

The transnational sphere of communications is significantly different from the domestic public sphere, which, as shown, is subject to forms of state action and intervention. No state is hermetically sealed, although some borders are more porous than others. For example, governments have always faced the challenge of developing an ability to police their borders and effectively enforce prohibitions on the import of unacceptable publications. With the development of broadcasting and electronic communications, Arab states have also developed means of restricting access. Some states choose to jam what they regard as hostile radio broadcasts from either other Arab states or international broadcasts such as the BBC and the Voice of America. Access to satellite broadcasts is restricted through the banning or regulation of dishes. Similarly, access to equipment for the Internet can be restricted and its use may be monitored. Enforcement is very uneven, however.[14]

Whether the ownership of broadcasting channels is public or private, inter-Arab competition for cultural leadership within the sphere of 'deterritorialized' communication has become quite fierce. This competition has some similarities with Nasser's aspirations, but today's new players contest

[13] Human Rights Watch, *The Internet in the Middle East and North Africa*, p. 22.
[14] According to Human Rights Watch the techniques used by governments in their efforts to restrict access to electronic media and to information are many and varied. Saudi Arabia, for instance, imposes censorship on the Internet by means of proxy servers that filter and block specified content, including politics and human rights issues. E-mail can be subject to surveillance. Qatar requires users to sign agreements to refrain from activities contrary to public order as part of service contracts. State-sponsored rival sites have also been established. See ibid., p. 1.

Egypt's claim to cultural as well as political leadership. Some of those contestants are small Gulf states which, through the new technologies, make their presence felt quite disproportionately to their political weight. In the Arab Gulf there is competition between al-Jazira of Qatar and MBC of Saudi Arabia. At this level, Arab competition dictates a quite different approach from that taken in domestic broadcasting, and technology makes the possibilities appear endless. The cost of technology is falling, and greater numbers of the population are keen to pay more for a dish, especially as they are steadily losing trust in their state television.

With the development of this 'deterritorialized' sphere of communications, we can begin to speak of two kinds of 'public sphere': one national and territorial, the other supranational. Broadcast media provide a public platform on which issues of general interest can be voiced and portrayed. The degree to which they contribute to a public sphere, in the sense of an arena in which political authority is accountable, depends on who is permitted access to the platform and on the terms of permissible discourse. It is clear that in respect of both the scope of discourse and those who may participate, a wide gap is opening up between the national and the supranational spheres. In the national sphere we hear the language and see the representatives of government, while in the supranational sphere the mass of the people and their sentiments have a much larger presence.

These tensions are most clearly visible in the contrast between the persistently dull output of territorially based broadcasting and what is available from satellite. Local television stations, such as those in Saudi Arabia, remain committed to domestic norms. National news programmes continue to show the royal family engaged in interminable gatherings in which its members use highly formalized ceremonial greetings and routine expressions of piety to portray their romantic and somewhat detached vision of the social order and hierarchy. These lengthy rituals are carefully staged in traditional tents and are elaborated with incense-burning and sword-dancing. They exemplify the way in which the use of domestic television is subordinated to the portrayal of stability and continuity for the purpose of symbolizing and strengthening a very particular conception of national identity.

More able to respond to their audiences, the 'deterritorialized' media are increasingly setting a new agenda for the existing local media. The old media are being forced to attempt to compete for audiences on these new terms, to catch up, albeit in small measure, with the powerful and overwhelming flow of information. However, formal correctness rather than social, cultural or political transformation remains the overwhelming concern of public servants in charge of the local media. Although they continue to function thanks to state subsidies, some degree of updating and easing of state control is essential in order to prevent these established media from becoming extinct or at least irrelevant.

The limitations of local programming were exposed at the very start of the satellite era. It was CNN that first announced the Iraqi invasion of Kuwait and gave it 24-hour coverage, while some Gulf television stations ignored this momentous event. Eventually Saudi television reported the Iraqi invasion – three days after it took place. Many omissions such as this have revealed a gap in the local Arab media's coverage of sensitive news. This has contributed greatly to an increasing loss of trust in the state media.

It is as a result of this declining confidence that state censorship of the media has become a lively issue of debate for young men and women, among whom attitudes towards censorship appear to be becoming more ambivalent. Although many accept that there is a legitimate role for state censorship to play in protecting Arabic and Islamic culture from the pressures of Western influence, there is an equally deep concern about the use of censorship as a means of domestic political exclusion. On the one hand, censorship is widely held to be legitimate when it is used as a means of defending a vulnerable culture from powerful and potentially corrosive forces. For example, one typical young Saudi regards satellite television with suspicion. He explains that those who watch Western satellite TV 'have lost their identity. It is as if a spell has been cast on them, transforming them into distorted figures'.15 This young man articulates a view held by those such as radical *salafis* (those who militantly promote the Wahhabi form of Islam), who fear for the contamination of Muslim Arab identity.

On the other hand, it is not apparent to many of the new generation that existing controls are being properly used to foster the interests of popular Arab culture. Controls, on domestic television especially, are experienced as too restrictive. Domestic output is widely regarded as promoting too narrow a conception of Arab identity, one that is too closely associated with the domestic political leadership. There is a widespread appreciation that stations such as al-Jazira meet a pressing need. It is through these channels of communication that people can become more keenly aware of the realities of their situation and of the political debates that concern them. The same young Saudi recognized this when he explained that in the mid-1990s people were broadly unaware of the real economic problems facing their country until they started to receive information from al-Jazira.[16]

[15] See Yamani, *Changed Identities*, p. 17. This book also contains more detailed discussion among young Saudis on this issue.
[16] Ibid., p. 17.

These apparently ambivalent attitudes towards censorship indicate how a sense of community is critical in framing popular political discourse. Attitudes on this issue are clearly not informed by an abstract 'principle' either for or against it. They are much better understood in terms of perceptions of the use of political controls for the promotion of the interests of a distinctive political community. When disagreements arise over the exercise of political power, they are driven not so much by differences of principle as by differing conceptions of the character and interests of a specific community. Political legitimacy is granted only to those in power and authority who use their position to further the interests of the community as a whole. Indeed, the moral standing of existing political authorities is poor precisely because the bulk of the population do not regard either the institutions or the personnel of the state as representing their community, whether national or pan-Arab. Throughout the past century populations across the entire Middle East have been drawn out of very local communities into much broader national and pan-Arab communities. The original social bases of national states in the region, however, were considerably narrower, and they are still understood to represent tribal or other sectional interests and/or to be beholden to foreign powers, especially the US.[17]

Limitations on satellite broadcasting: ownership, affiliations and agendas

The new satellite television channels have not completely overturned the older forms of broadcasting and public language. It is noteworthy that most satellite channels are owned by rich Gulf Arab states such as the United Arab Emirates, Qatar and Saudi Arabia, and private ownership is frequently in the hands of individuals close to the ruling elite. To a certain extent, the nature of competition in satellite broadcasting means that both state-owned and private satellite channels are obliged to show images that stir the emotions of the young Arab population, for example those of Mohammad al-Dura and other young Palestinian martyrs. But although this could rebound on certain states if politically charged responses were to become unmanageable, there appears to be no stopping the rush to develop the new media. And although these media have expanded the boundaries of what occurs in the public sphere, clear limits on them remain in place, and a range of strategies for minimizing political controversy and externalizing the objects of political anger and frustration is still evident.

[17] Ibid., pp. 33–44.

While messages disseminated through state satellite channels seem to be in favour of the Arabs and in some cases dwell upon the intifada, they continue to cover up many issues that remain taboo. It is far easier for these channels to address problems in foreign relations than the domestic problems of Arab states. Sharon's atrocities are easier to denounce than the Saudi judicial system. When it comes to explicitly political issues rather than the apparently more innocuous cultural ones, transnational identity continues to be defined negatively, against outsiders, rather than in positive terms that would have implications for the legitimacy of regional governments. The limitations on news agendas remain very narrow. There are a number of issues such as human rights, democracy or women's calls for equality which do not receive a great deal of coverage. Nevertheless, there are signs that sustaining even the current boundaries within the transnational sphere will not be as easily achieved as in domestic spheres. For instance, initial steps have been taken to raise issues of immediate political importance, such as coverage of the political conflict over human rights issues in Algeria. More significantly, the 'professional' ethos behind live talk shows has worked hard to increase the plurality of views aired, allowing considerable access to the airwaves for ordinary voices.

Islamization and modernization: paradoxes facing young Gulf Arabs

There is a certain paradox in all this. Young Arabs want to express their dissatisfaction with America's hegemony in the region and especially its support for Israel, and yet the technology and culture of the Arab satellite television that sharpens these feelings is largely a product of the West. The majority of Arab youth in the Gulf are using and relying on Western culture and technology, and yet are rejecting its source. The more radical religious or ideological groups, those towards the margins of political and cultural life, are all the more reliant on these Western technological sources for their shared sense of community. This paradox is partially reconciled by the fact that the satellite TV news they rely on is increasingly broadcast in Arabic. The new channels use their own language and are making greater efforts to develop distinctive programming directed at an Arab audience. As a result, these channels have gained the trust of many in the Arab world, displacing CNN, for example, as a source of reliable information.

It has been a long-standing commonplace that modernization entails secularization and individuation. The process of modernization was understood as the spread of specifically Western cultural forms and values. Societies in which these values did not develop were considered to have remained 'traditional'. Globalization clearly does entail adopting practices and technologies that have originated in the West but, as we can see, integrating them into Arab societies entails their continual negotiation. The terms of this negotiation change continually. They are dependent on the events in both the international and domestic spheres. Modernization across the Arab world has been mediated more and more through the predominantly Islamic culture, and has thus taken on an ever clearer Muslim appearance. As 'deterritorialized' communication develops, it joins with and further encourages the growth of a 'deterritorialized' Muslim community across the region. Research into the attitudes of the new generation in the Gulf has revealed a very widespread adherence to Islamic idioms in discussions of political and cultural affairs.18 Distinctions can be made within this Islamic discourse among three broad strands: 'liberal modernist', in which consistency with Quranic teaching is important but ritual practices are of diminishing significance; 'traditionalist' or 'conservative', in which traditional family practices and the policies of the ruling regimes in the Gulf are supported; and 'radical', in which a more distinctively Islamic response to modernization is articulated. What we speak of as 'Islamization' is really a series of wide-ranging and continual attempts to develop, articulate and dispute the Islamic terms by which the character and qualities of social relations will be transformed under modernization. However, satellite television, especially the broadcasting of the intifada, has tended to subordinate these divergent strands to a common Arab identity.

As modernity is mediated through Islam, so being an Arab and a Muslim is mediated through modernization. The 'deterritorialized', imagined community of the Arabs is engaged in a distinctly modern process of contested self-definition. Although the community is often concerned about Westernization, the form it is taking is thoroughly modern, in respect of communication and much else.19 The continuing contrast between the West and the Islamic world, so central to this discourse, has real value, but it obscures at least as much as it discloses. For the Arab world, globalization entails both Westernization, in the sense that cultural institutions and practices are increasingly like those of the West in some ways, and a process of Arabization and Islamization. This entails the development of a modern but distinctive sense of community that carries its own moral and political discourse. The

18 'Religion: Reviving Islamic Identity', in ibid., pp. 115–31.
19 For a more detailed discussion of this issue across the Middle East, see especially Charles Tripp, 'Islam and the Secular Logic of the State in the Middle East', in A. Ehteshami and A.S. Sidahmed (eds), *Islamic Fundamentalism* (Boulder, CO: Westview Press, 1996).

processes of globalization across the Middle East encompass convergences with Western culture and norms but also distinctive divergences, with the development of modern but specifically Arab and Islamic cultural forms.

The effects of 'deterritorialized' communications and community on the streets and palaces of the region

There should be little doubt that the development of a new, transnational sphere of communication is having a significant impact on the Arab world and on the Gulf in particular. There was an instantaneous reaction across the length and breadth of the region in response to the coverage of the al-Aqsa Intifada by transnational television channels, as demonstrating voices echoed from Morocco to Oman. Would similar demonstrations have taken place had satellite television not been there? The answer is probably yes, but the new media were a catalyst for a special kind of reaction, fuelling the fires of popular reaction that were already smouldering. In the longer term they also contributed to the possibility of this reaction.

These demonstrations had many unusual features, and the impact of globalization was particularly striking in the Gulf Arab countries. Demonstrations in the GCC countries saw both Islamists and more secular groups taking a common stance, their shared sense of Arab belonging overriding other differences. In some cases there were spontaneous reactions by people who had not previously taken a public political position. The six conservative states of the GCC were perceived in the region and beyond as relatively isolated from the rest of the Arab world, and for the decade since the Gulf war they had been quiescent, their populations largely keeping their reputation for political passivity. But taboos were broken when, for the first time in Saudi Arabia, there was a series of demonstrations in which women also took to the street and expressed their sympathy with the Palestinians.

In Jeddah, for instance, some forty educated Hejazi women from prominent families stood in full national veils in a main square holding banners and chanting for the liberation and protection of the Palestinians. As women in Saudi Arabia are forbidden to appear in public unaccompanied by a male guardian or even to drive a car, this was bewildering for the authorities. These women were standing for a morally and religiously justifiable cause, but as women they were breaching the codes of custom and law that prohibited them from taking a stand in public. The female demonstrators were detained for a few hours at a police station, but they were not severely punished, as those involved in the 1990 driving demonstration had been.[20] Instead, these women were released after signing a document in which they promised not to demonstrate again. Their appearance in public could not be condoned; but neither could it be condemned, because of the justice of their demands and the political sensitivity of their cause.

The women in Jeddah created a specific local difficulty for the Saudi authorities, but they were also part of a wider pan-Arab movement. In standing up for Palestine, those taking part in demonstrations across the region took upon themselves the mantle of the just. By demonstrating in public they questioned the claims made by the palaces to represent the interests of the people. (The Riyadh government has responded to these public concerns by, among other things, establishing the Al Aqsa Centre in Jeddah. It contains models and exhibitions relating to the dome, and opens up a space for a more acceptable form for solidarity with the Palestinian cause.) Some features of the reactions across the Arab world to the al-Aqsa Intifada were unprecedented. There were popular demonstrations in support of the Palestinians that occurred extremely quickly, and in some places entirely new groups of people were brought into public political life and voiced their collective dissatisfaction with the lack of active support shown for the Palestinian cause by the 'palaces'. To some, it seemed as if popular opinion across the Arab world was being given a single voice. The characteristics of these recent protests can be understood more clearly in the context of globalization.

Conclusions

Since the outbreak of the second intifada in September 2000, the satellite channels have constantly broadcast images of the fierce struggle of the Palestinians. This has been collectively perceived as the humiliation of the Arabs. Satellite television has played the key role in unifying the 'Arab street'. In doing so it has exposed the gap between the regimes and their populations. The combination of long-term cultural broadcasting and short-term political coverage indicates some of the potential for unintended and uncontrolled social change caused by globalization. Specifically, it shows the inherent possibilities for forms of globalization to undermine the ability of states to control cultural changes and the consumption patterns of their populations. This can have very real political consequences. Within all GCC states, a different dimension of transnational Arab allegiance is

[20] See Mai Yamani, 'Some Observations on Women in Saudi Arabia', in Mai Yamani (ed.), *Feminism and Islam: Legal and Literary Perspectives* (London: Ithaca, 1996).

gradually forming alongside a deepening sense of a national identity, and it both threatens and attracts the population. This creates a sense of confusion about what should be the relations between state and society.

Owing in part to 'deterritorialized' media, many young people throughout the Arab world have been emboldened, and perhaps empowered, with knowledge, information, awareness and a renewed sense of solidarity with their fellow Arabs. This enhanced sense of solidarity draws on a conception of the sheer scale of their collective being. However, this self-awareness tends to lead to a growing frustration with their inability to do anything about what angers them most – their states' unwillingness or inability to turn popular sentiment into political action on the world stage. Although Arab identity has developed in the supranational sphere of communications, it has not been translated into an assertive political identity in the territorially based regional or international realm. People are aware of a potential, but also of their weakness. This situation produces a blend of dissatisfaction, ambition and fear. Although some overestimate what can be done, it is nonetheless possible that a real gap may open up between the Arab regimes and the people. All this creates difficulties for domestic governments that, until recently, have been able to exert a high degree of control over established forms of media and communications in their efforts to maintain political stability. Governments now have to contend with new modes of cultural competition in the supranational sphere, which disturbs the basis on which domestic strategies have been built.

This examination of globalization and its effects, of the emergence of a supranational community and a renewed sense of pan-Arab identity in the Arab Gulf region, has brought a number of issues to the fore. Relatively long-standing territorially based relations at the domestic, regional and international levels have all been affected to some extent by the 'deterritorialization' of community and communications brought about by satellite broadcasting's permeation of regional populations.

This developing 'space' of communication has evolved as an arena of competition with a set of rules significantly different from those employed within states. Within this new public arena a different range of issues has been raised, breaking taboos. Although the 'Western' media culture of news and discussion has become relatively well established, limits to this development remain in place, and many of the more sensitive cultural and political issues are still subject to very careful handling, if they are mentioned at all. At the same time, the rules, both formal and informal, for the broadcast media in the 'territorial' sphere and those in the new 'transnational spaces' are sufficiently at odds with each another for the conservative role of the domestic, land-based services to be clearly exposed.

A new 'space' for the pan-Arab community, on the other hand, has clarified the difference between the 'street' and the 'palace'. Popular support for the Palestinian al-Aqsa Intifada urges national states to be true to the shared sense of Arab identity and to distinguish themselves by their actions more clearly from the 'others', be they Israeli, American or Western. These states, however, remain firmly embedded in territorially based domestic, regional and international relations and, for the most part, are deeply reluctant to disrupt them.

As 'deterritorialized' relations develop, they increase the potential for tensions within each of the existing territorial spaces, just as they increase the potential for tensions to emerge between the states and the developing transnational sense of community. Means of communication beyond the control of governments are becoming ever more widely entrenched in the day-to-day life of the population, and as they do so they are sustaining a richer and more complex imagined community of Arabs. It is this community to which the 'Arab street' gives voice. As it makes its presence felt, this supranational Arab community comes into conflict with the rulers of the Arab world. Here, at least, globalization is a source of inspiration for the new generation, and of greater instability in already difficult territorially based relations. Modernization encompasses a wide range of processes of social transformation, including those of globalization, that engender 'deterritorialized' social relations. The development of a transnational imagined community of Muslim Arabs, for all its antecedents outside the West, is a distinctively modern process. States across the region possess many of the means, developed in the West, for social regulation, and they are having to grapple with difficulties of modernization that gradually, persistently are engulfing them.

6 Cultural transmutations: the dialectics of globalization in contemporary Iran

Ali M. Ansari

'... if you speak to a student of theology about your concerns over the ideal society, he might say "I have heard about globalization from one of my friends. It is a prelude to the reappearance of Imam Mahdi (May God hasten his reappearance). Therefore we must welcome this development."'[1]

Introduction

Globalization is a term that may be fairly characterized as 'essentially contested'. It is a term that has gained wide currency not only in social science literature but also in the media, through which it has embedded itself in popular discourse. This popularity, of course, almost ensures a wide variety of interpretations and an ambiguity that tends to hinder rather than help its productive application. Thus, there are many who dismiss the concept as a convenient cloak intended to disguise and in some cases justify the continuous expansion of Western values and economic modes of production throughout the globe. Others reject the concept altogether, pointing to the realities of localization and particularization, and argue that the world is less unified today within a global political or economic system than it was in the nineteenth century, at the height of European imperialism. Yet arguably, it is the very fractures in the post-colonial global order that have assisted the development of the complex dynamic now defined as 'globalization'. Indeed, drawing on the transformationalist thesis I shall argue that what distinguishes the process of globalization from that of imperialism, which preceded it, is the reciprocal and dialectical nature of this process at work. Where advances in military technology once assisted the formation of European empires which imposed a particular cultural

---

[1] Hojjatoleslam Nabavi, quoted in a roundtable discussion, 'The Effects of Globalization on the Islamic Republic of Iran', *Discourse*, Vol. 2, No. 2, fall 2000, p. 13. See also page 46 above.

vision on the world, contemporary advances in media technologies are providing the 'weak' with a means to gain access to the developed world and to appropriate and in a very real sense reciprocate cultural transmissions.

Although there can be little doubt that in economic terms the global initiative lies with the West, the impact of cultural globalization is much more nuanced and complex, and it is on this aspect of globalization that this chapter will focus. This is not to argue that the West does not dominate the transmission of cultural norms throughout the globe but simply to point out that the reception and appreciation of these norms varies enormously and that in some cases a process of reciprocation is beginning.[2] One place where this process may be witnessed is the Islamic Republic of Iran. At first sight Iran seems an unlikely subject in which to explore the appropriation and reciprocation of cultural globalization, given the widespread assumption that it has somehow managed to isolate itself from the world. Yet observers have already noted the apparent impact of globalization not just in the field of economics – Iran has already applied to join the World Trade Organization – but also, and most interestingly, in the cultural sphere. Travellers to Iran are often shocked at the level of Western cultural penetration, especially among the country's youth, and hold this up as a prime example of the inexorable march of globalization. Yet in their haste to characterize and justify a process, they fail to appreciate the complex dynamic at work.

Islamic revolution and globalization

For many in Iran, the Islamic revolution of 1979 was essentially an act of national resistance to a particular type of globalization, in this case Americanization.[3] That the shah had to be overthrown was almost incidental to this process of cultural retrenchment and assertion. He was widely seen as the prime vehicle for the process of Americanization, and therefore he had to be removed.[4] The Islamic revolution can therefore be characterized as ideological and cultural in determination and counter-hegemonic in construction. All aspects of Americanization had to be rooted out, however brutal the consequences of this policy might be, and replaced with an authentic culture that was both Islamic and Iranian.

[2] See J. B. Thompson, *Ideology and Modern Culture* (Cambridge: Polity Press, 1990).
[3] Hence the use of the term 'global arrogance' by Iranians to define the United States.
[4] See, for example, M. Reza Behnam, *Cultural Foundations of Iranian Politics* (Salt Lake City: University of Utah Press, 1986).

Two factors made this policy of cultural retrenchment difficult to accomplish. First, there was the reality of Iran's international situation and the technological changes that had increasingly penetrated its cultural defences. For all the genuine, if misplaced, efforts to 'purify' the country, it was clear to the new government that international relations had to continue and that trade commitments had to be honoured. Thus although the war with Iraq (1980–88) fostered a sense of isolation and self-reliance, military needs necessitated contacts with the outside world. If anything, the Western arms embargo ensured that Iran had to pursue links to countries it had hitherto had negligible contact with in order to broaden its supply base. In this sense, therefore, Iran was far from isolated in the 1980s. These contacts were developed and expanded in the aftermath of the war. An example of this was Iran's trading links with Europe. They developed to such an extent that it soon became apparent that the protestations of European countries anxious to internationalize the human rights agenda could not be ignored. Iran's response, which in many ways foreshadowed its reaction to globalization, was to appropriate and reinterpret the agenda in terms of *Islamic* human rights.

The attempted universalization of these ideas was, of course, not new. The pursuit of a human rights agenda had, after all, done much to undermine the authority of the last shah and had given encouragement to his opponents. Yet the intensity of cultural transmission – the mode of global interaction – had now changed. This was in large part because of the advent of new technology, which made the control of information much more difficult. But, in addition, one must not neglect the consequences of massive emigration in the aftermath of revolution and war, which ensured that most Iranian families had a relative in an at least one major international city. It is estimated that at least two million Iranians have emigrated, mainly to the West, since 1979, although the figure could be considerably higher if second-generation Iranians are included in these statistics. These migrants have not only justified and, to some extent, excused the vastly increased use of international networks of communication but also facilitated the transmission of cultural ideas. Moreover, their presence abroad has often encouraged further travel by relatives in Iran, which again increases cultural interaction. This trend more than compensates for the comparative lack of Iranian students studying abroad since 1979. At its peak the number reached 75,000, of whom 50,000 studied in the United States.[5] Students remain an important source of cultural transmission, but the proportion going overseas is now much smaller, and their destinations are much more diverse.

[5] See James A. Bill, *The Eagle and the Lion* (New Haven: Yale University Press, 1988) p. 211.

Technology is the key determinant that has allowed these geographically diverse but culturally affiliated communities to maintain contact with
one other. Although the Islamic Republic has sought to prevent 'cultural
pollution' through its rhetorical battle against the 'onslaught', its practical
means of control have been less than effective. The needs of trade and
international interaction rapidly predominated over the desire to maintain
cultural isolation, and it also became increasingly impractical to monitor
the use of electronic media of cultural exchange. Initially, one had to hold
a licence in order to operate a fax machine. This injunction was swiftly
ignored, found to be impossible to monitor and subsequently abandoned.
Next came the video machine, whose use was rapidly endorsed when what
was widely known became officially apparent: that many members of the
ulama (the Shia clergy in Iran) were in possession of the machines,
ostensibly to watch reruns of Ayatollah Khomeini's speeches! After fax
machines and videos came the debate over the use of satellite dishes,
regarded by many in authority as the most powerful tool of cultural
imperialism. Having failed so dramatically to prevent the use of faxes and
videos, the government took an initial attitude to satellite dishes that was
ambivalent and non-committal, with the result that many people acquired
the dishes. There were even instances of poorer communities clubbing
together to purchase the equipment, and it was widely believed that some
government agencies were actively involved in their procurement and
distribution. Nevertheless, conservative elements within the clerical
hierarchy ensured that eventually the Majlis ratified a formal ban. This did
not have the desired effect: several years on, satellite dishes still exist in
abundance throughout the country.[6]

This failure has been well reflected by the determination to promote and
encourage the use of the Internet. All political factions use the Internet, to
acquire and also to disseminate information. Attempts have occasionally
been made to shut down undesirable sites, but there has been no concerted
effort, as, for example, in China, to control what appears on the servers. On
the contrary, Internet cafés have mushroomed, especially in Tehran, and
provide the country's youth with immediate access to a world of information. The Internet has provided a means of access to dissident ayatollahs
under house arrest, and also a tool for a press corps under severe pressure.
Iranian students established their own news-wire service in response to the
mass closure of the country's newspapers in April 2000.[7]

[6] For a detailed analysis, see S. Barraclough, 'Satellite Television in Iran: Prohibition, Imitation and Reform', *Middle Eastern Studies,* Vol. 37, No. 3, July 2001, pp. 25–48.
[7] See, for instance, the 'Iranian Students News Association' (ISNA) or the discussion forum of Amir Kabir University: *clubs.yahoo.com\club\akunews.*

The second significant factor working against cultural isolation was (and is) the determination and, arguably, the inexorable logic of the revolution to export its ideas. Those promoting both 'Iran' and 'Islam' have been universalist in their pretensions. Although this fact is often ignored or dismissed by Western analysts,[8] it is a historical reality that begs reassessment. Iran or 'Persia', to use the culturally more palatable term, has always sought to disseminate its ideas regionally and internationally. Commentators are often struck by how Iranian communities abroad, while eager to adapt, have at the same time stubbornly retained a high level of cultural homogeneity that they have sought in turn to impart (if not impose) on others. A major aspect of this 'cultural imperialism' has been in the field of religious ideas, with Islam forming the second universalizing element. In fact Islam shares with Christianity an evangelizing and total vision of the world that is absent from other major religions. It is this tendency that has made it the fastest-growing religion in the world. Combine both Iran and Islam and one has a highly intense and determined motor for the globalization of an ideal. In the early days of the revolution this was appreciated, if wilfully misinterpreted in the West, to suit political needs, in the fear of a 'fundamentalist wave' overturning regimes in the Middle East. When the impact of Iranian ideas seemed to be wholly negative, they appeared to be a very real threat to the stability of the region. Latterly, as the revolution has matured and its ideas have become more nuanced and complex, it is curious how this transmission of ideas has suddenly become irrelevant and unrealistic.

For Iran, however, the dissemination of its ideas continues to be a central aspect of its cultural and revolutionary heritage. Thus it has appropriated the means of dissemination and transmission with considerable enthusiasm, including the development of a satellite television network and, most of all, the use of the Internet. Iran's appreciation of the technological revolution and its response to it was well expressed by President Khatami in 1995, when he was the head of the National Library:

In its contemporary, complex forms, information technology represents one of the highest achievements of modern culture which uses its control over information to solidify its domination of the world. Thus,

[8] Consult, for example, D. Held, A. McGrew, D. Goldblatt and J. Perraton, *Global Transformations: Politics, Economics and Culture* (Cambridge: Polity Press, 1999), p. 332. The authors make the curious assertion that while Christianity and Judaism 'have spread their adherents to most corners of the world' and 'Hinduism, Buddhism and Confucianism are all more tightly concentrated in their regional strongholds ... Islam occupies a middling position.' Islam's universalizing tendencies are probably more accurately reflected in Huntington's essay on 'The Clash of Civilizations', although his emphasis is somewhat mischievously laid on the antagonistic and conflictual aspects of this process.

inquiry into the nature of the information world is inseparable from uncovering the nature of modern civilisation itself. And until we address this important question we will not be able to muster the confidence and wisdom to understand our relationship to modern civilisation. Otherwise, we will live in a world whose rules have been set by others, at the mercy of circumstance, not as masters of our fate ...

... This does not mean that we must isolate ourselves from the Western-dominated information world. Such a thing is undesirable and practically impossible as the global reach of information constantly expands. Awareness of today's world events is an imperative for understanding our place in the world and planning our future in it. Being isolated from the world's information networks can only turn us into pawns of others because it is they who control the flow of this vital and strategic resource.[9]

The reformist world-view

When Khatami was elected president in 1997, his chief of staff Hojjat-ol-Islam Abtahi pointed out that Iran now had a chief executive who knew Iran and, importantly, understood Iran's place in the world. Khatami, while symbolic of the reformist tendency in Iran, also reflected it, and in many ways he was the political manifestation of an intellectual renaissance that had captivated the Iranian intelligentsia and youth over the previous decade. This renaissance was itself a product of the fractures in authoritarian rule that had emerged after the revolution and the experience of war. They encouraged people to be more critical of their relationship with the state, and also to re-evaluate Iran's relationship with the global order. Indeed the war with Iraq and the devastation it caused, both materially and psychologically, was a major factor in forcing intellectual reflection. The somewhat simplistic (if reassuring) notions of revolutionary fervour were increasingly questioned and challenged. Although some continued to cling tenaciously to notions of cultural purity and glorious isolation, others, including some senior ayatollahs, were acutely aware that Iran was not an island which could be easily quarantined and that some form of engagement was needed.[10] It was argued that Iran could not resist globalizing trends, even if they were characterized as a 'cultural onslaught'. Instead, the country had to accom-

---

[9] M. Khatami, 'Observations on the information world', in *Hope and Challenge: The Iranian President Speaks,* trans A. Mafinezam (New York: Binghampton University Press, 1997), pp. 61 and 65.
[10] Interview carried out by the author, Tehran, Iran, September 1999.

modate, appropriate and respond. Interestingly, it was understood that for this to occur, there first had to be a fuller appreciation of 'Western culture'. This movement took its cue from Khomeini himself, who had taught aspects of Western philosophy, if only to show their inadequacy. Of even greater influence was the chief ideologue of the Islamic revolution, Ayatollah Motahhari, who had explicitly referred to Marx and Engels in unusually sympathetic terms as thinkers who, although clearly incorrect in their conclusions, had at least tried to *do* something about the nature of the world. Many Iranian intellectuals, including clerics, decided to immerse themselves in the Western intellectual tradition. Some seminaries even took the decision to send their students abroad.[11] Cultural globalization was, in this respect, not so much imposed on Iran as fully endorsed but then transformed by it.

This was not, of course, an uncritical immersion. It was, on the contrary, a strategy for inclusion. Rather than be the object of globalization, as many would have argued was the case during the time of the shah, the new Islamic Republic wanted to *participate*. In order to participate, it had to learn and to integrate itself in the international intellectual community. This view was well expressed by the noted clerical intellectual Mojtahed Shabestari as far back as 1988:

> The fact that our seminaries have separated their path from that of the social sciences and are minding their own business without any aware-ness of the developments in these disciplines has brought us to the present condition in which we have no philosophy of civil rights or philosophy of ethics. [Furthermore] we have neither a political nor an economic philosophy. Without having a set of solid and defendable theories in these fields, how can we talk of universal or permanent laws and values? How can we [even] gain admission to the international scientific communities?[12]

By gaining 'admission', Iranian intellectuals hoped to understand and appropriate Western ideas and to refashion them in a manner suitable to Iranian culture. By internalizing global cultural norms, these ideas could then be re-exported, both regionally and internationally. An interesting case study of this process in operation is that of the appropriation of democratic values. Not only have Iranian intellectuals sought to reinterpret 'demo-cracy' within the context of Islam, they have also offered a challenge to the

---

[11] Interview carried out by the author, Shahr-Rey, Iran, July 1997.
[12] Quoted in M. Borujerdi, *Iranian Intellectuals and the West* (New York: Syracuse University Press, 1996), p. 168.

normative ideas of democratic development, which rely heavily on a particular conception of secularism. This is, to be sure, the beginning of a challenge, but there is little indication that ideas of 'religious democracy' have as yet impacted on the global (Western-defined) consciousness. It remains an interesting challenge nonetheless, and given the religious roots of the Western intellectual tradition, it may yet fall on fertile ground.

In the same manner, although for different reasons, Iranian culture has proved to be remarkably receptive to the ideology if not the practice of democracy. For the better part of a century, and largely through the infusion of ideas from the West, Iranian intellectuals have sought to limit the powers of the shahs and to implement some form of elective constitutional government. Although these ideas have in the main been the province of a limited circle of intellectuals, the advent of mass media communication has allowed their dissemination to a much wider section of society. Several historical periods have witnessed a particularly vibrant press culture, and the low level of literacy did not prevent the transmission of ideas through group readings.[13] But far more influential in the preparation of the popular consciousness was the development and use of the radio, which did not depend on literacy. Mass political movements such as the National Front during the oil nationalization crisis (1951–3) lent further popular credence to the idea of an accountable elected government. That this did not materialize did not extinguish the idea. Nor did it prevent Mohammad Reza Shah from paying lip service to expressions of democracy, such as in the retention of a parliament and senate. The Islamic revolution itself was in part the heir of a growing democratic tradition, and it was expected to fulfil its promise in this respect. Certainly the constitution, which was ratified in 1979, contained enough assertions of democratic intent to lead some justifiably to believe that this would indeed be the case.

This belief was sustained through the early years of the revolution and war, when to all intents and purposes it appeared that anarchy had facilitated the re-establishment of authoritarian government. Certainly there were those who were anxious to rid the revolution of any democratic tendency and impose a particularly harsh interpretation of authoritarian Islam. Unsurprisingly, these groups were the most enthusiastic about maintaining the purity of the revolution and defending against any sort of cultural penetration. They were unable, however, to silence fully their critics, who continued to maintain that the state was an Islamic *republic* and therefore had to fulfil its popular as well as its Islamic character. Indeed, the republican element of the constitution and the title of the post-revolutionary

---

[13] Note the comments of the British ambassador in Tehran in FO 248 1427, 24 April 1943.

Iranian state proved to be extremely difficult for conservative authoritarians to deal with; they complained that despite Ayatollah Khomeini's clear
sanction of the term, it was wholly imported and possessed no Islamic
pedigree.[14] Such were the difficulties that some of the more extreme
elements sought to dispense with the term 'republic' altogether and argued
for an 'Islamic State' over an 'Islamic Republic'.

In terms of cultural authenticity, if not political justice, there was much
to commend their argument. It was indeed curious that this term should
have entered the Iranian political lexicon at a time when cultural retrenchment and isolation seemed to predominate, and it should have served
notice that even at this time, Iran was not immune to cultural penetration.
Nevertheless, by the late 1980s and the early 1990s an intellectual debate
began to emerge over the direction of the Islamic Republic and, in particular, over the precise nature of its republican content. In order to authenti-
cate and legitimize this consequence of cultural globalization, some
Iranian thinkers decided to redefine the boundaries of East and West in
such a way as to make the latter a part of the inheritance of the former.
Thus the first step in cultural appropriation and reinterpretation was the
'Iranianization' and, to some extent, the 'Islamization' of Western discourse, removing the exclusive subject–object dichotomy and replacing it
with an inclusive tradition applicable and belonging to all. Arguably, by
localizing the idea of 'republic' they accelerated its internationalization
and global penetration. Central to this process was the Iranian lay religious
philosopher Abdolkarim Soroush.

Soroush: the forging of an intellectual synthesis

Soroush, like many Iranian intellectuals, had absorbed many ideas from the
Western intellectual tradition and had sought to reconcile them with those
he had inherited. A student of the philosophy of science at London University,
Soroush was influenced by the writings of such diverse thinkers as Karl
Popper and Thomas Kuhn.[15] On his return to Iran, his first important task
after the Islamic Revolution was the deconstruction and de-legitimization
of what may be termed 'vulgar' Marxist doctrine as espoused by the various
left-wing secular political groups that were then active in Iran, in particular
the Communist Tudeh Party. This intellectual encounter was to have a last-

[14] See, for example, Mehdi Karrubi's comments in *Salaam*, 24 Aban 1376/15 November 1997, pp. 1–2.
[15] For a more detailed exposition and interpretation of Soroush's ideas, see A. M. Ansari, *Iran, Islam
and Democracy: The Politics of Managing Change* (London: Royal Institute of International Affairs,
2000), pp. 71–9.

ing influence on Soroush's political views, and left him with a suspicion and dislike of what he considered 'monopolistic', insular and exclusive ideologies, which to all intents and purposes seemed to stifle the progress of knowledge. He recognized that these closed ideologies were predicated on assumptions that had achieved the status of doctrine and that such doctrine could be undermined only if one challenged and deconstructed those root beliefs.

After the successful intellectual deconstruction of the secular left in Iran, Soroush turned his sights on the increasingly authoritarian and dogmatic religious right, which in his view harboured similar monopolistic and exclusive tendencies. He was struck by the extent to which this group relied on constant antagonism with an apparently monopolistic and exclusive Western 'cultural onslaught'. The parallels between the intellectual construction of the religious right and secular left were striking. Each sought to impose a world vision on the other and each resolutely rejected, effectively in absolute terms, the admonitions of the other. This was a 'clash' in a very real sense, and even if one succeeded in imposing its will on the other, it had already forfeited its social and cultural legitimacy. The solution, according to Soroush and his supporters, was to integrate existing traditions in a new inclusive intellectual discourse that would not only facilitate the legitimate penetration of Iranian culture by Western ideas (a reality his critics were quick to point out) but also allow a degree of counter-penetration. His first task was to challenge the notion of a unified, impenetrable 'West': 'Where do you draw the boundaries of the West? Is this moral decline present where-ever there is the West, or where-ever there is the West is there moral decline? Should we know the "Western spirit" based on the West or should we distinguish the "West" from the "Western spirit"?'[16]

Developing this argument further, Soroush added that far from being positioned in contradiction to Western culture, Iranian (and Islamic) civilization had in fact contributed to it, and therefore was a legitimate heir. 'We Iranian Muslims are the inheritors and carriers of three cultures at once. As long as we ignore our links with the elements in our triple cultural heritage and our cultural geography, constructive social and cultural action will elude us ... The three cultures that form our common heritage are of national, religious, and Western origins.'[17] This view was echoed by President Khatami in his speech to the Islamic Conference Organization in December 1997 on the issue of an 'Islamic civil society':

[16] Quoted in Borujerdi, *Iranian Intellectuals and the West,* p. 161.
[17] A. Soroush, 'The Three Cultures', in A. Sadri and M. Sadri (trans and ed.), *Reason, Freedom and Democracy in Islam* (Oxford: Oxford University Press, 2000) p. 156.

The civil society which we seek to establish in our country – and would also like to recommend to other Muslim countries – is fundamentally different to the civil society born out of Greek classical philosophy and the Roman Empire's political heritage; that is to say a civil society which has passed through the Middle Ages and has now gained its special identity in the modern world. However, the two concepts of civil society should not necessarily contradict each other as far as their manifestations and outcomes are concerned. For this reason, we should never downplay the importance of learning – without imitating and copying – from the positive achievements of Western civil society.[18]

In short, the very ambiguity of cultural boundaries made globalization and its political scion democratization a legitimate process. This legitimation was enhanced by a process of deconstruction and synthesis by which Soroush also sought to challenge and undermine Western assumptions about development as generally summarized within the 'modernization thesis'.[19] This thesis argued in robust terms that development was predicated on the secularization of society and the elimination of religion as a social and political force. Soroush understood that this thesis was unlikely to endear its conception of modernity to its critics in the Muslim world in general and Iran in particular. Inclusivity could be achieved and globalization encouraged only if the relationship between East and West were redefined, and this could be achieved only if the 'West' were understood in terms familiar to the East. This process had already begun with the study of Western philosophy and a greater appreciation of those philosophers who were considered 'religious' in their orientation. In a dialectical response to globalization, Soroush, among others, sought to remind the West of its religious roots and the spiritual foundations of its social and political structures. 'Secularism' was redefined in much more ambiguous terms. For Soroush, exclusivist definitions were incorrect. He endorsed 'secularism' insofar as the rigorous scientific questioning it fostered reinvigorated religious thought. Thus:

The notion that the new world gradually rids itself of religion is only half true. It is true insofar as the modern world condemns ignorant and vulgar religiosity to extinction. However, it also shows a different kind of religiosity, a learned and examined religion, to prosper on a higher

[18] BBC Summary of World Broadcasts (SWB), ME/3099 S1/4–9, 11 December 1997 and Iranian Television, 9 December 1997.
[19] See N. Keddie, 'Secularism and the State: Towards Clarity and Global Comparison', *New Left Review*, No. 226, 1997, pp. 21–40.

level. Scientific treatment of political and economic affairs does in no sense preclude a well-defined role for God and religion in political, social and natural affairs. Determining the limits of that role and the exact form of that relationship remains to be worked out by scholars. The least we can say in this respect is that religiosity, or the lack thereof, do[es] not enter the essence of government. However, as an external reality, government is subordinate to society and constitutes one of its forms of realisation. If a society is religious, its government too will take on a religious hue.[20]

Religious democracy was therefore not absent from the West, contrary to popular assertions; its existence depended on the will of society. Echoing views held by Muslim scholars over the past two centuries, Iranian intellectuals pointed to the continuous use of religious imagery, symbolism and justifications by 'secular' Western democracies and asked why the use of Islamic justifications within political discourse should, in contrast, be interpreted as backward. Was not (in theory at least) the United Kingdom, with its established Church and its monarch as 'Defender of the Faith', a Christian democracy?

Far more telling, and with no little irony, was the model of religious democracy used by Iranian intellectuals to show how a religious society would be reflected in government – the United States. It was in the United States that Iranian intellectuals found evidence of the compatibility between religion and democracy, a point stated quite categorically by President Khatami in his interview with CNN in January 1998, when he drew attention to the writings of Alexis de Tocqueville.[21] In legitimizing the use of Western ideas in Iran, Soroush and other like-minded thinkers were of course involved in a far more reciprocal process insofar as they drew attention to the ambiguities in Western thought. While this reciprocation might have been slight, President Khatami's use of the international media to highlight his views reflected globalization in action. In its possession of a large portion of the world's means of mass communication, the West is not only the largest producer of knowledge but arguably also its greatest consumer. President Khatami, in appearing on CNN, was able to gain access to a far greater proportion of the American population than any of

[20] A. Soroush, 'The Sense and Essence of Secularism', in Sadri and Sadri (trans and ed.), *Reason, Freedom and Democracy in Islam*, p. 61.

[21] See A. Soroush, 'Tolerance and Governance', in Sadri and Sadri (trans. and ed.), *Reason, Freedom and Democracy in Islam*, p. 153; and also President Khatami's interview on CNN, 8 January 1998, BBC SWB ME/3210 MED/2, 9 January 1998. For the relevant passage in de Tocqueville, see his *Democracy in America* [first published in 1835] (London: Everyman Library, 1994), Part I, ch. 17, pp. 300–14 and Part II, ch. 5, p. 22.

his predecessors, and although it is difficult to ascertain the precise reception of his views, there were reports that sales of de Tocqueville's *Democracy in America* had indeed received a boost following his comment that he hoped all Americans had read the book.

The impact of this aspect of cultural globalization on Iranian political life has been much easier to evaluate. There is little doubt that in legitimizing the argument for greater democratization, Soroush and other thinkers have encouraged its indigenous development. As what is essentially a product of Western political thought has been localized, the pursuit of democratization becomes culturally valid, and Iranian thinkers and political activists have pursued it with some determination. Although the visual, and arguably superficial, aspects of global culture have caught the imagination of foreign observers, it is in the field of intellectual appropriation and political mobilization that the profundity of cultural globalization becomes truly apparent. A popular appreciation of 'Madonna & McDonald's' may indeed have penetrated youth culture in Iran, although significantly, for all its imitators, an 'authentic' McDonald's restaurant has yet to be granted permission to open; and 'Madonna & McDonald's' may reflect the palpable weakness of central government to contain the influx of cultural icons from abroad. But these icons are a symptom rather than a cause of the real impact of Western political philosophies and activism. The impact is, again, one of degree. It is generally recognized that student activism against the Vietnam war in the 1960s and 1970s and the student activism that galvanized France in 1968 had a profound influence on a generation of Iranian students, who later sought to emulate their predecessors by seizing the American embassy in Tehran in 1979.

The political activism which accompanied the rise of President Khatami has been similarly influential, and on a hitherto unprecedented scale.[22] Student numbers had increased dramatically, nearly tenfold, in the two decades since the Islamic revolution. And the means by which students could communicate with one another and the outside world had also improved exponentially. Besides the fax machine, students could now use both the Internet and the mobile phone, and it is significant that during the widespread student demonstrations which gripped the country in July 1999, one of the first moves of the authorities was to switch off the mobile phone network, through which student 'cells' had been communicating and coordinating. The Internet and other computing facilities such as desktop publishing allowed students to produce their own literature much more

---

[22] For the importance of the student movement in Iran, see Ansari, *Iran, Islam and Democracy*, in particular pp. 116–18.

easily and to disseminate it more widely and with much greater rapidity. Technology was facilitating the growth of civil society and undermining the pillars of the authoritarian state.

It is also increasingly clear that technology is facilitating the absorption and appropriation of ideas from abroad. Iran's resistance to intellectual property rights, a major aspect of legal globalization, has allowed the speedy reproduction of knowledge. Books and articles are read avidly, translated and reprinted in the Persian language, providing a broader reading public access to the great philosophical and political discourses of the West. It is true, of course, that the writings of Nietzsche, Marx and Weber are unlikely to have been read or indeed understood by the wider public. But it is remarkable how well-embedded the ideas of these writers (among others) have become among the literate and intellectual public and how these people in turn have sought to disseminate them in an accessible manner through the organs of the mass media.[23] That some Western commentators have criticized the interpretation of these thinkers in Iran misses the point entirely. There can be no single reading of these large and complex texts. In order to make them relevant to Iran's historical experience, they must be interpreted in the light of relevant events. In order to be truly globalized, they must first be localized and particularized; and this, as noted above, was well understood by Iranian intellectuals. Encouraged by thinkers such as Soroush, Iranian students and activists saw no contradiction in adapting the democratic theories, along with the symbolic values, of the West for their own purposes. It has become commonplace, for instance, for the authoritarian right to be described as 'fascists', a term that has no intellectual pedigree in the Iranian political tradition. More particularly, the investigative journalist Akbar Ganji has drawn from Arendt's *Banality of Evil* in order to try to explain the actions of right-wing vigilantes.[24]

On a more practical level, Iranians also avidly watched and learned from the experiences of other countries, which were relayed with relative immediacy via the new tools of media technology. Not only were vast events such as the collapse of the Soviet Union and the 'velvet revolutions' of eastern Europe digested with increasing curiosity by Iranians of all political

[23] See, for example, A. Ganji, *Tarik-khaneh-ye Ashbah* (The Cellar of Phantoms) (Tehran: Tar-e No, 1378/1999), p. 68. The book is a collection of his articles that have appeared in the mainstream press. In this particular article Ganji explicitly discusses Weber's concept of 'charisma' and its possible trajectories into 'patrimonialism' or 'rational/legal' structures.

[24] Ibid., pp. 26–8. More metaphorically, and with much more popular success, Ganji has managed to apply the phrase 'His Red Eminence' (an allusion to the 'Machiavellian' Cardinal Richelieu) to Hashemi Rafsanjani. This identification has done Rafsanjani an enormous amount of political damage.

shades, but issues of finer detail were also studied for the lessons they may yield. Students watched the unfolding of political movements in other countries with great interest. The fall of Milosovic was studied carefully, and the differences and similarities with the incumbent regime in Tehran identified, so that lessons could be learned. Both sides of the political divide in Iran drew their own lessons. The Palestinian intifada is an interesting case in point. Iranian state television relentlessly showed pictures of unarmed Palestinians in combat with the might of the Israeli Defence Force, in an effort to show 'Muslim' resistance. However, the message received by Iranians depended very much on their political position. There is little doubt that while activists drew comparisons between themselves and the hapless if heroic Palestinians, the authoritarian establishment drew succour from the apparent reality that 'might' seemed very much to equal 'right'. A similar analogy was drawn from the anti-apartheid struggle. Again the Iranian authorities sought to draw a favourable comparison between their own battle against 'global arrogance' (i.e. the United States) and the anti-apartheid movement. Of course, the manner in which the establishment sought to draw international comparisons and social interpretation often varied dramatically. For conservatives, Iran's struggle with the United States was universalized as part of a wider international contest. For reformists, on the other hand, international struggles were internalized in order to show how the domestic struggle for reform was part of the grand narrative of the unfolding of freedom and consciousness.[25] Both reflected a particular conception and perspective on the process of globalization.

The reformist interest in de Tocqueville's *Democracy in America* has already been noted, but far more specific interest is shown in developments in the United Kingdom, which is regularly held up as a model of political stability. Iranians of all political hues have long enjoyed an essentially schizophrenic relationship with Britain, at once fearful of political manipulation while unashamedly admiring what they perceive to be the astute management of the state by its political establishment. For reformists Britain represents a successful example of a state that has managed a peaceful transition from an authoritarian monarchy to a democracy. For the authoritarians, much more emphasis is placed upon the establishment's ability to maintain its power and traditions, reflected in both the monarchy and the distribution of wealth and, by extension, power. The former concentrate on Britain's ability to manage change while the latter emphasize the continuity. The election victory of New Labour in 1997 and the apparent

---

[25] See, for example, ibid., pp. 291–301, in which parallels with transitions in apartheid South Africa, eastern Europe and Chile were increasingly drawn.

attack on tradition, symbolized by the reform of the House of Lords, that ensued were therefore viewed with great interest by the reformists and with some dismay by the authoritarian right, which discovered that its source of political reference had begun to shift. These are of course idealized impressions mediated through time and space, and there is clearly an argument for New Labour's avowed support of tradition from which the right in Iran can draw some reassurance. Yet the palpable changes are having an impact. People viewed with great interest the developments in both the David Shayler case and the extradition proceedings against former Chilean president Pinochet. In the former, analogies were drawn with Iran's own intelligence ministry. In the latter, there is little doubt that the Iranian leadership viewed Pinochet's predicament with some consternation. Rafsanjani ceased to be a modern Cardinal Richelieu (see footnote 24) and now became Iran's Pinochet.

Conclusions

The fact that there is a debate on the nature and limits of globalization in contemporary Iran is itself an indication of the reality of the process at work. In intellectual terms at least, it is a development whose recognition and comprehension are central to the Islamic Republic's identification of itself within the global order. Indeed, the political debates that have galvanized Iran over the past two decades can be defined, and understood, from the perspective of the wider emerging debate on the nature of globalization. Thus the Islamic revolution can be understood as a rejection of the 'hyper-globalists', those who believe in a global culture, largely defined by the Western experience, which had to be imitated and adopted wholesale. The subsequent debate between reformists and conservatives similarly can be defined as a struggle between 'transformationalists' and 'sceptics', those who see the development of cultural interaction between Iran and the West and those who reject this process as simply an extension of imperialist subjugation that must be resisted at all costs.[26] While one side seeks to engage and the other to disengage, both want to be active in shaping the future direction of globalization.

Their key battleground is over culture, for in economic and migratory terms the contest would appear to be singularly unequal. Even the 'sceptics' are anxious to utilize fully the growing facility to travel, relocate and, crucially, export capital. (The ease with which money flows out of the

[26] See Held, McGrew, Goldblatt and Perraton, *Global Transformations,* p. 7.

Islamic Republic is one of the most significant and most serious problems facing any Iranian government determined to retain as much of the national wealth as possible within its borders and to encourage investment.) In cultural terms the relationship is more nuanced and subtle. Among many in Iran, there is a growing realization that the best way to deal with the process of cultural globalization is to engage with it and seek to reshape it in a manner that is acceptable to the local environment and to some extent beyond. Thus Iranian intellectuals have sought to deconstruct the cultural icons and myths of global culture through a process of absorption, appropriation and synthesis, which arguably facilitates the internalization of global culture while changing it. In this sense, Iran seeks to reiterate its historical role not only as a consumer but also as a producer of cultural norms, and it is this conviction that underpins the development of the concept of the 'dialogue of civilizations'. This reciprocation is in its infancy, but as we move increasingly towards the 'mediasation of modern culture',[27] its potential may yet be realized.

---

[27] Thompson, *Ideology and Modern Culture,* pp. 12–20.

PART III
Globalization and the wider Arab Middle East

7 Between the market and God: Islam, globalization and culture in the Middle East

Maha Azzam

Introduction

There are inherent difficulties in defining the position of a universal religion in relation to a particular economic or ideological trend or movement. This is especially true of Islam and globalization. It has become commonplace to discuss Islam in connection with a wide range of subjects without clearly defining the context and specifying which aspect or interpretation of the religion is being addressed. This chapter intends to map out a framework for further research. It focuses on how globalization is perceived to impinge on Islamic religious and cultural identity. It then looks at the Islamist responses to globalization in the context of Islam's historical legacy and of current political and economic dynamics.

Globalization is considered here primarily as an economic challenge that has particular political and cultural significance in the Middle East because of the nature of state power and the region's history of religious and cultural resistance to Westernization and secularization. The history of Islam is replete with examples of how Muslim society absorbed various influences, such as that of the Byzantine bureaucracy, and synthesized Greek philosophy and arithmetic from India. Trans-border trade and commerce have also been an essential part of the Muslim world's power and influence. Throughout the nineteenth century the Ottoman Empire made various attempts to modernize the military and the education system. These attempts reflected its struggle to reform and stem decline. The nationalism and socialism of the twentieth century in the Middle East were in themselves attempts at resistance, independence and reform that have resulted mainly in weak and poor states in relation to the present international order.

The contemporary assertion of political Islam is in itself part of the struggle with modernity, and both an outcome of it and a response to it. Muslim societies, while maintaining traditional features, have struggled to adapt to the world around them in order to integrate Islam in their daily lives but also to benefit from modernity. They cannot avoid being affected by and connected to the processes of globalization. However, Muslims are not the authors of today's globalization. They are unsure that they can gain sufficient control over it to benefit economically and technologically while suppressing any threat to the religious and cultural make-up of their societies. Islam as faith, *daw'a* (call, invocation to Islam) and law is, as its followers proclaim, universal; the message transmitted in the Arabic language is in itself transnational. The Muslim community (*umma*), the spread of Islam and the various channels it uses are therefore essentially global. Islam's appeal as a dynamic religion, and not merely as a culture, has continued in the midst of increasing secularization in the twentieth century and into the twenty-first. The fact that it places politics at the centre of its philosophy and that it is concerned with power as a means of asserting the faith fully through the establishment of a divinely inspired law means that it offers its followers an alternative in the face of contemporary challenges.

Islam historically was the main ideology and basis of law in advanced Middle Eastern empires and societies. 'Muslims and the West have been interconnected through international trade and economic exchange (or exploitation), together in what has been referred to as the "economic world-system".'[1] Muslims' belief in a golden past, combined with their present political and economic weakness, means that many of them do not want to fall further behind by opting out of that system. However, attitudes towards globalization are influenced by the experience of colonialism and by the widespread belief that Western hegemony and interference, particularly on the part of the United States, continues to plague the Muslim world, as clearly represented by support for Israel and the US presence in the Gulf.[2]

Doctrinally Islam is neither for nor against globalization. Islam's emphasis on universalism and unity opens the way for a dissolution of barriers. Free markets and free trade arguably coexist well with a strong Muslim mercantile tradition. The creation of wealth is not shunned as long as it falls within the laws and regulations of responsibility regarding the wider community and social justice. However, it is this stress on social justice that provides ammunition for Muslim critics of globalization.

Opposition to and fear of globalization derive largely from the fact that the majority of Muslim populations have not seen an improvement in their economic status and may feel even less secure than a generation ago. The

---

[1] See I. Wallerstein, *The Modern World System* (New York: Academic Press, 1974) and I. Wallerstein, *The Politics of the World–Economy* (Cambridge: Cambridge University Press, 1984).
[2] M. Azzam, 'The Gulf Crisis: Perceptions in the Muslim World', *International Affairs*, Vol. 67, No. 3, July 1991, pp. 473–87.

problem remains that Muslim societies are continuing to lose out in terms of growth and development in the twenty-first century, rather than catching up.[3] This has little to do with Islam and more to do with political and economic factors, given that Muslim governments that have failed to deliver have not necessarily carried out an 'Islamic' agenda and share some of the political and economic problems of non-Muslim states in Africa and Latin America.

The complex and rapid transmission of ideas, influenced in varying degrees by the new technologies, has contributed to a potent mixture of secular political notions and cultural influences. The individuals and groups espousing Islam today have crossed geographical boundaries, and although they carry a rich historical legacy they also possess new ideological leanings. The result is a mixture of modern-day travellers and messengers who are rooted in the Islamic tradition of the search for knowledge and the spreading of the faith. *Du'a* (those who invite others to Islam and spread its teachings) and Muslim travellers have historically been important features of the Muslim world's religious and cultural legacy.[4] Against this background, Muslim society's view of itself and the world around it is, on one level, influenced by its search for recognition, independence and lost power and, on another level, permeated by political lethargy, economic despair and cultural dislocation. At both these levels globalization adds to the challenges and frustration.

Identity and social change

At the very heart of the debate about globalization for Muslims is how it impinges on their ability to remain pious and practising believers. Therefore the challenge is perceived primarily as religious and secondarily as cultural. Globalization is perceived to be contrary to certain Islamic principles and norms of behaviour. Equally, for many secularists globalization is considered to be an encroachment on indigenous culture, although by their very secularism they have adopted one of the main cornerstones of Western values. The forms of resistance to globalization involve a return to strict religious practice, expressed through, for example, the segregation of the sexes and an 'Islamic' mode of dress. Critiques tend to be rhetorical, and are generally in the form of writings and publications by intellectuals

---

[3] See H. Hakimian and Z. Moshaver (eds), *The State and Global Change* (London: Curzon Press, 2001).
[4] See D.F. Eickelman and J. Piscatori (eds), *Muslim Travellers: Pilgrimage, Migration and Religious Imagination* (London: Routledge, 1990).

as well as by religious and political leaders. There are a number of central questions. What exactly is the cultural or religious threat? What channels does it use and what form does it take? Do Muslims really have a problem with embracing new technology, or is their fear related mainly to how the ever-increasing penetration and diffusion of Western knowledge and laws (set in motion in the nineteenth century) will affect religious and moral precepts that are fundamental to the very fabric of society and family?

Of course it is how culture (whether in the form of laws, rules and regulations, education, the media or literature and music) is translated, used and made indigenous that gives it different meanings among various groups and classes which allow or reject its influence. As Westernization has been making inroads into Muslim societies for over a century, there is nothing inherently new about the latest 'innovation' or 'assault' except for its speed of transmission and its ability to reach far larger numbers of people. Generally, 'new' or 'foreign' imports tend to be viewed as suspect in most social contexts, not only Islamic ones. Within a single group, globalization can result in confusion and rejection or acceptance and assimilation. Although Islamic law has specific injunctions in the social realm that continue to permeate the social fabric and behaviour patterns of many Muslims, the boundaries of social conduct and jurisdiction have nevertheless become increasingly unclear.

Many broad areas are affected, including the position of women in relation to education and employment. The images of women in the public sphere and in the media have of course had an impact on women's self-perception and expectations, both social and economic. However, increasing levels of education and governments' encouragement or discouragement have had the most immediate impact on the debate over women's rights and their public role. This is evident in the different way that, for example, Iran, in contrast to Saudi Arabia, has actively integrated women in the public and political sphere as part of its political agenda while maintaining its emphasis on Islamic values and the importance of the mother's role. Globalization too has had an impact, by helping to create both greater transparency about the role of women and policies towards them worldwide through, for example, NGOs and international conferences. Nevertheless the principal factors for change or lack of it appear to lie on the domestic front, and are political decision-making, ideological orientation and economic pressures.

In the context of the Muslim societies of the Middle East, the impact of change on the role of women (and this tends to apply to non-Muslim women who share common societal constraints of what is considered right and wrong) seems more apparent, and takes on a moral significance, because of the nature of their central position in the social and family structure and within the honour code. Women, like men, are believers in Islamic law and uphold their position primarily as mothers and wives in the face of perceived challenges to this role. In the majority of cases there is little outward rejection of this role, but there is a search for a comfortable duality. In this process Westernization and globalization have had an influence. Women seek to improve their and their families' material well-being and to extend their education and possibly their public role while also maintaining their traditional role. This duality is of course present in most societies. What differentiates Muslim societies from Western ones is that whatever the changes, welcome or unwelcome, there continues to be a widespread defence of religious principles and a public denial of Western values, which are seen as leading to promiscuity and a breakdown of family values.

The impact of globalization on young people is another important area to consider. In the Middle East, where illiteracy levels remain high, its influence on the lives of the majority of youth has remained detrimental. Young people have heightened expectations encouraged by advertising, the media and their own governments' promises, but they lack the ability to work towards achieving a better living standard. The result is unrealized ambition for material goods. Naturally, this has frustrated many. While there is a sense of deprivation among the very poor, there is anger and an inability to make ends meet among the lower middle classes and even the middle classes, which see the gap between themselves and the 'mega-rich' increasing. In addition, moral and social pressures exist across classes, with some people rebelling against the traditional limits of what is permitted (*halal*) and what is prohibited (*haram*). The traditional strictures being challenged involve, for example, the rights and wrongs of mingling with the opposite sex or of drug use, especially among the wealthy. The increasing use of drugs is seen as a direct result of globalization, which has resulted in the accumulation of large financial resources by some but also in a breakdown of values.

The Islamist path provides an alternative route. It supplies a rigid and morally strict code of practice for many throughout the Middle East and beyond, even though it may also have helped to turn them towards radical politics. Islam offers a framework of behaviour that is all the more relevant in times of uncertainty and when the available alternative is far from clear. In addition, its message appeals to all social strata and to those who have benefited as well as those who have suffered from globalization. Over the past three decades the social and cultural climate in much of the Middle East has become increasingly one in which the race for wealth has become the norm, despite this being resented by many, particularly by those who are part of a generation that once espoused socialist values.

The indigenous critique

A great deal of this resentment and anger is expressed by writers and intellectuals and is directed at globalization. (This criticism was levelled in similar, if not identical form, against the West before the current debate.) The combination of political and cultural encroachment and economic exploitation are attacked through the use of rhetorical language. Globalization is presented as limiting the freedom of countries and societies and ultimately as colonialism in a new guise.

One well-known writer and intellectual is Hassan Hanafi. He is a one-time socialist who turned to Islam in the 1970s and represents a strand of intellectuals who have attempted to fuse Islam and socialism. He describes the divide within the Arab world as between two groups:

> [those who] surrender to the existing order and see the world as a single order and [accept] the end of history and who see that globalization is a pre-determined and a historical law. This applies to all – whether Islamists who wish to trade with the West, with oil money and enjoy its consumer values, or a secularist who places himself on a path to which he does not belong and a civilisation that does not represent him out of a feeling of inferiority. And ... those who resist surrender and who see that globalization is a new ideology, a new wrapping to an old form of dominance and that it is only a stage, whether short or long until an alternative develops out of Asia, Africa and Latin America at the heart of which is the Arab-Islamic world which straddles Asia and Africa. That is why it is being concentrated on through sanctions on Iraq and Libya, threats against Iran and Sudan and a stab in the heart of Palestine and the marginalisation of Egypt. Both these views include Islamists and secularists and the difference between independence and dependence.[5]

According to Hanafi the battle with the West is not new, despite its present political and economic features. Globalization is 'not only a political, economic, technological or IT phenomenon but ... essentially a continuous historic manifestation of the North's wish to control the South, since the war between Rome and Carthage and the West's wish to control the East, since the war between Greece and Persia'.[6] It 'manifests itself mainly as an economic bloc for the main powers to invest global wealth,

---

[5] H. Hanafi and S.D. Al-'Athm, *Ma'l 'Awlama* (What is Globalization?) (Beirut: Dar al-Fikr al-Muassir, 1999), pp. 12–16.
[6] Ibid., p. 18.

their commodities and their markets to the detriment of the poor nations. And to contain the elements which try to escape from it through the liberation movements of the 1950s and 1960s and which were not successful in building the nation-state ... And in its political dimension globalization is a form of political domination following the collapse of one of the two camps. So that in the name of globalization, independent nationalism can be eradicated.'[7] Hanafi's point of view reflects the ideological legacy of 1950s and 1960s nationalism and socialism in the Middle East. Despite his sympathy for the Islamist trend he remains rooted in a primarily nationalist and anti-Western tradition that was part of the non-aligned movement and that survives in some quarters of the Middle East, particularly Algeria, Egypt and Syria.

The following expression of anti-globalization (made in an article in the widely circulated *al-Quds* newspaper, published in London) conveys economic, political and moral strands that are all anti-Western. The author expresses similar concerns to those of the Islamists and shares a common attitude towards social and moral issues. However, he is at odds with the Islamist position over the bombing of Yugoslavia insofar as the article reflects little sympathy for the plight of the Bosnian Muslims. In criticizing American and European economic dominance the writer ignores the fact that Sony, Toyota and Hitachi are world-dominating Japanese companies, and therefore he finds in the West's political and cultural encroachment the fuel for his antagonism to globalization.

The largest and most important twenty companies in the world belong to the countries of NATO, eighteen American and two European. And since the start of capitalist activity at the end of the eighteenth century to the present, not once has there been a company that came to prominence in the world markets from outside the American European circle. What this means specifically is that the flow of commerce and capital in today's world which is the most important aspect of globalization, remains as it was in the past, a reflection of the balance of world powers.

While the other and more important dimension of the balance of world powers is the struggle over values, which gives things and concepts their meaning. For example, is it the whole of human society with the totality of human inheritance that defines terrorism, or a small group of people? Who categorises state leaders or defines which states as being outside international law? How can Milosevic alone be a criminal against humanity while they bombed Yugoslavia ninety consecutive days without

---

[7] Ibid., pp. 22–3.

giving the Yugoslavs the right of reply? And this without going into the issue of Iraq and the sensitivities that engenders. Most of all there is the question of virtue and how to define it.

In today's world nations are being asked to abandon their historical and religious values, states are being asked to abandon sovereignty, while one state alone has been responsible for hindering fourteen international projects to protect humanity from itself in the past year alone. It is this same state that leads the train of globalization, that is to say the United States. From the project of the International criminal court to the world conference on biological weapons, from the Kyoto project to the initiative to limit small arm[s] sales which results in the death of millions of Africans, the Americans have hindered global consensus, including that of their friends the Europeans, without batting an eyelid. And a few days ago, the USA withdrew from the world congress against racism which was scheduled to be held in South Africa after the Arabic-Islamic bloc insisted on a couple of clauses connected to the racist nature of Zionism and compensation for slavery. Under such an imperialist regime, how can Egypt or any Arab or Islamic country abandon laws that reflect its religious and social values? This is not only related to homosexuality, but to the fundamental right of nations to pass laws that respond to its beliefs and values. The penetration of the internet or mobile telephones should not mean that homosexuality (lit. sexual deviance) develops by necessity from a crime to a virtue, in the same way that the invention of electricity and telegraph did not make theft or rape acceptable.[8]

A significant reading of the Islamist response to globalization is that of Burhan Ghalyun, for whom the option of isolation and a retreat to early Islam has not, in reality, been espoused by the majority of Islamists. 'Even Khomeini who extolled the nation for the creation of an Islamic Republic relied on the creative use of cassettes.'[9]

I do not believe there is a single Islamist in Palestine, in Iran or any other place who believes opposing American domination can only come through a rejection of modern technology, be it military, economic, the media or ideological. It is true that Islamic discourse (moderate or extremist) concentrates on the shortcomings of modernity and exaggerates what they believe to be the despair, lack of logic, crime, corruption and decadence

[8] B.M. Naf 'a, 'Al-sira' hawl al-kiyam wa'l mafahim tatruk al-abwab al-'Arabiyya wa'l-Islamiyya' (The struggle over principles and meanings), *al-Quds*, London, 2 August 2001, p. 19.
[9] B. Ghalyun and S. Amin, *Thaqafit al-'Awlama wa 'Awlamit al-Thaqafa* (The Culture of Globalization and the Globalization of Culture) (Beirut: Dar al-Fikr al-Muassir, 1999), p. 115.

in Western civilisation but the core of their thinking is not about the comparison between modernity and tradition as with their predecessors, but rather a comparison between socio-political systems (and in this they are closer to the communists). So they believe that regimes that derive their principles from a secular culture are open to corruption and injustice. While Islam represents the highest morals for a socio-economic system based on liberty, equality and justice. It is as if they believe that true modernity can only be achieved through Islamic laws. ... It might be said Islamists although affected by modernity only accept its technical side and refuse to accept the human and political values within it. But in reality Islamists dream of the main values of this movement, at the forefront of which is consumerism and in a more fundamental way self-determination.[10]

This is a valid argument, but it is through the new technology of satellite television that images and messages, which may be contrary to Islam, are transmitted. Therefore the questioning or fear of globalization and its cultural and ideological message are not unfounded.

One of the most important perspectives is that of mainstream Islamic scholars represented by *Azhari* opinion (those who are based or who studied at Al Azhar University in Cairo). Sheikh Yusuf al-Qaradawi is a respected *Azhari* who is well known throughout the Muslim world and whose opinions tend to bridge the moderate and extremist trends. His starting point, like that of many Muslims, is that Islam, as a universal religion, has little problem with looking to and connecting with the outside world and those beyond its boundaries.

It is the nature of Islam that it is an open faith [which does not favour] East or West. It is also part of its nature that it is a proselytising faith that addresses all peoples and the whole world. It does not differentiate between peoples because of their countries, their regions nor because of ethnicity, colour, language or class. All that exists is that Muslims are cautious in their dealings with the West because of the many wrongs the West has done to Islam in the past and during the modern colonial era.[11]
... Another issue which makes our opening up to the West an inevitable one is that we live in an age of greater contact (*takarub*) especially post the communications revolution.[12]

[10] Ibid., p. 123.
[11] Y. al-Qaradawi, 'Al-infitah 'ala al-Gharb: Muktadyahu wa Shrutuhu' (The Opening up to the West: what it involves and its limits), in M.A. Abu Shamal (ed.), *Risalet al-Muslimin fi bilad al-Gharb* (The Message of Muslims in the West) (Dar al-Amal, n.p., 2000), p. 8.
[12] Ibid., p. 19.

Al-Qaradawi puts forward conditions for opening up, which include the need for the West to abandon its enmity towards the Muslims and to do away with the legacy of the crusades that continues to permeate Western views of Islam. He asks,

> Are we talking of an intellectual and cultural clash or a political and military clash? If we are talking of an intellectual clash we welcome this – each one can put forward what he believes in and set out his argument and what will survive in the end is the better one. But we prefer to call this a dialogue or interaction between civilisations rather than a clash. Not forcing their culture on us. We do not wish the West to use material force for we are not slaves to be driven with a lash. We wish that force and the arrogance of might are abandoned and the attempt of imposing one culture upon another through the use of material and military power. What we wish for is that we are treated as free men and equally.
>
> ... Islam is a threat to materialism and atheism, it is a threat to tyranny, it is a threat to corruption but it is not a threat to humanity and it is not a threat to morality and it is not a threat to justice, liberty and the rights of man.[13]

Here al-Qaradawi deploys the very labels 'materialism and atheism' attached to capitalism by Islamists and most notably by the late Sayyid Qutb, the intellectual guide and mentor to much of the modern Islamist movement.[14] Al-Qaradawi argues:

> ...what we want from the West if it wants to open up, is that we do so as equals, that we co-operate to build a new future for humanity. And so our first condition remains that the West gives up its enmity toward us which is nourished by ancient hatred and modern fears. That the West abandons its greed for our wealth ... for the age of colonialism is over and the West should be satisfied by what it has already pillaged from our resources and what it has taken from our countries. As regard[s] Western civilisation and progress the West benefited from the East ... let us start a new chapter. The West should abandon its arrogance which is an outcome of its view of itself as the master of the world.[15]

[13] Ibid., pp. 23, 24.
[14] S. Qutb, *Sayyid Qutb and Islamic Activism: A Translation and Critical Analysis of Social Justice in Islam* (Brill, 1996).
[15] Al-Qaradawi, 'Al-infitah 'ala al-Gharb', p. 26.

In the following commentary al-Qaradawi calls for the West to accept the Muslims' desire for an Islamic system of law in Muslim countries, which Muslims identify as an essential criterion of their identity and independence.

That the West accepts our message. We wish the West as well to acknowledge that we are a people with a message and a history and that this message is global – from the Lord to all humanity. And that we have the right to achieve our destiny in our own land. The problem is that the West does not wish us to establish Islam or spread our message even on Muslim soil. ... So what is it that disturbs you Westerners? That the Muslims wish to apply Islam on themselves on their own soil. We say that it is neither just nor good that the irreligious, the atheists, the corrupt should rule Muslim countries. On the contrary it is in everyone's interests that Muslim countries are ruled by people who keep their word and their treaties ... We wish the West to acknowledge our message, our essence and our identity. [For the West to acknowledge] that we have an individual identity and that it is our right to live within it and to live for it and die believing in it ...[16]

Finally al-Qaradawi turns to the West's support for Israel, a recurring point of contention between Muslims and the West which, whether under the umbrella of international relations or human rights, remains a point of friction in the debate over Muslim rights and the West's 'double standards'.

We wish the West to recognise our rights and not to stand with our enemies as it has with the Zionists and as it does even today ... [W]e are advocates of tolerance ... [I]t is true that there are some Muslim[s] who are extremists but this extremism is born out of Western aggression and Western tyranny. If the West had been fair in their dealings they would not have found this extremism because tolerance is an essential issue for us because it is based on God's will.[17]

Unlike many of Islam's followers and apologists, al-Qaradawi reflects a more confident and more traditional interpretation of Islam, coupled with the familiar concerns over Western encroachment and exploitation. He believes Islam's message can and should be relayed to the outside world, and essentially places Islam on an equal (or even superior) standing to the dominant 'Western world-view'. There appears to be little contention with the West over the question of progress, but there is a strong sense of having

[16] Al-Qaradawi, 'Al-infitah 'ala al-Gharb', p. 26.
[17] Idem.

been dominated and that this domination continues. However, globalization is not a one-way process, and therefore it has not only resulted in antagonism and enmity towards Islam but also in a greater curiosity about, familiarity with and even conversion to Islam by growing numbers in the West.

The political dimension: control versus liberalization

A recurring question since the 1970s, which has remained unanswered, is whether there can be economic liberalization without political liberalization. The sovereignty of the state (despite ambiguities regarding the idea of the nation-state) is paramount both for leaders, desperate to protect their power and the continuity of their regimes, and for societies, which often perceive any encroachment on the state's independence or legitimacy to be a return to interference and domination. This strength of nationalist fervour exists equally among governments and their opponents. Attempts at reform and structural adjustment, although slow and limited in the states of the Middle East, have nevertheless raised questions about the role of the state itself. The state, although not a monolithic structure and possessing different characteristics from one part of the Middle East to the other, has succeeded in establishing political control and political containment and in restricting political freedoms, despite the success of democracy in other parts of the world.

One of the main promises and supposed by-products of globalization, as represented by the dominant influence of the US as a world power, is democracy. Why, then, has democratization eluded societies in the Middle East? It is true that structural adjustment has been limited, but is there also an inherent incompatibility between Islam and democracy that will continue to affect Muslim societies despite strides that might be made by modernization and globalization?

There are two principal sides in the debate within Muslim opinion about Islam's compatibility with democracy. On one side there are those who believe that Islam is in essence democratic and that principles such as *shura* (consultation), *baya* (granting allegiance) and *ijma* (consensus) lend themselves to a democratic system. This position argues that there is nothing in the Quran and the *hadith* (sayings of the Prophet) that is opposed to democracy. The alternative position reflects the uniqueness of Islam and dislikes the assimilation of other ideologies, whether democracy or socialism. This view stresses the centrality of the *shari'a*, arguing that sovereignty lies with God and not with the people, who cannot change the divinely inspired law. This is the particular point that divides a religious system and a secular one.

Despite the influence of Westernization, the *shari'a* continues to have an impact on the daily lives of Muslims, be they in Saudi Arabia, Morocco or Egypt. This means that democratic values, particularly those impinging on social liberties, cannot coexist easily with Islam's own social rules. However, there is more room to manoeuvre in the political, as opposed to the social, sphere. Here greater accountability on the part of rulers, political participation and respect for the rule of law would find popular resonance and appeal. Therefore, democratic practice in a Muslim context can be only partial in comparison with Western-style democracy unless globalization brings with it greater secularization of society itself. Since the demise of the Ottoman Empire and the end of the Caliphate in 1924, very different groups and individuals have called for a return to the implementation of the *shari'a*. The contemporary resurgence of Islam, particularly among the young (despite the persecution of those calling for an Islamic system of government), reflects this continuous search for an identity based on an 'authentic' set of laws, values and rituals.

The argument for the universality of human rights is challenged and unpopular at the state level in most Muslim countries because of the authoritarian nature of regimes. This argument is challenged also on the basis of arguments for cultural exceptionalism.[18] The promotion of respect for human rights has influenced a variety of Islamic thinkers and activists; but as is the case with views of democracy, the basis of all rights is perceived as God-given. However, superimposed on a body of dogma is a host of rights and references that are in keeping with contemporary notions of human rights and social justice.[19]

On the whole, there has not been sufficient external or internal pressure to bring about political reform. Calls for the respect of human rights by international organizations and by NGOs such as Amnesty International and some pressure for political liberalization from the World Bank and the IMF have gone largely unheeded in the Middle East. Only when domestic pressure has been intense and regimes have feared losing power or authority have there been moves towards political liberalization. These moves have frequently been reversed (as in the case of Algeria, Egypt and Jordan) when regimes have felt strong enough to clamp down or to hinder the process. Political liberalization has to recognize and accommodate the Islamist trend, a process that most governments are reluctant to implement. Under political systems as different as those of Algeria and Turkey, the participation of Islamists, whether in extremist or moderate guise, in the

---

[18] See, for example, T.M. Franck, 'Are Human Rights Universal?', *Foreign Affairs*, January–February 2001, Vol. 80, No. 1, pp. 191–205.
[19] Islamic Council, *Universal Islamic Declaration of Human Rights* (London: Islamic Council, 1981).

democratic process has ultimately been rejected, and without any real pressure on governments by the West to alter this situation.

The contemporary Islamist movements are essentially a modern phenomenon. They have been involved in different degrees in a power struggle with Middle Eastern regimes and have been an integral part of the politics of the region. The history of the Muslim Brotherhood, for example, is one of a political movement that emerged in 1928 in the full throes of nationalist politics and interacted with the main political parties of the day. The Muslim Brotherhood has many of the features of a modern political movement. It engages in opposition politics while its ideological basis and message remain religious. The smaller extremist Islamist groups are also a product of modern political dynamics, and have resorted to violent political protest as a means of weakening particular regimes. It is in their interpretation of Islam that the various Islamist groups are at odds with the premises that capitalism brings prosperity and that competition is to be encouraged. This is partly a result of Islam's own emphasis on social justice and of the necessity for strict adherence to a curb on interest and usury, which in principle is thus at odds with the Western financial system. In addition, a legacy of socialist values and principles continues to permeate the outlook of many in the region, including the Islamists.

In practice it is not Islam *per se* but the practice of state control that creates resistance to capitalism. It is the legacy of the socialist experiment in Egypt under Nasser and in Algeria under Boummedienne that, combined with fear of political and social unrest, constrains action by governments, even if they are eager to implement economic reform. Where the state has been reluctant to relinquish authority and control, as in the case of Saudi Arabia, and resists aspects of globalization on religious and ideological grounds, structural adjustment has been limited. Where there is political will for change, as in the case of some of the Gulf states, the prospects for economic and political liberalization are greater.

Global power and the international order

Different political movements in the Middle East view international relations and international economics as beyond the influence and control of Muslim states, and their responses to international pressures vary from accommodation to opposition. Opposition to the United States permeates much of the political climate across the region. In these circumstances the national interest is seen as being served best by opposing US influence. Muslims and the radical Islamist trend believe power and salvation do not reside in globalization or any other Western import but in the establishment of the *shari'a*, in Muslim unity and in a rejection of the West. There is a belief that despite the assertion that globalization marks the 'end of the age of ideologies', its economic and social ramifications cannot but take into account its ideological content.[20] The 'new world order' is viewed as relying on three pillars: first, American military might; second, *al-shar 'iyya al-dawliyya*, the legitimacy of international law, which is connected to an alliance of the capitalist states; and third, the utilization of capital for the objectives of the 'new world order'.[21]

In seeking to oppose the United States and its allies, some Islamist groups have resorted to the use of globalized networks for terrorist activity. Some of the fighters who went to Afghanistan or Chechnya from different parts of the Muslim world have established links or contacts with Osama bin Laden. They have developed a commitment to an Islamic system that knows no national boundaries.[22]

The perception of a threat exists in both the Islamic and the non-Islamic world and is seen as global. For those in the Middle East it is rooted primarily in domestic and regional politics; while for the United States and Europe it has both a domestic dimension, because of the fear of terrorism on home territory, and an international dimension, because of their influence and interests beyond their borders. It is not only perceptions but also actual policies and strategies that have aggravated the situation on both sides, whether these are the West's policies regarding the Palestine question or Iraq or Muslim responses which have involved terrorism, despite the fact that acts of violence have been carried out largely by a minority.

The perception of a material and economic threat posed by globalization raises many familiar concerns. The debates in the Muslim world over modernization, from the late nineteenth century and throughout the twentieth century, are strikingly similar to those today about globalization. Islam is viewed as promoting progress and welcoming modernization as long as Westernization and secularization are kept at bay. Although it is generally acknowledged that attempts at socialism in the 1950s and 1960s in the Middle East failed to deliver, they still left the legacy of an ideological rejection of capitalism among many non-Islamists and Islamists alike. This is coupled with a prevalent anti-Americanism at the popular level and contributes to a distrust of globalization.

---

[20] G. Kanan, 'Al-'Arab wa Tahdidat al-Nizam al-'Alami', *Al-Mustakbal al-_Arabi*, 16 (Beirut: Markaz Dirasat al-Wahda al-'Arabiyya, October 1999), p. 138.
[21] Ibid., p. 140.
[22] S. Reeve, *The New Jackals: Ramzi Yousef, Osama bin Laden and the Future* (London: André Deutsch, 1999).

The disparity between the haves and the have-nots in societies ridden with corruption creates an ambiguous conception of globalization. There is, on the one hand, a desire to partake in and perhaps reap the rewards of capitalism but, on the other hand, a rejection of the emphasis on materialism. This tension exists in Muslim societies as in non-Muslim ones, as does distrust of the IMF and the World Bank, institutions that many believe should be made more accountable.[23] Of course there are positive responses to globalization in Muslim states and among committed Muslims. There is a strong belief that they must not be left behind, that there is no real alternative and that there will be many benefits. Essentially it is the changes brought by globalization, whether through its rewards or losses, that engender anxiety. Many Muslim from the Middle East and Asia share a desire to partake in the rewards of globalization but they are resentful and angry at the imbalance between the North and the South.

A reflection of the tenor of critical scholarly debate about globalization among those more familiar with economic issues is summed up by M. Atrash in the following argument:

From 1840-1914 Britain forced free trade and free capital movements on areas it colonised which was disadvantageous to the Third World, such as China, India and the Ottoman Empire. After the Second World War they did the same, but since the 1980s direct investment by Western governments increased and that is how they control other countries. But has national sovereignty been eradicated? 1) States still have a major economic role. 2) What is called financial globalization is exaggerated because most multinationals achieve much of their value added in their home base. 3) There is no true globalization in the labour movement. 4) The globalization of capital represented in direct investment is very limited. And in any case much of this direct investment is not economic investment but financial investment and secondly the value added is primarily in the investing company. Finally what is called financial globalization does not include the majority of the world and is concentrated on the advanced [states] since most countries in the world do not allow floating exchange rate[s] and free movement of capital.[24]

Atrash's economic analysis typifies the position of those who think there is still room to manoeuvre in furthering national interests. They argue

---

[23] J.S. Nye Jr., 'Globalization's Democratic Deficit', *Foreign Affairs*, Vol. 80, No. 4, July–August 2001, p. 3.

[24] M. Atrash, 'Al-'Arab wal-'Awlama: Mal 'Amal' (Arabs and Globalization: What is to be done), *al-Mustaqbal al-'Arabi*, Vol. 3, March 1998 (Beirut: Centre for Arab Unity Studies), p. 103.

that the current stage of economic development does not limit the economic choices of the Arab states with which they are concerned. Direct and indirect inward (stock) investment is minimal, as the Arab states are net exporters of investment. American political dominance can be resisted by Arab unity, as was shown in 1973.[25] Atrash goes on to call for the creation of an Arab common market relying on Arab identity and nationalist assertion and to emphasize the importance of supporting national Arab security and the common economic good.[26]

This argument takes little account of the political predicament faced by Middle Eastern countries, in which there is limited or virtually no access to political decision-making, which then limits the economic choices presented to the majority of the population. The stress placed on Arab nationalism assumes the continuous ideological appeal of pan-Arabism. Despite the previous failings of Arab nationalism, there remains a strong economic and political imperative for cooperation and integration across the region.[27] For societies in which poverty affects the majority and in which deprivation in terms of adequate housing, health and education is the norm, the promise of improved economic conditions remains elusive. However, the problem with any system of a Western provenance is that it is frequently viewed with mistrust. There are those in the Middle East who acknowledge the benefits of globalization and see it as a means of personal prosperity and wealth, but the wider society remains to be convinced that globalization will do more than widen the gap between the rich and the poor.

Conclusions

Globalization offers economic opportunities for Muslim states. The real issues, however, are how governments and societies respond to and participate in globalization, and how they can overcome a history of political and economic mismanagement and an absence of the rule of law, all of which have impeded development. Criticism of globalization on the basis of economic exploitation and cultural domination goes beyond the boundaries of the Middle East and is also voiced in various forms in the West through debate and violent protest. Worldwide protest against globalization encompasses the poor and disenfranchised as well as the rebellious young people and the educated who are concerned about poverty and the 'world'.

[25] Idem.
[26] Ibid., p. 111.
[27] G. Nonneman, *The Middle East and Europe: An Integrated Communities Approach* (London: The Federal Trust For Education and Research, 1992).

The gap between the North and the South has increased and with it a resentment of anything offered or emanating from the already rich and powerful. Although many in the non-Western world seek to join in and benefit from globalization, the process seems too full of obstacles, some new and some inherited. These include foreign interference but also political mismanagement and corruption.

'Empowerment' and 'choice' are key words that recur in the debate over globalization and are used by both its supporters and its detractors. Nevertheless empowerment and choice have eluded the vast majority of those living in the Middle East. The protest against political, economic and cultural domination, whether through an Islamist movement or in another way, has been a search for empowerment, not only in relation to domestic governments but also internationally. An alliance between Islamism and globalization may offer Muslims an ideological and an economic route that could deliver a sense of religious and cultural independence coupled with greater prosperity.

8 Bringing the bourgeoisie back in: globalization and the birth of liberal authoritarianism in the Middle East[*]

Toby Dodge

Introduction

The attacks on the United States on 11 September 2001 have paradoxically engendered a degree of hope in the intelligentsia of the Middle East. In discussions among liberal activists across the region and their colleagues in exile in Europe and America there is an optimism that the atrocities committed in New York and Washington will act as a catalyst for long-awaited political change. The response of the American government and of international society will put pressure on the region's dictatorial regimes. It is anticipated that this will result in democratic transformation. These liberal arguments predict that the outmoded and anachronistic rulers, embarrassing relics from the post-colonial Cold War era, will finally succumb to the inexorable forces of globalization. The hoped-for result will be the rise of democratic government long awaited in the salons, *diwaniyya* and lecture theatres of the region.

This heightened sense of optimism closely resembles the mood after the Gulf War of 1990–91. The then nascent ideology of liberal globalization was deployed to predict the results of outside intervention. In the early 1990s, with the fall of the Berlin Wall, it was the combined forces of the allied troops sent to tackle Saddam Hussein and the technocrats of the International Monetary Fund and the World Bank that were to be the catalyst for change. Then as now, radical transformation was predicted. The dictatorial regimes of the region would be swept away by a wave of democratization. Sadly, the hopes of the early 1990s were not realized. The liberalization delivered by globalization has been very limited, and has been concentrated in the economic sphere.

[*] This paper has benefited from a round-table discussion on the future of the Middle East held at the Institute for Middle Eastern and Islamic Studies, Durham University on 30 November 2001. I would like to thank all those who took part, especially Dr Ali Ansari, Professor Anoush Ehteshami and Dr Emma Murphy. They may not agree with my conclusions but I thank them for helping me to reach them.

There is general agreement in the large and diverse academic literature on globalization about its effects on the state. Although authors disagree about the nature and extent of the state's transformation under globalization, the state has changed, and will continue to do so. Whether we live in a 'post-Westphalian' international system or a 'borderless world', the state is perceived to be the main target of globalization. The states of the Middle East, however, have stubbornly resisted their predicted transformation. The vast majority of regimes that entered the 1990s still exist. Indeed, with the apparently successful dynastic change of power in Syria from father to son it can be argued that the dictatorships of the *Mashreq* are stronger today than they were a decade ago.

The Middle East is *not* somehow culturally or politically immune to either democracy or globalization. Its democratic transformation under globalization has failed to materialize because the basic presuppositions of the prediction were misconceived. Most of the literature on globalization theory identifies the international economy as the key agent of change. It is argued that the international economy's dynamism forces domestic economics, and thus domestic politics, to change. In reality, however, regional governments have maintained a much greater degree of political autonomy in the face of global economic change than was predicted a decade ago. They have been forced to react to the changing nature of the world economy, but as with most regimes in the developing world, this reaction has been political, not economic. Regime survival has long been the chief priority of Arab governments, and, unsurprisingly, Arab leaders have worked hard to secure it. Economic reform has been slow and piece-meal. Serious political reform, which might undermine or threaten a regime's existence, has not happened. In the face of economic globalization the republican regimes of the Middle East have simply brought the bourgeoisie back in. Faced with economic crisis the ruling regimes have sought new sources of revenue by allowing indigenous capitalists to become junior members of the ruling elite. This has resulted in the birth of a 'liberal' authoritarianism: the state has retreated from the economic sphere in order to guarantee its dominance of the political sphere.

Theories of globalization and the predicted transformation of the state

The leading explanations of globalization argue that the distinction between what has traditionally been conceived of as 'national' or internal to the state and what has been seen as 'international' and external to the state has broken down.[1] Increased financial, cultural and political interaction has made countries heavily interdependent. Individuals across the world find themselves interacting with each other and the market beyond the territorial boundaries of their separate states. These increasingly important transactions are carried out above and below states that in the past have been the coherent political, economic and social units within which people organized their lives.

Social science understands the process of globalization to be driven primarily by the growth of an integrated global economy. It is the huge increase in the speed and size of financial transactions that has led the way to a global market in communications, industrial production and also cultural consumption. In a globalized world the 'national economic space no longer coincides with national territorial borders'.[2] Besides financial transactions, industrial production too has been globalized: factories have become increasingly mobile and are able to move to wherever the price of labour is the most advantageous.

This economic process is understood to have had profound effects on the state, internationalizing it along with its population.[3] As individuals' prosperity becomes increasingly tied to global markets, the state has had to act as a 'transmission belt' for global capitalism, facilitating its interaction with the society it traditionally sheltered from international economic instability. Governments have had little choice but to compete with one another in the global economy for the fickle investment of multinational companies. As these companies become more mobile, states are put at a disadvantage as they try to make their workforce and economy as attractive as possible. National prosperity is dependent on the ability of the state to please an increasingly powerful globalized market.

The effects of globalization on politics, local, regional and international, are considered to be far-reaching. A globalized world is an increasingly complex one. States, through increased economic interdependence, have been involved in a myriad of overlapping and constraining relationships that have a great deal of influence on how they conduct their affairs. These relations are with other states, but also with multinational companies, different international markets and intergovernmental and non-governmental

[1] See, for example, Roger Tooze, 'International Political Economy in an Age of Globalization', in John Baylis and Steve Smith (eds), *The Globalization of World Politics: An Introduction to International Relations* (Oxford: Oxford University Press, 1998), p. 215.

[2] David Held, Anthony McGrew, David Goldblatt and Jonathan Perraton, *Global Transformations: Politics, Economics and Culture* (Cambridge: Polity Press, 1999), p. 8.

[3] See Robert Cox, 'Multilateralism and World Order', *Review of International Studies*, Vol. 18, No. 2, 1992, p. 178.

organizations. These complex transnational networks of interaction force states to be outward-looking, to project their power and influence into the world in order to function efficiently. Under globalization, policy-making has become internationalized.

The involving of states in a web of complex relationships has transformed not only their autonomy but also their sovereignty.[4] In order to control their interactions with a complex world, states are voluntarily joining regional and international organizations whose aim is to manage the effects of interdependence. In the environmental, economic and political realms, it is argued, states are ceding their rights to unfettered action so as to guarantee a degree of order and stability.

Along with the rise of structures of international governance, the whole notion of sovereignty has been transformed, according to liberal promoters of globalization. The post-colonial right to self-determination that came to the fore in the 1950s and 1960s is now increasingly balanced with the responsibilities of statehood; '... a new "sovereignty regime" is displacing traditional conceptions of statehood as an absolute, indivisible, territorially exclusive and zero-sum form of public power.'[5] Liberal theorists of international relations argue that the normative conception of political sovereignty now places much greater responsibility on governments to treat their populations in accordance with internationally accepted norms of human rights. The advent of a putative international human rights regime means that states now cannot obtain international legitimacy without being to some degree accountable to the national community that they claim to represent. This new and conditional notion of sovereignty is reflected in international law, with the increasing recognition of the rights of individual citizens alongside if not equal to the rights of sovereign states.[6]

It has been suggested above that social scientific explanations of globalization view the growth of global markets and globalized production as the engine driving increasing interdependence. It has also been suggested that political globalization, the transformation of the state and its relations with domestic society, follows inexorably in the wake of economic globalization. Although the majority of analysts would not go as far as Kenichi Ohame in predicting the end of the nation-state, liberal theorists of globalization do see the rise of a normalizing rationality at the heart of

[4] Held et al., *Global Transformations*, p. 81.
[5] Ibid., p. 9. For its practical ramifications, see Bruce W. Jentleson, 'Coercive Prevention: Normative, Political and Policy Dilemmas', 'Peaceworks' series (Washington, DC: United States Institute of Peace, 2000), pp. 9–36.
[6] See Antonio Cassese, *International Law in a Divided World* (Oxford: Clarendon Press, 1986), Chapter 4.

global governance.[7] This is formally embedded in the growing autonomy of international institutions and, increasingly, of international law. Governments can no longer abuse their populations with impunity, claiming the sovereign rights of an autonomous state.

It is this liberal teleology, the notion of political convergence resulting from economic globalization, that liberals in the Middle East and beyond deploy to predict the imminent decline of autocratic regimes in the Arab world. The rise of a transnational liberal economic and political culture is perceived to be the vehicle that will bring democratization to the weak but 'fierce' states of the region.[8] There is apparently no alternative to the minimal but representative state of the neo-liberal model.

The arrival of democratic government in the Middle East has long been predicted, but appears perennially to be delayed. A review of the Arab world since the fall of the Berlin Wall and the end of the Gulf War does not show one regime that has voluntarily given up power in the wake of free and fair elections.[9] From the mid-1980s the neo-liberal economic solutions of the International Monetary Fund (IMF) and the World Bank have been imposed on Egypt, Tunisia and Jordan. In the 1990s elections became almost commonplace, with parliaments sitting in many of the major capitals of the region. But despite the trappings of economic globalization and the window dressing of political participation, very little of substance has changed. The predicted effects of political globalization appear to have passed the region by. What can explain this apparent anomaly? Is the Middle East on the verge of a series of democratic revolutions? Are its governments engaged in a last-ditch, but ultimately futile, attempt to keep the liberal forces of globalization at bay? Or is there instead something faulty with the supposed predictive ability of globalization theory itself?

At the heart of liberal theories of globalization is a set of largely unspoken assumptions about the causes and effects of the phenomena they purport to describe. These assumptions can be divided into two interconnected subsets. First, as with classical liberal theory, the economic and the political spheres of social life are conceived of as separate. The economic sphere is then assigned the dominant role, with its unfettered dynamics imposing a rational reforming logic on the political sphere. The pressures a globalized economy puts on states are perceived to be broadly similar and unavoidable.

[7] See Kenichi Ohame, *The End of the Nation State: the Rise of Regional Economies* (London: Harper Collins, 1996).
[8] On their weak but 'fierce' nature, see below, p. 177.
[9] See Gerd Nonneman, 'State of the art. Rentiers and autocrats, monarch and democrats, state and society: the Middle East between globalization, human "agency" and Europe', *International Affairs*, Vol. 77, No. 1, January 2001, pp. 141–62.

The second subset of assumptions concerns the reactions of governments to the restrictions placed on them by globalization. Globalization theory, generalizing from a European model of the state, assumes that governments share a universal logic of action that will prevail in the face of globalization. States are seen as rational utility-maximizers. The state will seek to preserve and increase its collective interests in all circumstances. As a state finds its political autonomy undermined, it will conform to a liberal economic logic in order to attract the maximum amount of inward investment. In turn this will result in a shrinking of the state's role in the domestic economy and a liberalizing of its attitude towards its population as economic and then political competition develops.

As the example of the Middle East shows, this has not been the case in the past, and it does not appear to be the case in the foreseeable future. The philosophical division between capitalism and the state at the heart of liberal understandings of globalization is difficult to substantiate empirically.[10] As Karl Polanyi's work on the growth of capitalism in Europe indicates, historically markets have had to be created by decisive state intervention in the economy.[11] What was true for Europe was even more so for the post-colonial Middle East of the 1950s. With a historically weak bourgeoisie tainted in the popular nationalist imagination by close links with the colonial powers, the state itself took the central role in the economy. Markets in the Middle East today still depend very much on the states that created them; as such they bear the hallmarks of their creators. The large-scale entrepreneurs who dominate the economy have been created by the state. It is these people who would be expected to take the place of the state as it retreats from the economic sphere. But they rely on the state for their existence and their ability to prosper. The division at the heart of liberal theory between the public and the private, between the state and the economy, is for this reason fragile in the Middle East.

The state in these circumstances is the dominant player both politically and economically. It has taken the leading role in shaping not only the market but also the terrain on which any economic reform is to be enacted.[12] The state's dominant role means that any reform process will be shaped by the logic of regime policy. Here too the presuppositions underpinning liberal theories of globalization are increasingly difficult to substantiate in analyses of the Middle East.

[10] See Leo Pantich, 'Rethinking the Role of the State', in James H. Mittleman (ed.), *Globalisation: Critical Reflections* (Boulder, CO: Lynne Rienner, 1996), p. 85.
[11] Karl Polanyi, *The Great Transformation,* (Boston: Beacon Press, 1957), pp. 63–73.
[12] See Charles Tripp, 'States, Elites and the "Management of Change"', in Hassan Hakimian and Ziba Moshaver (eds), *The State and Global Change: the Political Economy of Transition in the Middle East and North Africa* (Richmond: Curzon Press, 2001), p. 214.

Liberal understandings of globalization propose a set of universal reactions to the economic pressures on states. Faced with increasingly mobile investment capital and industrial production, states will reduce their interference in the domestic economy in order to guarantee continuous economic growth and societal quiescence. Markets will be allowed to function autonomously, releasing entrepreneurs to meet the demands of the population with greater efficiency and equity. The rational economic logic of the state is taken for granted. States ultimately have to serve the needs of their populations. In a globalized economy the only way to achieve this aim is to give greater autonomy to domestic markets and entrepreneurs.

But this economic logic is not evident when the effects of globalization on the Middle East are studied. Regimes there are much more concerned with their own day-to-day survival than they are with the long-term economic well-being of their populations. With the paucity of political representation in the Middle East, threats to regime survival are much more likely to come from intra-regime conflict than from societal revolution.[13] In the short to medium term, political logic is much more influential in the calculations of rulers than the long-term economic logic that theories of globalization assume.[14]

It would be difficult to overestimate the political and economic influence of globalization. Capitalism has become universal in its reach and also (in the years immediately after the end of the Cold War) in its legitimacy. However, those trying to understand the ramifications of globalization for the states of the Middle East mistakenly assume an ahistorical universalism when seeking to understand globalization's effects as well as its causes. In trying to gauge the influence of globalization, it is all too easy to forget that states and societies differ greatly across the world.[15]

Globalization is clearly a universal phenomenon, but to understand its effect with greater clarity and accuracy, the different nature of the states it is interacting with has to be understood. The states of the Middle East have their own distinct history. Like many states in the developing world they share the common heritage of colonialism. But in order to understand how they react to the pressures of globalization, their post-colonial evolution has to be understood. Only when the indigenous political institutions of the Middle East are explored shall we be better able to understand what effects globalization will have upon them.

[13] See Joel S. Migdal, *Strong Societies and Weak State: State–Society Relations and State Capabilities in the Third World* (New Jersey: Princeton University Press, 1988), pp. 206–25.
[14] See Tripp, 'States, Elites and the "Management of Change"', pp. 225–9.
[15] Michael Mann, 'Has globalisation ended the rise and rise of the nation-state?', *Review of International Political Economy*, Vol. 4, No. 3, Autumn 1997, pp. 479, 494.

The rise of the post-colonial state in the Middle East: revolution from above and the growth of patronage

The post-colonial states of the Middle East entered the international system at a specific economic and ideological moment. They bear the heritage of this entry both in the economic policies that regimes applied until recently and in regime type and leadership methods. The seizure of power by Nasser and fellow young officers in 1952 signalled not only the abolition of the Egyptian monarchy but also the rise of radical republicanism at the heart of the Middle Eastern state system.

The republican states of the *Mashreq*, Egypt, Iraq and Syria, distanced themselves from their former colonial masters in the 1950s and 1960s. The independence they strove to establish was influenced by then dominant international economic and political trends that gave legitimacy, financial support and technical assistance to state-driven modernization. Both Eastern-bloc and capitalist aid donors favoured the state-led development model. Academics in the developing world also promoted the state's dominance of the economy as a way of increasing national autonomy for late-industrializing countries.[16]

As these regimes strove to consolidate their power, they faced indigenous economic classes that did not have the financial power or social coherence to challenge effectively the state's dominance of its population.[17] The military bureaucrats that now staffed the main institutions of the state were comparatively unrestrained by domestic interest groups as they attempted to transform society by unleashing a 'revolution from above'. Their aim was to 'modernize' the economy and society without mobilizing a mass political movement that could threaten their newly obtained political power.[18]

The 'revolution from above' by the republican regimes in Iraq, Syria and Egypt was to be pragmatic and pursued in a step-by-step manner. However, the economic goals of state-driven development also served political ends. By intervening directly in the economy, by instigating land reform in the name of national development, the republican regimes were directly

---

[16] See Colette Chabbott, 'Development INGOs', in John Boli and George M. Thomas (eds), *Constructing World Culture: International Nongovernmental Organizations Since 1875* (Stanford, CA: Stanford University Press, 1999), p. 238; Mustapha Al-Sayyid, 'International and Regional Environments and State Transformation in some Arab Countries', in Hakimian and Moshaver (eds), *The State and Global Change*, pp. 157–9, 167; and Nazih N. Ayubi, *Over-stating the Arab State, Politics and Society in the Middle East* (London: I.B. Tauris, 1995), p. 191.

[17] Lisa Anderson, 'The State in the Middle East and North Africa', *Comparative Politics*, Vol. 20, No. 1, October 1987, p. 11.

[18] E.K. Trimberger, *Revolutions from Above: Military Bureaucrats and Development in Japan, Turkey, Egypt and Peru* (New Brunswick: Transaction Press, 1978), pp. 3–4.

attacking the power of the *ancien régime*. The policies of state-driven development were intended to destroy large landowners whose prestige and economic wealth had provided the unstable social base of the previous regimes. In addition, by taking the dominant role in the economy the military regimes were effectively denying space for an indigenous bourgeoisie to grow in economic size or political influence.[19]

The legacy of this political and economic approach is ambiguous. After taking power, the republican states quickly developed all the trappings of modern government, with large bureaucracies and powerful armies, urbanization and a degree of welfare provision. But, as has been persuasively argued, although they acquired the ability to deploy violence frequently against their populations, they still lacked the institutional capacity to extract resources from society regularly and efficiently. In this sense they are certainly 'fierce' states, but not necessarily strong ones.[20] They lack the institutional power and political legitimacy to implement government policy effectively and regulate society throughout their territory.[21] State intervention in society is often not welcome; it is seen at best as a necessary evil and at worst as an illegitimate intrusion.

Governments involved in post-colonial state formation that were unable or unwilling to institutionalize legal-rational bureaucratic links with most of their populations had to resort to more informal and personal networks of social control and mobilization. And individuals were forced to rely on personal contacts with people in positions of power in order to guarantee their economic survival when state institutions and market mechanisms alike failed to provide the resources needed. As a result, neo-patrimonial structures of political organization arose and dominated state–society relations. Clientelism provided the link between the ruling elite and its immediate trusted circles and, by way of widening circles of patron–client relationships, the majority of the population. This system does not link politicians with the 'public' in a democratic contract, but ties patrons personally with their associates, clients and supporters.[22]

---

[19] See Anderson, 'The State in the Middle East and North Africa', p. 11; and Raymond A. Hinnebusch, 'Syria', in Tim Niblock and Emma Murphy (eds), *Economic and Political Liberalisation in the Middle East* (London: British Academic Press, 1993), pp. 177–202.

[20] See Ayubi, *Over-stating the Arab State*, p. 3, and Migdal, *Strong Societies and Weak States,* p. 5.

[21] On the distinction between violent 'despotic' power and 'legal-rational' infrastructural power, see Michael Mann, *States, War and Capitalism: Studies in Political Sociology* (Oxford: Blackwell, 1988), pp. 5–7.

[22] For a more detailed examination of this process in action, see Robert H. Jackson and Carl R. Roseberg, *Personal Rule in Black Africa: Prince, Autocrat, Prophet and Tyrant* (Berkeley: University of California Press, 1988).

Neo-patrimonialism is inherently unstable. It is based on unequal access to government resources and it constantly creates constituencies of the dispossessed and resentful. However, it does have advantages for Middle Eastern leaders, who control the top of the neo-patrimonial networks. By the very nature of neo-patrimonialism, the relations between state and society that it nurtures are unofficial, diffuse and for the most part implicit. This means they are organic and flexible, changing to suit the needs of both patron and client in times of political turmoil or economic scarcity. Ultimately, access to state patronage has defined the shape of the public sphere in the Middle East. Economic opportunities, group loyalties and social and political identities have all been shaped and reshaped, based upon where a specific individual stands in relation to the state-sponsored patronage networks.[23]

The combination of official state-driven development policies and dependence on neo-patrimonialism to secure the political loyalty of key constituencies resulted in the economies of Middle Eastern states being shaped in the image of the regimes that came to power in the 1950s and 1960s. An already modest private sector, perceived as economically unable to deploy the resources needed to drive development, was swept aside. The state gradually took more and more responsibility for the economy, moving from a planning and coordinating role to direct investment in and management of industrial production. This worked well as a strategy for increasing regime power, either integrating potentially influential entrepreneurs directly into the state or making their success heavily dependent on state favours. But it also had the effect of politicizing the performance of the economy. Post-colonial Arab governments that promised speedy modernization in return for loyalty were taken at their word.[24] When success in the economy was meagre the blame was placed firmly on government policy.

The consequences of globalization and the crisis of the Arab state

A convergence of events from the mid-1980s to the 1990s appeared to herald the arrival of globalization in the Middle East. The contradictions of the statist revolution began to impact severely on government policy in the late 1970s and the 1980s. This was exacerbated by the oil price collapse in the mid-1980s and the end of the Cold War in the early 1990s. The result

---

[23] See Tripp, 'States, Elites and the "Management of Change"', p. 220 and Hinnebusch, 'Syria', p. 183.
[24] See Ayubi, *Over-stating the Arab State*, p. 33.

was a widespread crisis among Arab states. As predicted by liberal theorists of globalization, the economic and political sovereignty of Arab states was placed under severe pressure.

Throughout the 1970s and 1980s Lebanon had been used by Middle Eastern regimes as an example of what would happen if post-colonial state-formation failed. Here was a state devoid of any domestic or international power. It was in a civil war, a conflict of all against all, consuming its population, and fuelled by neighbouring states that intervened with impunity. In an era dominated by the protection of sovereignty and the projection of state power, Lebanon was a potent symbol. In the 1990s, a different era with different ideological concerns, Algeria took Lebanon's place as the spectre haunting Arab states and societies.

The lessons taken by Arab leaders from Algeria in the 1990s were different from those of Lebanon. Independent Algeria was the quintessential radical post-colonial state aggressively defending its sovereignty and building state power. After violently expelling its colonial masters, it initiated non-aligned statist policies that were to be the model for Third World leaders everywhere.[25] Its descent into bloody civil war was used by other Middle Eastern regimes to highlight the damage to be done by ill-conceived liberal reforms hastily enacted in the face of international pressure and societal dissatisfaction. As Lebanon represented failure in the era of state formation, so Algeria came to represent the dangers inherent in the era of liberal globalization. States that had to a large degree staked their legitimacy on social and economic progress found it increasingly difficult to deliver on their revolutionary rhetoric. This lack of legitimacy developed into a widespread crisis when the resources derived directly or indirectly from oil revenue dwindled and the availability of external credit declined.

Internationally, two related phenomena highlighted the political impact of globalization on the sovereignty of Middle Eastern states. First was the increasing influence of neo-classical economics in the IMF and the World Bank as the non-oil-producing states became indebted. By the mid-1980s the Bretton Woods institutions began insisting that the economies of recipient states be 'structurally adjusted' as a condition of borrowing. The economies of Tunisia, Jordan and Egypt all succumbed to the prescriptions of market reliance at the heart of the 'Washington Consensus' in the 1980s and 1990s. In return for receiving large loans these states had to limit their involvement in the economy, removing import quotas, cutting tariffs and

---

[25] See Bahgat Korany and Saad Amrani, 'Explosive Civil Society and Democratization from Below: Algeria', in Bahgat Korany, Rex Brynen and Paul Noble (eds), *Political Liberalisation and Democratisation in the Arab World, Volume 2: Comparative Experiences* (Boulder, CO: Lynne Rienner Publishers, 1998), p. 11.

interest rate controls and moving towards the privatization of state industries. Even states such as Syria that fought hard to maintain control over
their economic sovereignty had to conform to some extent to the new economic Zeitgeist in the face of poorly performing economies and increasing
indebtedness.

The second and in many ways more shocking effect of globalization was
the ramifications of operating in a unipolar world. A number of republican
regimes, notably Syria and Iraq, had come to depend on the Eastern bloc
for weapons and technology and, more importantly, for diplomatic leverage in their relations with Israel, the United States and the United Nations.
With the sudden demise of their Communist allies they knew that their
international autonomy had been radically curtailed. Diplomacy was now
a much more delicate operation; it had to be carried out unilaterally and
with a greater sense of vulnerability. Political globalization looked to be
ushering in an era in which a state's relations with its own population and
its immediate neighbours would be subject to a level of international
scrutiny absent in the years of the Cold War.

The treatment of Iraq after its invasion of Kuwait in 1990 appeared to
typify this threat to sovereignty. With the Soviet Union in its death throes
there was no counterbalance in the international community, and this
enabled the United States quickly to build a political and military coalition
that isolated the Iraqi regime and allowed the unrestrained deployment of
America's superior weapons technology. More portentous than the reimpo-
sition of regional order was the sustained economic and military isolation
of Iraq in the 10 years since the liberation of Kuwait. The sacred role of
sovereignty in post-colonial international society counted for little as Iraq
was placed under international supervision: its imports and exports were
now controlled from New York and United Nations weapons inspectors
were given international authority to roam across Iraqi territory in search
of weapons of mass destruction. The fate of Iraq in the past 10 years, still
under a comprehensive sanctions regime and subjected to regular bombing
by Anglo-American planes, has become a powerful symbol of the limits of
sovereignty in the era of globalization.

International threats to the political and economic sovereignty of the
Middle East were compounded by the fall of the price of oil, which had a
very strong effect at the regional level. State-driven development strategies
pursued from the 1950s onward had been directly and indirectly sheltered
from the dynamics of the global economy by increasing oil wealth and its
associated inter-Arab aid and worker remittances.[26] By the mid-1980s this

[26] Although there are degrees of economic autonomy, 'Virtually no state in the region relies solely on its
domestic production for resources …'. Anderson, 'The State in the Middle East and North Africa', p. 14.

oil-based autonomy was in serious doubt. OPEC had become a victim of its own success. The high cost of oil forced consumer economies to improve fuel efficiency while it made exploration for oil in non-OPEC areas more cost-efficient. Oil as a percentage of global energy consumption dropped along with OPEC's share of global production. In 1985, on the eve of the oil price collapse, OPEC was supplying just 19 per cent of the world market's needs.[27]

The extent of the economic shock of the oil price collapse of the mid-1980s can be gauged by noting the dependence of non-oil-producing states on inter-Arab aid and worker remittances sent home from the Gulf states. For Syria and Jordan the assistance they received from the oil producers was equal to 25 per cent and more than 30 per cent respectively of the state budget. The value of Arab aid to Jordan dropped from a high of $1,256 million in 1981 to $427 million in 1988. The Middle East's real gross national product in the 1980s fell by a yearly average of 2.4 per cent.[28] The end of bipolarity, the increased power of the IMF and the World Bank and the collapse of oil prices placed severe pressure on both political and economic autonomy. Regimes were forced to search for alternative sources of finance, thus further limiting their ability for autonomous policy-making.

Domestically there seemed to be little alternative to the liberal prescriptions for the socio-economic woes facing Middle Eastern states. The failure of the statist model was as apparent to Arab populations as to their leaderships. Trade imbalances and increasing foreign debt forced governments to cut back expenditure, which further depressed the economy. State-imposed austerity highlighted the structural crisis of the economy, the ineffectual nature of previous government policy and the state's dependence on external sources of funding.

The inability of regimes to maintain, let alone improve, living standards directly affected their legitimacy. The collapse of the Soviet Union and its Marxist ideology undermined comparable regional ideologies, and the liberal triumphalism at the end of the Cold War began to influence domestic Arab political opinion. The Arab socialism of the Baath Party in both Syria and Iraq looked increasingly anachronistic in the face of domestic economic failures and the declaration of the victory of international capitalism.

---

[27] See Peter Kassler, 'Developments in the global energy market and the implication for Gulf producers', in Rosemary Hollis (ed.), *Managing New Developments in the Gulf* (London: Royal Institute of International Affairs, 2000), p. 19.

[28] See Raymond A. Hinnebusch, 'Calculated Decompression as a Substitute for Democratization: Syria', p. 229 and Rex Brynen, 'The Politics of Monarchical Liberalism: Jordan', p. 81 in Korany, Brynen and Noble (eds), *Political Liberalisation and Democratisation in the Arab World*; and Hassan Hakimian, 'From MENA to East Asia and Back: Lessons of Globalisation, Crisis and Economic Reform', in Hakimian and Moshaver (eds), *The State and Global Change*, p. 82.

By the early 1990s, in the immediate aftermath of the Gulf War, the predictions of liberal promoters of globalization seemed to be justified. The republican regimes of the Middle East did indeed appear increasingly anachronistic. State-driven development had failed to deliver economic modernization to the vast majority of the population. The large numbers of graduates produced by ambitious education programmes were facing a very bleak future as urban unemployment rose rapidly. The states themselves were increasingly indebted, and were imposing austerity measures to meet balance-of-payments crises. Food subsidies were cut and the Jordanian and Egyptian governments faced bread riots.

Internationally things looked even bleaker. Iraq languished in diplomatic and economic quarantine, with its population impoverished and its sovereignty destroyed. In a unipolar world the intrusive political liberalism favoured by the Clinton administration appeared to pose a direct threat to the continuance in power of the non-democratic Arab regimes. The triumph of liberal democracy (if not the 'end of history' predicted by Francis Fukuyama) appeared as a well-grounded prediction, not just the bombastic celebration of market capitalism.

A decade later, however, the political and economic transformation of the Middle East driven by globalization has yet to take place. The regime in Baghdad, a symbol in the first half of the 1990s of Arab powerlessness in a unipolar world, has in the past five years managed not only to survive but also to grow in strength. Although Egypt, Jordan and Tunisia have all undergone structural adjustment, their leaderships remain in place. The structures of political power have not, as predicted, become more representative or less repressive as a consequence of globalization. Even the retreat of the state from the economic sphere has been halting and has had ambiguous results. The autonomy of Arab leaders has proved to be very robust in the face of sustained political and economic challenges from the international system.

The state fights back: neo-patrimonialism and globalization

It has been shown that in the early 1990s the non-oil-producing states of the Middle East, in particular, faced economic and political problems indicative of a globalized international system. Challenges at the international, regional and domestic levels had come together to place restrictions on their ability to act autonomously. But a decade later these regimes are still in power. Economic reform has been minimal and political reform, resulting in democratic structures that place meaningful restraints on the leadership, is negligible. The domestic autonomy of the *Mashreq* regimes has proved to be much more robust than the situation 10 years ago or than liberal theories of globalization had led analysts to believe.

Governments' survival strategies worked because the challenges they faced were neither constant nor homogeneous. Regimes muddled through successfully by partially or temporarily addressing problems in one sphere while ignoring or using intimidation in another. Key players in the international system could be bought off with limited but well-timed diplomatic initiatives. Syria's role in the coalition against Saddam Hussein brought it renewed Gulf aid, and a period when the United States ignored its human rights record. Domestically, Jordan's experimentation with limited democracy allowed for the mollification of East Bank anger at time of government austerity.

Egypt's much longer flirtation with restricted economic and political liberalization became both a template for others and a warning about the threat to regime autonomy if strict limits were not placed on the whole process. Egypt's *infitah* or economic opening up, declared in April 1973, was the result of state economic failure but also the availability of regional assistance and international support. Its problems sprang from the collapse of the statist economic model in the mid-1960s and an accompanying foreign exchange crisis that effectively brought import substitution to an end.[29] Opportunity sprang from President Sadat's courting of finance from the Gulf states in the immediate aftermath of the 1973 oil price rises. Egypt's move away from non-alignment to close relations with the United States was based on his correct judgment that the Americans would be able to broker a favourable deal with the IMF and the World Bank in return for a strategic alliance.

Domestically, Sadat's move away from statist dominance of the economy allowed him to forge a new alliance with the entrepreneurial stratum of the middle class. The breaking of the political and economic power of the landowners and bourgeoisie under Nasser enabled Sadat to integrate a weak and dependent business class into the lowest levels of the patronage system without threatening his power base. This limited economic liberalization was accompanied by elections and the installation of a parliament. However, the dangers involved in this political process, and also the bounds of liberalization, were highlighted when the new bourgeoisie

---

[29] See Robert Springborg, 'Egypt', in Niblock and Murphy (eds), *Economic and Political Liberalization in the Middle East*, p. 145.

developed autonomous links with the international economy and social unrest flared as a result of unequal distribution of the new financial resources. The resulting crackdown on society by the state set the template for Egypt's *infitah* – slow and limited liberalization followed by authoritarian state action when the process appeared to be moving beyond the state's ability to control it.

Egypt's pioneering if ambiguous experimentation with liberalization highlights the dynamic interaction that has developed between the political and economic effects of globalization and the Arab states. Those states have maintained their autonomy because they have put political survival above economic success. Middle Eastern states have over the past 50 years created the economic setting within which any economic liberalization will unfold. The bourgeoisie, identified by theories of globalization as the shock troops of reform, are highly dependent upon the state. The result is that political and economic changes are managed by incumbent regimes for their own ends. Liberalization is never allowed to threaten a regime's power base or its ability to dominate its population.

Economic reform in the Middle East has tended to unfold in two stages. The first is heralded by government attempts to instigate reform domestically and internationally by opening up the economy while simultaneously cutting back on domestic expenditure. The resulting social tensions have led to a more cautious and less overt strategy whereby liberalization is gradual and unpublicized.[30] The initial wave of economic reform is marked by the government's adoption of managerial rhetoric. After years of statist propaganda focusing on the inequity of capitalism, the full implications of reform are disguised by the indigenization of the process, which stresses its origins from within the country. States continue to possess and run industrial production, but they try to attract investment by liberalizing export regulations and banking laws. The results in Egypt and Syria have been meagre, with inward investment remaining comparatively mobile and concentrating on commerce and tourism. If anything, changes in banking law have encouraged greater indigenous capital flight.[31]

Of necessity, the second stage of liberalization involves attempts to commercialize the state sector and to open up the economy to international commercial capital.[32] In Egypt and Jordan this has been coupled with signing up to IMF structural adjustment packages. As noted above, political

---

[30] Ibid., p. 151.
[31] Raymond Hinnebusch, 'The Politics of Economic Liberalisation: Comparing Egypt and Syria', in Hakimian and Moshaver (eds), *The State and Global Change*, pp. 119–21, and Hinnebusch, 'Syria', p. 188.
[32] N.N. Ayubi, 'Political Correlates of Privatisation Programmes in the Middle East', *Arab Studies Quarterly*, Nos 2 and 3, spring–summer 1992, pp. 39–56.

stability, not economic reform, is the regimes' paramount interest. Egypt's liberalization gained momentum only when Western and GCC governments wrote off $50 billion of its debt after the Gulf War. Jordan's attempts at reducing state subsidies were derailed by rioting in 1989 and 1996.[33]

The main goal of the reform process is to deal with economic imbalances without damaging political autonomy. To that end financial resources have been sought from donors who would minimize conditionality. Up to the mid-1980s the Gulf states filled this role, especially for Syria. But the oil price collapse forced Egypt and Jordan to agree to the above-mentioned IMF adjustment packages. Syria managed to avoid that drastic action by forging limited alliances with indigenous private capital until it could again tap into aid from the oil-producing states after the Gulf War.

The most attractive source of financial resources is indigenous capital that has been moved out of the domestic economy in order to escape the reach of the state. This capital often belongs to elements of the bourgeoisie and landed classes decimated in the early years of state-building. Ironically, the very regimes that set out to destroy the power of the *ancien régime* have now based a major element of their survival strategy on them. Expatriate capital is tempted back by the opportunities of benefiting from the state's reduction of its economic role. The hoped-for economic growth would then lessen the social tensions involved in austerity measures.[34]

There is a delicate balance to be struck between liberalizing banking and investment laws enough to make the economy attractive while retaining the power to control and direct the investment so as to strengthen the regime's support base. This is done through the maintenance of tariffs and import restrictions that favour the regime's chosen entrepreneurs without risking the danger of a full free market developing. The resulting crony capitalism brings the bourgeoisie back into the domestic economy but heightens their dependence on the regime and its maintenance of the status quo.

The privatization process in Egypt and in Iraq before 1990 was dominated by a small set of businessmen with close links to the highest echelons of the regime. The relationship became symbiotic, with those in positions of political power developing economic interests. This process went a step further as the old Nasserist elites in Egypt were sidelined in the

---

[33] Yezid Sayigh, 'Globalisation Manqué, Regional Fragmentation and Authoritarian-Liberalism in the Middle East', in Louise Fawcett and Yezid Sayigh (eds), *The Third World Beyond the Cold War: Continuity and Change* (Oxford: Oxford University Press, 1999), p. 221; and Rex Brynen, 'The Politics of Monarchical Liberalism: Jordan', in Korany, Brynen and Noble (eds), *Political Liberalisation and Democratisation in the Arab World*, p. 93.

[34] See Hinnebusch, 'The Politics of Economic Liberalisation: Comparing Egypt and Syria,' pp. 113, 116 and 118, and Hinnebusch, 'Calculated Decompression as a Substitute for Democratization: Syria', pp. 233, 236.

1980s and replaced by economic technocrats. The change in personnel and in government rhetoric indicated a realignment of the social coalition on which the regime was based. The urban working class and the peasantry, previously mobilized to support the regime, were marginalized as the newly empowered bourgeoisie were integrated into the regime as subordinate partners.

Conclusions

At the core of academic theories of globalization is the idea that capitalism is now a truly global force that is transforming, for better or worse, all it comes into contact with. This is certainly the case: developed and developing countries are finding it increasingly difficult to shelter their populations from the instabilities and inequities of international market forces. But theories of globalization have difficulty in understanding the ramifications of this transformation. Although capitalism is global, its effects are certainly not uniform or universal. The interaction between international markets and national societies is mediated by the specific history and geography of each country. To simply project a liberal political and economic model onto different states and societies is to ignore the specific complexities of each case.

A majority of Middle Eastern states have existed for a little over a century. The fact that their national economies and political systems were constructed out of the wreckage of the Ottoman Empire highlights a very different historical trajectory from that of Europe. Their state-building strategies, especially those of the post-colonial republican regimes of Iraq, Syria and Egypt, put them at the heart of their economies: they mobilized resources, chose investment strategies and managed both supply and demand.

The distinction between the political and the economic, between the private and the public, is empirically very hard to maintain in the Middle East. Even after years of poor economic performance, its states still have a great deal of influence in their economies. Liberalization is thus driven by a political logic in which the goal of regime survival is paramount. Like state-building in the 1950s and 1960s, economic liberalization in the 1980s and 1990s has been a highly centralized and top-down process primarily for cementing the regime's control over its population. The entrepreneurs who have been enriched by this process are tied to and dependent on the state. Because of this they have benefited from the restricted nature of liberalization and have not sought to push it any further than the regime itself wants to take it.

The result has been the birth of a 'liberal' or more plural authoritarianism in the Middle East. The state has given up some of its economic roles, but only in order to consolidate its political position. The ruling coalition has been broadened and the bourgeoisie have been brought back in. Having been given a large stake in the status quo, they are not inclined to push for democratization. Thus it can be argued that globalization, far from causing democratization in the Middle East, has made it much less likely. Instead, regimes have adopted a theatrical approach to representation. Elections are held and parliaments are stocked with representatives who have debates and pass laws, but the locus of power has never moved from the presidential palaces. The day-to-day management of politics is largely untouched by democratic trappings contrived more to please the international community than to fool a cynical, demobilized population struggling to get by in a poorly performing economy.

9 The challenges of the global economy for Middle Eastern governments

Rodney Wilson

Introduction

Globalization is usually regarded as an economic phenomenon character-ized by the increasing international interdependence in trade and capital flows and by a reduction in information barriers that economists categorize as transactions costs. In the case of the Middle East the process can arguably be described in terms of trade and financial dependence on the advanced industrialized countries and a conflict of civilizations in the economic sphere that is related to, and arguably one facet of, wider religi-ous and cultural conflicts.[1]

It is asserted here that although the trade and capital dependence of the Middle East places limitations on the economic sovereignty of govern-ments, this is not a new situation, and in many respects it parallels develop-ments in the nineteenth century. Furthermore, data on trade and investment flows show that in some respects the region is becoming more detached from the international economy rather than more integrated in it. Quanti-tative measures of economic variables tell only part of the story, however. Factors such as differences in economic culture and the implications of Islamic teaching point up the uniqueness of the region and its resistance to being absorbed into a global capitalist system based largely on indivi-dualistic and material values.[2] These differences leave governments in the Middle East with much freedom of manoeuvre and discretion, as the experiences of Egypt and Saudi Arabia, discussed later in this chapter, show.

---

[1] Samuel P. Huntington, *The Clash of Civilizations and the Remaking of the World Order* (London: Touchstone Books, 1998), pp. 109–21.
[2] Akbar Ahmed, *Postmodernisation and Islam* (London: Routledge, 1992), pp. 207–8. In this work he discusses 'mosque versus mall', spirituality versus consumerism. See also Akbar S. Ahmed and Hastings Donnan, *Islam, Globalisation and Post-modernity* (London: Routledge, 1994), p. 3.

Globalization and economic power

In the economic sphere the impact of globalization on governments is complex and multifaceted. It is tempting but too simplistic to suggest that there is a trade-off between globalization and the power of governments to manage their economies. The premise here is that power is transferred from governments to unelected international bodies such as the International Monetary Fund (IMF) or the World Trade Organization (WTO), or even to multinational investment banks through forums such as the Paris Club that determine the fate of debtor states. This implies not just a loss of freedom for governments with respect to fiscal and monetary policy but also limitations on industrialization, trade and investment policies and even on welfare and social security spending.

For governments in the Middle East their position in relation to international institutions is more equivocal, as it cannot be understood without reference to the domestic constituents whose interests the governments represent or are seeking to represent. Some of these constituents, notably merchants, traders, distributors and financiers, as well as private contracting firms, have an interest in the government applying the type of liberalization policies advocated by the IMF and the WTO, provided they can be modified appropriately to suit local circumstances. This gives the government a role as a negotiator and facilitator, increasing both its international and domestic legitimacy.

At the same time, other domestic economic interests may be threatened by IMF and WTO policies, notably those of civil servants and workers in state-sector industries, the landless in the rural areas and the beneficiaries of state education or basic medical services. These poorer constituents may pose a potential threat to governments seeking to pursue so-called structural adjustment and economic liberalization policies that result in relatively less state spending and the creation or opening up of markets. Governments can attempt to pacify these groups by demonstrating that they can modify or slow down the implementation of such policies, thus serving as a buffer between the rigours of international competition and the more protected domestic market.

This view of the role of the state supports the position recently set out by Charles Tripp.[3] He rejects the notion of the state as a prime mover in directing economic activity and sponsoring capital formation. He sees the

[3] Charles Tripp, 'States, Elites and the Management of Change', in Hassan Hakimian and Ziba Moshaver (eds), *The State and Global Change: The Political Economy of Transition in the Middle East and North Africa* (Richmond, Surrey: Curzon, 2001), pp. 211–31.

state instead as providing the boundaries within which elites and essential groups take political and economic action. The state is the site for conflict and contestation, and can be regarded as a community, a hierarchy and an apparatus for coercion. Therefore, to view the effect of globalization on the state simply in terms of state enfeeblement is incorrect, as there is much more to the state than the narrow economic role of exploiting and distributing resources. The state is multifaceted, imaginative and resilient, and the sharp distinction drawn in the West between public and private realms is less relevant for regions such as the Middle East. The economically powerful blur the distinction between the two, their main aim being to keep in place systems of privilege and exclusion for the defeat or cooptation of those who would challenge their position.

Even authors such as Michael Mann who see globalization as slightly weakening the countries of the North, and the European Union states in particular, believe that economic development should strengthen Middle Eastern, along with other, Southern nation-states.[4] He sees a decline in 'hard geo-politics' in Northern states, but not in the South. Mann identifies a rise in 'soft geo-politics' as new state functions emerge and as states play the major role in maintaining international networks. Although he does not consider the Middle East in particular, his analysis is consistent with that of Tripp and the analysis presented here.

Martin Shaw builds on Mann's analysis and believes it is erroneous to counterpose globalization to the state; he considers it appropriate to examine how globalization results in state transformation.[5] However, he sees the state in the West no longer as a nation-state but as 'a massive, institutionally complex and messy agglomeration of state power centred on North America, western Europe, Japan and Australasia',[6] which he calls the 'Western state'.

If Shaw's hypothesis is correct, the question arises where this leaves states in the Middle East when confronted with this dominant Western form of global state. The answer is obviously in an economically weak position internationally, but not necessarily internally. The state's internal power must derive from the differences of its economy from that of the West. As this is more likely to be based on differences in economic attitudes and behaviour than on economic structures, it is important that the economic culture should be examined, not least because those structures

[4] Michael Mann, 'Has globalisation ended the rise and rise of the nation-state?', *Review of International Political Economy*, Vol. 4, No. 3, 1997, pp. 472–96.
[5] Martin Shaw, 'The state of globalization: towards a theory of state transformation', *Review of International Political Economy*, Vol. 4, No. 3, 1997, pp. 497–513.
[6] Ibid., p. 497.

have been affected by so-called IMF-imposed structural adjustment pro-grammes. What international bodies such as the IMF have been less successful in influencing is economic behaviour.

The historical context

Economic historians largely agree that capitalism was far from being an isolated development in northwestern Europe: although it was still in the process of being formed in the fifteenth and sixteenth centuries, it increas-ingly involved other areas of the globe in material exchanges.[7] By the seventeenth and eighteenth centuries, economic historians suggest, there was a significant shift in the balance of economic power between the Middle East and the nation-states of western Europe.[8] The opening of the trade route around the Cape of Good Hope adversely affected the region's transit trade and the ability of the Ottoman authorities to collect revenues, but merchants and traders proved remarkably adept at adjusting to change and developing new business, and there is little evidence of general economic decline.

The struggle to gain economic sovereignty has always been difficult in the Middle East, and has never wholly succeeded. The challenges posed by globalization and the issues they involve are familiar to the region, even if the actors and the theatre have changed. In the nineteenth century the British thwarted Mohammad Ali's efforts to industrialize Egypt,[9] and both the French and the British exacted major economic concessions from the Ottomans in return for limited debt relief.[10] Christopher Clay's study of the debt issue reveals in detail the link between the bankruptcy of the Ottoman government in 1875 and the enfeeblement of the state and the loss of its European provinces in 1877–8. This enfeeblement, and the penetration of Western capital through the Public Debt Administration, resulted in the further disintegration of the empire after 1908 and its ultimate collapse in 1918.

A central question in Clay's study is the extent to which foreign banks and bankers pushed the Ottoman administration into accepting loans on onerous terms that should never have been accepted in the first place.[11] It is

---

[7] Ankie Hoogvelt, *Globalization and the Postcolonial World: The New Political Economy of Development* (London: Macmillan, 2001), p. 14.

[8] Roger Owen, *The Middle East in the World Economy, 1800–1914* (London: Methuen, 1981), p. 8.

[9] Charles Issawi, *The Economic History of the Middle East and North Africa* (London: Methuen, 1982), pp. 154–5.

[10] Christopher Clay, *Gold for the Sultan: Western Bankers and Ottoman Finance, 1856–1914* (London: I.B.Tauris, 2000), pp. 229–78.

[11] Ibid., pp. 132–228.

clear that the exploitation was mutual between the Ottoman authorities and the foreign banks rather than being one-sided. There was much competition among the banks for government business, with one willing to undercut the others in the terms offered. Consortia of banks were formed, largely because of the limited size of the institutions in relation to the loans being sought, but there was no grand alliance that would have given the Ottomans little choice in securing financing. The Imperial Ottoman Bank won few loan contracts in the 1860s and 1870s largely because it was unable to match the terms offered by some of the smaller institutions and was always very cautious in its response to funding requests.

Clay shows also how the Ottomans were formidable negotiators, being tenacious in their arguments and willing to delay negotiations whenever necessary if an advantage could be secured through such tactics. Western governments and their ambassadors were reluctant to get involved in Ottoman finance, leaving the bankers largely to their own devices. There is little evidence that foreign governments and bankers exploited the political and financial weakness of the Ottoman government or that there was a conspiracy between these two groups. Indeed, with the arrival of foreign banks the Ottomans obtained financing on better terms than previously. Far from being incompetent, the Ottoman administrators are shown to be skilled negotiators. In the end they were doomed by the enormity of the problems the empire faced, but arguably the involvement of foreign financiers postponed rather than advanced the ultimate, probably inevitable, demise of the empire.

In the first half of the twentieth century the European powers placed severe restrictions on Middle Eastern governments' freedom of economic manoeuvre. For example, the nominally independent Egyptian government lacked the autonomy to set tariffs until 1930, and it was not allowed to impose new taxes, which might have affected the foreign community living there, until 1937.[12] Egypt, Sudan, Palestine, Jordan and Iraq, as well as the Gulf emirates and sheikhdoms, were part of the sterling area,[13] while Syria, Lebanon and the Maghreb states were part of the French Franc zone. The resultant limitations on currency convertibility meant that their trade was tied to the colonial power, which also determined the amount and allocation of investment,[14] and even domestic monetary and fiscal policy.[15]

[12] Roger Owen and Şevket Pamuk, *A History of the Middle Eastern Economies in the Twentieth Century* (London: I.B.Tauris, 1998), pp. 35–6.
[13] Paul W.T. Kingston, *Britain and the Politics of Modernisation in the Middle East, 1945–1958* (Cambridge: Cambridge University Press, 1996), pp. 31–6.
[14] Bent Hansen, 'Capital and lopsided development in Egypt under British occupation', in Georges Sabbagh (ed.), *The Modern Economic and Social History of the Middle East in its World Context* (Cambridge: Cambridge University Press, 1989), pp. 66–88.

There are many parallels between the colonial or neo-colonial experience of the governments of the Middle East in the first half of the twentieth century and their experience in the second half, the main difference being in the shift of global power from European- to American-based institutions with global pretensions.

The exposure of the Middle East to the global economy

Economic openness is one measure of the extent to which states are becoming more integrated into the global economy. Openness can be measured by examining the extent of international trade in relation to gross domestic product (GDP) and by the magnitude of foreign investment flows. If the economies of the Middle East are becoming more integrated into the global economy, the share of trade in relation to GDP, deflated into purchasing power parity (PPP) terms to allow for inflation, would be expected to rise. Similarly, the value of net foreign direct investment might be expected to rise in developing countries requiring capital, especially in those, such as the many Middle Eastern states, that had liberalized their investment laws.

In the 1990s trade as a share of purchasing power parity gross domestic product fell in most countries in the Middle East and in the region as a whole, as Table 9.1 shows. The figures refer to the sum of exports and income divided by PPP GDP. Far from becoming more open, the economies of the Middle East were becoming more internally orientated, the exceptions being Israel, Morocco, Turkey and Yemen. In the case of Egypt the rise was so marginal that it should not be considered significant. Some of the decreases reflected declining oil prices, although in 1999 prices had recovered from the slump of the previous year and were not much different from average 1990 levels. In any case the decline was most rapid in some of the non-oil economies, notably Syria, which was supposedly opening up its economy to the West. Admittedly the Syrian trade figure may have been distorted by the failure to record smuggling through Lebanon, but there is no reason to suppose that this was relatively worse in 1999 than a decade earlier.

Despite its proximity to Europe, the Middle East has received relatively little foreign direct investment in recent years in comparison to other

[15] Rodney Wilson, 'Economic Aspects of Arab Nationalism', in Michael Cohen and Martin Kolinsky (eds), *Demise of the British Empire in the Middle East: Britain's Response to Nationalist Movements, 1943–55* (London: Frank Cass, 1998), pp. 64–78.

Table 9.1: Trade as a percentage of PPP GDP for Middle Eastern countries, 1990 and 1999

Country	1990	1999
Algeria	19.9	14.3
Bahrain	128.3	76.5*
Egypt	8.9	9.1
Iran	15.4	8.4
Israel	45.9	52.4
Jordan	34.2	29.4
Lebanon	45.1	39.0*
Morocco	15.9	18.6
Saudi Arabia	45.9	36.0
Syria	22.0	10.4
Tunisia	28.4	25.5
Turkey	13.0	16.2
UAE	85.3	106.7
Yemen	25.9	34.1
Middle East	23.5	16.8

*1998.

Source: World Bank, *The Little Data Book* (Washington, DC: World Bank, 2001).

regions of the developing world such as Southeast Asia or Latin America. Indeed, most of the investment flows have been outward, with the value of private Gulf wealth invested in Western financial markets possibly exceeding $1,200 billion, of which about $700 billion may be accounted for by Saudi Arabia alone.[16] For East Asia and the Pacific region, net foreign direct investment increased from $11 billion in 1990 to $56 billion in 1999, despite the decline from the 1997 peak after the Asian financial crisis. The total for Latin America increased from $8 billion to over $90 billion over the same period, while that for the Middle East excluding Turkey declined from a mere $2.5 billion to below $1.5 billion, as Table 9.2 shows.

Insofar as governments in the Middle East are attempting to encourage investment inflows by liberalizing foreign investment laws, their policy clearly is not working. The IMF defines foreign direct investment as net inflows of investment in order to acquire a lasting management interest, which is interpreted as 10 per cent or more in the voting stock of a company.[17] Not only is foreign direct investment very limited but Western

[16] Brad Bourland, 'Outward flows, inward investment needs in the GCC', *Arab Banker*, Vol. 16, No. 2, 2001, pp. 49–51.
[17] The World Bank, *The Little Data Book* (Washington, DC: World Bank, 2001), p. 233.

Table 9.2: Net foreign direct investment flows ($m) for Middle Eastern countries, 1990 and 1999

Country	1990	1999
Algeria	0	7
Egypt	734	1,065
Iran	−362	85
Jordan	38	158
Lebanon	6	250
Morocco	165	3
Syria	71	91
Tunisia	76	350
Turkey	684	783
Yemen	−131	−150
Middle East	2,504	1,461

Source: World Bank, *The Little Data Book* (Washington, DC: World Bank, 2001), pp. 9, 11 and 12.

portfolio investment in company shares quoted on regional stock markets is also minimal, partly because some markets are closed to foreign investors, notably the Saudi market, the largest in the region, while others are small and volatile.

The explanation for low investment flows may reflect government restrictions and political risk factors perceived by Western multinational companies and investors, but this shows that Middle Eastern states are effectively resisting globalization despite the lip-service paid to economic liberalization and the opening up of markets. The reality seems very different from the rhetoric, although it is worth asking whether this is because of government duplicity or because the governments themselves wish to liberalize but are constrained by the cultural and religious environment of the region, which hampers economic integration with the West. To answer this question, consideration must be given to whether the region has a distinctive economic culture that resists change and whether Islam is a factor in explaining the rejection of a capitalist system shaped by Calvinist thinking.

Globalization and economic culture

The implications of globalization for the economic role of the state are of course not unique to the Middle East, as they apply also to other areas of the developing world. What makes the experience of the Middle East different, however, is the cultural and religious context, notably the Arab states' sense of Arab identity and, in the case of the great majority of the Muslim population, shared Islamic values.

Despite the Arabs' common language and shared culture there is no Arab economic community, as inter-Arab trade is minimal: investment mostly flows out of the region into international markets, and there are no developed regional institutions to foster regional economic links, the Arab League being a powerless organization with few resources. Even the more successful sub-regional institutions such as the Gulf Cooperation Council have little executive power.

What is significant, however, is the exchange of ideas on economic issues, including globalization, and the extent of inter-Arab debate, which help to shape attitudes and responses at all levels of society. Millions of ordinary Egyptians and Jordanians have first-hand knowledge of the functioning of the economies of Saudi Arabia and the Gulf through working there. At the government level there are frequent meetings between Arab finance and national economy ministers at sessions of the Arab League and in other multilateral and bilateral forums. Central bank staff meet under the auspices of the Abu Dhabi-based Arab Monetary Fund, while economists attend conferences and workshops organized by the Cairo-based Economic Research Forum for the Arab Countries, Iran and Turkey.

Common agreement is not necessarily reached, but there is a dynamic to the debate that creates its own culture. Among economists and policy-makers this culture is likely to be expressed in economics terminology – what has even been described as the 'rhetoric of economics'.[18] This response to the dominant global social thought in economics has been described less eloquently by the translator of Samir Amin's work as 'economistic', in the sense that economic laws are viewed as being 'inconvertible' in 'dictating the functioning change and progress of systems of production, which among other things imposes increasing interdependence of national sub-systems at the global level'.[19]

The dilemma for economists in the Middle East is that the more they identify with their professional colleagues in the wider world, the less likely they are to be listened to by their own governments, or to have much impact on economic policy-making. Regional governments emphasize form rather than substance. This emphasis includes encouraging the growth of economics departments within state universities, and even funding staff members to go to the West for doctoral research. However, respect for the expert does not extend to the substance of what he or she suggests, and

[18] D.N. McCloskey, *The Rhetoric of Economics* (Madison, WI: University of Wisconsin Press, 1985).
[19] Samir Amin, 'The challenge of globalisation', *Review of International Political Economy*, Vol. 3, No. 2, summer 1996, p. 218.

economists who believe that the government will heed their policy prescriptions on issues such as the need for greater competition in local markets are in for a shock. What matters is local politics – the vested interests of established suppliers whose interests the governments seek to serve rather than to challenge.

Jan Aart Scholte's concept of global communities of difference is of relevance here, as he suggests that globalization helps to reinvigorate or invest with new meaning a diverse array of trans-border solidarities.[20] These have, he suggests, prompted a number of nationalistic reactions. Although it would be an exaggeration to depict the conflict between Western-educated and -influenced economists and governments in the Middle East in these terms, conflict with those who govern society is more likely for social scientists than for those in the physical sciences. However, there is a tendency for many Middle Eastern economists, perhaps the majority, to try to avoid confrontation. They retreat from policy debates, concentrate on theory or on the technicalities of econometrics and avoid political economy if they wish to progress in their careers.

In the workings of the Middle Eastern economies there is more emphasis on personal connections than on institutions and formal processes. The mentality of the bazaar or the souk economy permeates all negotiations, with intense bargaining the norm among parties who know each other.[21] Loyalty is much more highly valued than the impersonal measurement of results through performance evaluation. In an insecure and uncertain environment where there is often a lack of information and transaction costs are high, private traders, and even those involved in the award of government tenders, prefer to deal with those they know and believe they can trust on the basis of past experience. This imposes entry barriers, and results in market inertia and the maintenance of the economic status quo.

Economic change, when it comes, tends to be the result of crisis, usually of a political rather than an economic nature, and is revolutionary rather than evolutionary. The 1950s and 1960s were turbulent political and economic times, but since then changes in much of the region have arguably been more cosmetic than real, and economic reform has been somewhat superficial, in spite of pressures from international institutions such as the IMF and the WTO. A number of economic anthropologists have traced the links between global and national developments and changing economic behaviour, notably James Toth in his work on Egypt, which highlights

[20] Jan Aart Scholte, 'The geography of collective identities in a globalising world', *Review of International Political Economy*, Vol. 3, No. 4, 1996, pp. 565–607.
[21] Rodney Wilson, *Economic Development in the Middle East* (London: Routledge, 1995), pp. 19–21.

popular resistances to change.[22] Some observers see governments in the Middle East as being themselves unenthusiastic about economic reform, which makes them only too willing to cede to populist resistance. Bradley Glasser suggests that it is foreign exchange crises that have brought neo-liberal reforms, as for example in Turkey, but also that where governments have been less hard-pressed, as in Egypt, they have been successful in resisting these reforms.[23]

There are few indigenous multinational companies in the Middle East, most businesses being family-owned and -controlled rather than publicly quoted companies. The major quoted institutions on regional stock markets are typically banks rather than manufacturing or retailing and distribution companies. This failure of larger businesses to develop can be attributed to the major role that governments and state-sector enterprises continue to play in most economies of the region, which crowds out the private sector. It can also be a consequence of the limited development of local or regional capital markets, and equity markets in particular. Perhaps the most important factor is the business culture that attempts to keep family control rather than seek market capital, as the concern is to maintain the business for future generations. Given the choice between seeking capital to expand and taking on more risk or remaining smaller through reliance on family resources and ploughed-back profits, most businessmen in the region choose the latter.

Business inertia and the tendency to operate on a very small scale is compounded by an aversion to takeovers and mergers, which would imply cooperation between families and perhaps one emerging as the dominant partner. There are also few exit routes, as the law in most states does not adequately provide for bankruptcy. This is largely because extracting interest from debtors in difficulty is regarded as *haram* (prohibited) by *shari'a* (Islamic law) religious courts, and civil judges are reluctant to give rulings that would conflict with fundamental Islamic teaching. The difficulty is that debtors may abuse their position and simply refuse to acknowledge debts, which creates moral hazard problems for the banks and other financial institutions and encourages risk-averse behaviour. Banks therefore often demand collateral or guarantees against personal wealth before

[22] James Toth, *Rural Labour Movements in Egypt and their Impact on the State, 1961–1992* (Gainesville, FL: University Press of Florida: 1999), pp. 220–34. See also James Toth, 'Beating plowshares into swords: the relocation of rural Egyptian workers and their discontent', in Nicholas S. Hopkins and Kirsten Westergaard (eds), *Directions of Change in Rural Egypt* (Cairo: American University in Cairo Press, 1998), pp. 66–87.
[23] Bradley Louis Glasser, *Economic Development and Political Reform: The Impact of External Capital on the Middle East* (Cheltenham: Edward Elgar, 2001), pp. 23–4.

making loans in countries such as Egypt,[24] even though this is also contrary to the *shari'a*.[25]

Islamic shari'a law, Middle Eastern governments and international business

Islam has its own economic laws, the best known of which is the prohibition of *riba*,[26] which can be interpreted as applying to all interest-based transactions.[27] Interest is the key pricing measure in global money markets and a major determinant of developments in global capital markets. Insofar as they adhere to the *shari'a*, the Muslim countries would appear to need to exclude themselves from such markets by avoiding international borrowings, the issue of bonds and the investment of dollars and other international currencies acquired through oil and gas exports in bank deposits, treasury bills or other instruments which earn interest.[28]

In practice most governments in the Middle East conveniently ignore *shari'a* teaching in their international financial dealings and both borrow and, in the case of the Gulf countries, earn income on the basis of interest. For almost a decade after the Islamic revolution Iran avoided borrowing in international markets; but needing to finance reconstruction after the end of the war with Iraq, it returned to these markets and relied increasingly on supplier credits from Western companies. Even the Islamic banking law of 1983 was applied only internally, to dealings between banks and their clients,[29] and there was no attempt to extend it to the dealings of the Central Bank of Iran or to transactions between Iran's commercial banks and foreign banks.[30]

[24] Ziad Bahaa-Eldin, 'Formal and informal finance in Egypt', in Baudouin Dupret, Maurits Berger and Laila al-Zwaini (eds), *Legal Pluralism in the Arab World* (The Hague: Kluwer Law International, 1999), pp. 205–18.

[25] Nayla Comair-Obeid, *The Law of Business Contracts in the Arab Middle East* (The Hague: Kluwer Law International, 1996), pp. 172–4.

[26] The Holy Koran, Sura 2: 275–6.

[27] Rodney Wilson, *Economics, Ethics and Religion: Jewish, Christian and Muslim Economic Thought* (London: Macmillan, 1997), pp. 124–8.

[28] M. Siddieq Noorzoy, 'Islamic laws on *riba* and their economic implications', *International Journal of Middle Eastern Studies*, Vol. 14, No. 1, 1982, pp. 3–17. Reprinted in Tim Niblock and Rodney Wilson, *The Political Economy of the Middle East*, Volume 3, *Islamic Economics* (Cheltenham: Edward Elgar, 1999), pp. 12–26. For international implications, see pp. 22–4.

[29] Mohsin S. Khan and Abbas Mirakhor, 'Islamic banking: experiences in the Islamic Republic of Iran and Pakistan', *Economic Development and Cultural Change*, Vol. 38, No. 2, pp. 353–75. Reprinted in Niblock and Wilson (eds), *The Political Economy of the Middle East*, pp. 432–54.

[30] These inter-bank transaction were valued at almost $11.4 billion by December 2000, of which $7.6 billion represented outstanding debt. There was a further $4.6 billion of liabilities on the part of Iranian companies, including the state-owned oil company, to international banks. See Bank for International Settlements, *Quarterly Review*, Basle, June 2001, pp. 20 and 31.

These international financial dealings by Muslim countries, including the Islamic Republic of Iran and Saudi Arabia (the latter supposedly governed in accordance with the *shari'a* law), can be justified by arguing that as the international financial system is based on Western norms, there is little alternative to dealing with the system, other than isolation and impoverishment as with the Taliban regime in Afghanistan. Hence the response is pragmatic, rather than ideologically pure. The Iranian government can argue that it has acted within its own territorial jurisdiction to implement Islamic financing, and the Saudi authorities can assert that they promote Islamic finance through their funding of the Jeddah-based Islamic Development Bank and their encouragement of Islamic commercial banking in the kingdom and world-wide, where it has become a $200 billion industry.

In all Middle Eastern states apart from Iran and the Sudan, conventional Western banking dominates; Islamic banks play a limited role at best. A number of states, including Syria, Lebanon, Iraq, Algeria, Libya and Yemen, do not permit locally owned Islamic banks to operate, and others, such as Turkey and Egypt, continue to curtail their activities. These restrictions on Islamic finance have been introduced not as a result of any pressures from international organizations but because local bankers, including those managing the state-owned banks, would prefer the status quo to be maintained. The international pressure is on states to open up their financial markets to multinational banks rather than to prescribe any particular financing method. But most governments in the region have also resisted the former because of the vested interests of local banks and other financial institutions, which wish to limit competition and avoid being taken over by foreign institutions that could threaten jobs.

Although most Middle Eastern states are nominally Muslim, there is a reluctance to see *shari'a* law implemented in areas that could limit the scope of governments' discretionary management, including over economic matters. The *shari'a* is usually applied to family matters and criminal offences rather than to commerce. Commerce is subject to Western codes of practice, or tax law; *zakat,* the Islamic wealth tax, is usually voluntary rather than imposed by the state. The countries of the region, apart from Israel, are all members of the Organization of the Islamic Conference and are represented in the Islamic Development Bank,[31] but there is a reluctance to cede any monetary sovereignty to that Jeddah-based bank that would undermine the position of national finance ministries or central banks.[32]

[31] Ibrahim Warde, *Islamic Finance in the Global Economy* (Edinburgh: Edinburgh University Press, 2000), pp. 74–5.
[32] Rodney Wilson, *Islamic Finance* (London: Financial Times Publishing, 1997), pp. 61–3.

Islamic economics is regarded with scepticism, if not outward anta-gonism, by government officials involved in economic policy-making. In regional universities there is often scant respect for departments of Islamic studies among those in the economics or business faculties, and where departments of Islamic economics have been established, relations are often fraught between their staff and those teaching mainstream economics and finance. This mirrors the harsh tone of some of the international critics of Islamic economics, notably that of Timur Kuran, who has published wide-ly on the subject.[33]

Globalization, however, is in many respects strengthening the position of Islamic economists and those who see the implementation of the *shari'a* as the state's prime political objective. There are many international confer-ences, both commercial and academic, on Islamic economics and finance, and they attract participants from throughout the Muslim world. There are dedicated academic journals[34] and banking journals[35] in the field and web-sites containing a wealth of information on the subject.[36] This has resulted in a development of the field and in a degree of engagement, not all of which has been constructive, with Muslims who adhere to neo-classical econo-mic ideas or conventional Western theories of finance.

Phil Marfleet, a specialist in cultural studies, makes the following pertinent observations, which could be applied to the resurgence of Islamic economics:

It is easy to see why Islam has been associated with globalization. Muslim activists' vision of a pan-Islamic *umma* which might link believers across national boundaries, ethnic and political barriers has the ring of a universalism in keeping with both the 'compression' of the modern world and as the apprehension of a totalising socio-cultural environ-ment. Its strong assertion of scripturalism and legalism also appears to offer certainties which answer the quest for fundamentals among those who face the greatest uncertainty in a world of rapid change.[37]

---

[33] Timur Kuran, 'The discontents of Islamic economic morality', *American Economic Review*, Vol. 86, No. 3, 1996, pp. 438–42, and Timur Kuran, 'Islamism and economics: policy implications for a free society', *International Review of Comparative Public Policy*, Vol. 9, No. 1, 1997, pp. 71–102.

[34] Notably *Islamic Economic Studies*, published by the Islamic Development Bank; *Islamic Economics*, a journal of King Abdul Aziz University; and the International Islamic University of Malaysia's *Journal of Economics and Management*.

[35] See *New Horizon*, produced by the Institute of Islamic Banking and Insurance, and *Islamic Banker*, both published in London.

[36] Useful starting points are *www.islamic-banking.com* and *www.islamiq.com*.

[37] Phil Marfleet, 'Religious activism', in Ray Kiely and Phil Marfleet (eds), *Globalisation and the Third World* (London/New York: Routledge, 1998), p. 207.

Islamic economic writers have noted the strength of their approach when confronted by globalization. Mohammad Ali Khan is worth quoting in this respect, as he speaks of:

> The articulation of an Islamic ethos and its role in providing restraints against what one sees as the deleterious effects of globalization, particularly financial globalization. At the same time the role of globalization in providing further insight on Islamic values. The importance of pluralism, and the realisation that there is not one 'scientific' way of doing things; but this realisation interpreted within the rubric provided by the Koran and the Islamic past.[38]

The appeal of Islamic economics to those in indebted Muslim countries can be seen in the writings of scholars such as Umer Chapra, who see conventional Western financing methods as bringing instability, inequality and injustice.[39] Being critical of international banks and the international financial order does not, however, imply being against all the activities of multinational companies. The extent to which Islamic law constrains businesses can be exaggerated, as many see the Islamic belief system as compatible with a market-orientated economy based on private enterprise.[40] According to Kavoossi, Islam can reconcile individualism with a deep sense of community, and it is compatible with a modern business environment.[41]

Egypt and Saudi Arabia: contrasting state responses

In order to examine the complexity of government reactions to the challenges of globalization it is useful to investigate in detail the recent experiences of Egypt, the most populous Arab state, with over 63 million inhabitants, and Saudi Arabia, the world's largest oil-exporting state, which has more than one-quarter of global oil reserves. Both governments are engaged in an intense relationship with the United States that impinges on domestic economic policy-making; both are members of the IMF; and Egypt is a member of the WTO, an organization that Saudi Arabia is in

[38] M. Ali Khan, 'Globalization of financial markets and Islamic financial institutions', *Islamic Economic Studies*, Vol. 8, No. 1, 2000, pp. 59–60.
[39] M. Umer Chapra, *The Future of Economics: An Islamic Perspective* (Leicester: Islamic Foundation, 2000), pp. 314–23.
[40] David L. McKee, Don E. Garner and Yosra Abu Amara McKee, *Accounting Services, the Islamic Middle East and the Global Economy* (Westport, CT: Quorum Books, 1999), p. 164.
[41] Masoud Kavoossi, *The Globalization of Business and the Middle East: Opportunities and Constraints* (Westport, CT: Quorum Books, 2000), p. x.

negotiations to join. Neither government is accountable to freely elected legislative bodies. Egypt is ruled by a strong presidency that has never been subject to a democratic change of power and Saudi Arabia is monarchical, with power in the hands of the ailing King Fahd and his brothers, Crown Prince Abdullah and Prince Sultan. In Egypt elections are held for both the presidency and the parliament, but Islamist parties are banned, and the National Democratic Party is largely a vehicle of the presidency rather than a popular political party. Saudi Arabia has an appointed consultative assembly, the Majlis, and a council of ministers, also appointed, that are drawn mainly from the House of Saud.

In the economic sphere those in power respond both to domestic constituencies and to other governments and international organizations. Much of the political energy and debate is taken up by economic matters, with the ministers of economy, finance, trade and petroleum and their senior officials playing a central role, along with the governor of the central bank, in Saudi Arabia the governor of the Monetary Agency. These ministers and officials respond to the demands of the managers of state-sector industries, owners of major private-sector industries, merchants and traders; they try to formulate policies that will serve the interests of these constituents and they intermediate on their behalf with international organizations.

Egyptian government policies, local economic elites and international organizations

In Egypt there are many examples of government actions that have been applauded by local economic elites, even though they are not necessarily popular with industrial workers or farmers or others living in the countryside. The recent economic performance of Egypt has been unimpressive; per capita GDP growth averaged only 2.4 per cent in the 1990s, reaching a mere $3,460 in purchasing power parity terms in 1999.[42] Most of the economic elites have done well from this growth, however: many in the private sector have amassed considerable fortunes, and even managers in the public sector are reasonably content with the government's defence of their position despite pressures from the IMF and the World Bank to speed up the privatization process.

Despite the rather mediocre performance of Egypt's economy – with relatively low economic growth, state industries suffering from a lack of investment, uncertainty over agricultural prices, stagnant labour productivity,

[42] *World Bank Atlas* (Washington, DC: World Bank, 2001), p. 44.

poor quality state education and illiteracy rates of 34 per cent for males and 57 per cent for females aged 15 and above[43] – the government's economic policies have been applauded by the IMF and the World Bank. The real economy may be marking time, but the country's finances are regarded as being in good shape. The overall budgetary deficit has been reduced to a mere 2 per cent of GDP, lower than that of most developed countries, as a result of government spending restraint. As a consequence inflation fell from almost 20 per cent in 1990 to below 2 per cent in 2000, which enabled the exchange rate to be pegged to the dollar at £E3.9 and kept within a 1.5 per cent band at least until 11 September 2001.[44]

This macroeconomic stability should create a good climate for investment and entrepreneurial activity, but the evidence suggests that local financiers are largely playing safe by purchasing government bonds yielding relatively attractive rates rather than taking business risks. Indeed much government spending is accounted for by the servicing of internal debt rather than education, health or other types of social expenditure.[45] Externally, Egypt's official debt has stabilized at about $24 billion, with all arrears cleared by August 2001 and debt-servicing charges of about $1.7 billion annually. Although the World Bank agreed to provide a further $1.5 billion from 2001 to 2004, aid per capita has declined, from $104 in 1990 to $25 in 1999. Consequently the government is seeking finance in international markets, and in July 2001 it secured the country's first Euro bond issue, which was underwritten by Merrill Lynch. Such financing is expensive, as the interest on the 10-year $1 billion facility is 8.34 per cent, while that on the $500 million 5-year facility is 7.58 per cent.[46] This cost reflects the perceived risks, as Moodys rated the issue as Ba1, a status comparable to that of Lithuania or the Philippines.[47] Increasingly the task for the government will be to prove the country's creditworthiness to these international agencies rather than simply to bargain by making political gestures in return for economic assistance from the United States.

As Egypt was already a signatory to the General Agreement on Tariffs and Trade it was admitted to the WTO as a founder member. As a consequence, pressures to liberalize trade are less strong than those on candidate states currently negotiating entry such as Saudi Arabia, especially as Egypt enjoys developing country status, which the kingdom's negotiators

---

[43] The World Bank, *The Little Data Book*, p. 80.

[44] See *www.egypt.se.com*.

[45] Rania A. al-Mashat and David A. Grigorian, *Economic Reforms in Egypt: Emerging Patterns and Their Possible Implications*, World Bank Policy Research Working Paper (Washington, DC: World Bank, September 1998).

[46] 'Egypt celebrates Euro bond success', *Middle East Economic Digest*, London, 13 July 2001.

[47] *www.moodys.com*, *Ratings List, Government Bonds and Country Ceilings*, 17 July 2001.

have still not secured. In 1999 the WTO conducted an extensive trade policy review on Egypt that urged further liberalization, pointing to the import ban on clothing and poultry products and to the average tariff rates of 26.8 per cent, admittedly lower than the 42.1 per cent rate that had applied in 1991.[48] Youssef Boutros Ghali, the minister of economy and foreign trade, has defended Egypt's position vigorously, however, indicating that he sees no rationale for 'negotiating trade rules for competition'.[49] He perceives no urgency in negotiations over transparency in government procurement, and has indicated his opposition to the inclusion of environmental issues and core labour standards as matters for the WTO. Corruption in state procurement, a lack of pollution controls and the exploitation of child labour are all, of course, features of contemporary Egypt.

These positions demonstrate how the Egyptian government is concerned in its international negotiations primarily with the protection of the position of its domestic elites. These elites include state-sector managers and even appointed trade union leaders, who are members of the National Democratic Party. The government's caution over privatization and its willingness to listen to its appointed trade unionists have been noted by external observers.[50] In contrast, in Saudi Arabia trade unions are prohibited, and efforts to form unions can result in dismissal, imprisonment and, in the case of expatriate workers, deportation. Yet Saudi Arabia was admitted to membership of the International Labour Organization in 1976, despite its refusal to ratify either Convention 98, the right to organize and collective bargaining, or Convention 87, freedom of association and protection of the right to organize.[51]

The House of Saud, local business interests and globalization pressures

The Saudi government also endeavours to serve its economic elite in its diplomacy, the difficult negotiations to join the WTO illustrating just how far it is willing to go to protect local vested interests, not least those of the royal family itself. The working party on Saudi Arabia's membership application was established on 21 July 1993,[52] but market access agreements for

---

[48] *www.wto.com, Trade Policy Review, Egypt,* 1999.

[49] Statement by Youssef Boutros Ghali at the Third Session of the WTO Ministerial Conference, Seattle, 30 November–3 December 1999.

[50] Marsha Pripstein Posusney, *Labour and the State in Egypt: Workers, Unions and Economic Restructuring* (New York: Columbia University Press, 1997), pp. 238–43.

[51] *www.worldbank.org, Saudi Arabia: System of Industrial Relations and Trade Unionism.*

[52] *www.wto.org,* Working Party on Saudi Arabia.

goods and services have proved to be difficult to negotiate, as there is a desire to protect the interests of Saudi joint venture partners in industrial ventures and the locally incorporated banks. The government continues to exclude foreign oil companies from upstream petroleum operations, which reinforces the monopoly of the Arabian American Oil Company (ARAMCO).

Sharaf Sabri's study of the role of the House of Saud in commerce sheds much light on just how extensive the royal family's business interests have become.[53] He provides a breakdown for each branch, and gender, of the Al-Saud family, and finds that princes invest in twice as many companies as princesses do, although there appears to be greater gender equality for the Al-Jilawi branch of the family. Prince Walid bin Talal bin Abdul Aziz is by far the largest investor, with over $10 billion invested in 25 companies. Princess Noha bint Saud bin Abdul Mohsin appears to be the largest female investor, with over $16 million invested.[54] Sabri also provides a generational analysis. This shows that the third generation of the House of Saud is the most actively involved in business both as investors and as active owners, although the fourth generation is fast catching up.

Other Saudi entrepreneurs do not appear to have been affected adversely by the business aspirations of royal family members. Indeed Sabri suggests that they have benefited, both directly, by being involved as partners with princes and princesses, and indirectly, by enjoying a favourable business climate, which the royal family has seen as in its own interest to ensure.[55] He suggests too that there is a generally positive attitude to economic liberalization and reform, including WTO membership for the kingdom, on the part of royal entrepreneurs, but that there is some caution to avoid their own domestic business interests being undermined by globalization.

Sabri predicts a stable future for the royal entrepreneurs, as all three of the most important groups in Saudi Arabia, the princes, the merchants and the 'ulama (Islamic leaders) have benefited economically from the existing system. It was from the 1960s that the royal family started to become more entrepreneurial. This was partly a result of the limited possibilities for most of the princes to secure political advancement, especially for the younger princes under a system in which brother succeeded brother. Increasing oil wealth presented opportunities to the younger princes with money to invest, and they regarded investment as almost a religious imperative, given the tradition of *mudharaba* (profit-sharing), which was seen as

---

[53] Sharaf Sabri, *The House of Saud in Commerce: A Study of Royal Entrepreneurship in Saudi Arabia* (New Delhi: I.S. Publications, 2001).
[54] Ibid., pp. 249–78.
[55] Ibid., pp. 285–6.

being more legitimate than simply making money from money through *riba* (interest).[56]

The entrepreneurial aspirations and success of the royal family have not benefited the larger Saudi population, however. With the population numbering almost 16 million and with rapid growth in the potential workforce, unemployment has emerged as a major issue.[57] In the oil-boom years of the 1970s and 1980s large numbers of Saudi citizens were absorbed into government employment, and land purchases by the government were a major method of redistributing oil wealth to local tribes and landowners. By the 1990s these policies were no longer possible, as the government ran a fiscal deficit[58] and expenditure on employment creation for its own sake could no longer be financed. Consequently, in the sixth and seventh development plans there has been much more emphasis on the need for the private sector, including companies owned by the royal family, to hire more Saudi citizens.[59] These companies have been reluctant to do this, as hiring migrant labour is cheaper and more flexible. Saudis command higher wages, require expensive training and cannot be easily dismissed under existing labour laws. There is no similar protection for migrant labour.

It is unlikely that the new investment laws introduced in Saudi Arabia will contribute much to employment creation, as most investment is likely to continue to be in petrochemicals, which depends on cheap feedstock supplies, and gas harnessing. Such capital-intensive projects have only a limited impact on local labour markets, and most are situated in the new industrial cities of Jubail and Yanbu, to which Saudi workers, with their extended family commitments, are unwilling to move. There seems to be a large gap between the aspirations of young Saudis[60] and what the new Saudi Arabian General Investment Authority is likely to be able to deliver. Its aim seems to be to protect the interests of existing Saudi investors, notably in the banking sector, rather than to open up markets to foreign entrants – a move that might possibly create employment for local citizens without privileged connections.[61]

[56] Adnan M. Adeen and Dale N. Shook, *The Saudi Financial System* (New York: John Wiley and Sons, 1984), pp. 188–9.

[57] Said Abdullah al-Shaikh, 'Demographic transitions in Saudi Arabia and their impact on economic growth and the labour market', *The NCB Economist*, National Commercial Bank, Jeddah, first quarter 2000, pp. 5–12.

[58] Khan H. Zahid and Khalid al-Bassam, 'Fiscal Developments', *Saudi Economic Review*, Riyadh Bank, third quarter 2000, p. 8.

[59] John Presley, 'The Seventh Development Plan', *Saudi Economic Bulletin*, Saudi British Bank, Riyadh, fourth quarter 2000, pp. 4–8.

[60] Mai Yamani, *Changed Identities: The Challenge of the New Generation in Saudi Arabia* (London: Royal Institute of International Affairs, 2000), pp. 70–90.

[61] Prince Abdullah bin Faisal bin Turki al-Saud, 'Going global in a quest for quality partners', *Arab Banker*, Vol. 14, No. 2, Summer 2000, pp. 14–17.

Conclusions

It is clear that globalization implies a different rather than a reduced role for governments in the Middle East and that, as the experiences of Egypt and Saudi Arabia show, states are remarkably adept at protecting and promoting the vested interests of local economic elites in the face of global challenges. The position of one Omani commentator perhaps typifies the more enlightened regional response:

> In the global free market Darwin's principle of the 'survival of the fittest in the struggle for existence' operates for the most part. Countries that do not have a comparative advantage will be eased out of the market. Therefore the main challenge posed by globalization is to avoid marginalisation. The problem for Oman like many other developing countries is how to create a niche for herself in the world market. International organisations and global trade negotiations cannot offer fully-fledged solutions to marginalisation. Like many of the world's developing countries Oman has still to build the human capital, the institutions, the physical infrastructure and pursue the policies necessary to seize the trade and investment opportunities of globalization. Therefore public policies will have to be reoriented to face the challenges of increased globalization.[62]

Furthermore, governments in the Middle East have the resilience to confront globalization if it does not serve the interests of their constituents. Temporary marginalization may not necessarily be unwelcome to regimes in power, as the cases of post-revolutionary Iran or of Iraq under sanctions both show. In a region with long experience of the rise and fall of many external civilizations, globalization, which many there equate with Americanization, may be only a passing phase. Paul Streeten's observation that history shows that globalization is easily reversible is a view widely shared in the Middle East, which gives comfort both to rulers and to those with powerful economic vested interests.[63]

---

[62] Ali Hamdan, 'Globalisation opportunities and challenges for Oman', *Al Markazi*, Central Bank of Oman, Muscat, Vol. 26, No. 2, April–May 2001, p. 10.
[63] Paul Streeten, 'Integration, interdependence and globalisation', in *Finance and Development* (Washington, DC: International Monetary Fund, June 2001), pp. 34–7.

THE ROYAL INSTITUTE OF | Middle East
INTERNATIONAL AFFAIRS | Programme

Iran, Islam and Democracy
The Politics of Managing Change
Ali M. Ansari

'This book makes compelling reading. It presents the most lucid and convincing account to date of the developments in Iran which led to the election of President Khatami in 1997 and of the 6th Majlis in 2000. In an original argument about the nature and pace of change in the Islamic Republic, the author identifies key processes underlying Iran's politics, which will shape the direction of this pivotal Middle Eastern state for some years. Sensitive to the links between ideas and action, the book happily avoids static, misleading stereotypes. Instead, it presents the reader with a fast-paced narrative, capturing the sense of intellectual excitement and uncertainty characteristic of current political struggles in Iran. This testifies to the author's skill in bringing out the diversity of this extraordinary country and the sense of possibility that informs its increasingly articulate political public.'

Charles Tripp
Head of Department of Political Studies,
School of Oriental and African Studies,
University of London

£16.95 ISBN 1 86203 117 7 256pp
Published 2000
Distributed by Brookings

For European orders contact:
Plymbridge Distributors Ltd, Estover Road, Plymouth, Devon PL6 7PZ, UK;
or call the credit card hotline +44 1752 202 301
For North American orders contact the Brookings Institution
Tel: 1 800 275 1447 or 1 202 797 6258, Fax 1 202 797 2960

THE ROYAL INSTITUTE OF INTERNATIONAL AFFAIRS | Middle East Programme

Changed Identities
The Challenge of the New Generation in Saudi Arabia
Mai Yamani

'In a fascinating study built on unique access and patient research, Dr Mai Yamani probes the outlook, expectations and frustrations of Saudi Arabia's younger generation struggling to come to terms with economic and social uncertainty, globalisation and the stark limits on political and intellectual expression.'
- **Paul Taylor**, Diplomatic Editor, Reuters

'No question will be more decisive for the Middle East and the Islamic world, as for the stability of the global energy market, than the future of Saudi Arabia. After eight decades, the old order cannot continue to hold, as pressures from within and without accumulate, and the young, now a majority, aspire to a future that avoids equally the paralysis of the present and the turmoil of other neighbours.

Hitherto we have analysed Saudi Arabia through a dark glass. Now, in what is perhaps the first direct investigation of what Saudis really think, we can read, in convincing detail, of the changes taking place within this society. The result is a picture at once compelling and challenging.'
- **Professor Fred Halliday**, London School of Economics

£14.95 ISBN 1 86203 088 X 192pp
Published 2000
Distributed by Brookings

For European orders contact:
Plymbridge Distributors Lt,d Estover Road, Plymouth, Devon PL6 7PZ, UK; or call the credit card hotline +44 1752 202 301
For North American orders contact the Brookings Institution
Tel: 1 800 275 1447 or 1 202 797 6258, Fax 1 202 797 2960